SUCCESSFUL GARDENING

GROWING YOUR
FAVORITE PLANTS

Staff for Successful Gardening (U.S.A.)
Editor: Fiona Gilsenan
Senior Associate Editor: Carolyn T. Chubet
Art Editor: Evelyn Bauer
Art Associate: Martha Grossman
Editorial Assistant: Joanne M. Wosahla

Contributors
Editor: Thomas Christopher
Editorial Assistant: Tracy O'Shea
Consulting Editor: Lizzie Boyd (U.K.)
Consultant: Dora Galitzki
Copy Editor: Marsha Lutch Lloyd

READER'S DIGEST GENERAL BOOKS
Editor in Chief: John A. Pope, Jr.
Managing Editor: Jane Polley
Executive Editor: Susan J. Wernert
Art Director: David Trooper
Group Editors: Will Bradbury, Sally French,
Norman B. Mack, Kaari Ward
Group Art Editors: Evelyn Bauer, Robert M. Grant, Joel Musler
Chief of Research: Laurel A. Gilbride
Copy Chief: Edward W. Atkinson
Picture Editor: Richard Pasqual
Rights and Permissions: Pat Colomban
Head Librarian: Jo Manning

The credits that appear on page 176
are hereby made a part of this copyright page.

Originally published in partwork form.
Copyright © 1990 Eaglemoss Publications Ltd.

Based on the edition copyright © 1990
The Reader's Digest Association Limited.

Library of Congress Cataloging in Publication Data

Growing Your Favorite Plants
       p.   cm. — (Successful gardening)
  Includes index.
  ISBN 0-89577-577-8
    1. Plants, Ornamental 2. Plants, Ornamental—Pictorial works.
I. Reader's Digest Association. II. Series.
SB407.G76 1993
635.9—dc20   93-20907

Printed in the United States of America

Opposite: Lush ferns and variegated hostas frame an early-summer scene of pink alliums,
cerise geraniums, and bright-eyed violas.

Overleaf: Thriving in moderate shade or full sun, long-lived, pest-free, and brilliant in
bloom, the daylily is one of America's favorite flowers.

THE READER'S DIGEST ASSOCIATION, INC.
Pleasantville, New York / Montreal

GROWING YOUR FAVORITE PLANTS

CONTENTS

Bedding pansies The varied blooms of violas come in solid or mixed-color selections.

Annuals and biennials

Although they flower through a single season and then die, the many varied types of annuals and biennials available to the gardener today compensate by bringing exuberant splashes of color to the garden. Annuals form dazzling flower beds whether a single species dominates the layout or a few different ones are displayed to eye-catching effect. These plants are also a perfect choice to fill the seasonal gaps in perennial beds.

The spring garden would seem incomplete without pots of smiling pansies — as would the summer landscape without the gleam of marigolds. And certainly the fall garden would not be the same without the sunny blaze of chrysanthemums. In addition to providing color, annuals can also solve intractable problems. For example, the owners of shady yards can depend on colorful impatiens to grow where few other flowers would flourish.

Each year, plant breeders introduce new strains of annuals with an ever-widening range of flower size, color, foliage variegations, or growth habits. Some of these join the hundreds of cultivars that have never lost their appeal; the popularity of others waxes and wanes with fashion. But whether you choose familiar or recently developed varieties, none of them are difficult to grow. Probably the most demanding care required by annuals is frequent deadheading, but you will be rewarded for this work by the continuous displays of flowers these plants yield when their energy is not wasted forming seeds.

The diverse menu of annuals and biennials offers delightful choices to the experienced gardener — and a perfect experience for the beginner. For what can match the pleasure of watching the miraculous (nearly effortless) transformation of a pinch of seed into a vibrant patchwork quilt of blooms?

French marigolds, orange and yellow, gild this dooryard planting of annuals.

SUNNY MARIGOLDS

Quick growth, easy cultivation, and a summer-through-fall display of brilliant color make these annuals a gardener's standby.

For many, a patch of marigolds is their first garden. The seeds are large and easy to handle, and they sprout quickly, in as few as 7 days from sowing. These undemanding and hardy plants are generous, with double or single blossoms in brilliant hues of gold, orange, and mahogany from early summer until the first frost.

Classes of marigolds

African marigolds, hybrids and cultivars of the Mexican species *Tagetes erecta,* are sturdy annuals that grow up to 3 ft (90cm) and carry yellow or orange (and occasionally white) flowers 2-5 in (5-12.5 cm) wide. Blossoms are typically double; some types have wavy or rolled petals resembling carnations, and others are globe-shaped, like chrysanthemums. They can fill seasonal gaps in a mixed border or be cut for flower displays. Good cultivars include the 'Discovery' and 'Lady' series of hybrids; a fine white is 'Snowdrift.'

French marigolds, cultivars and hybrids of *T. patula,* grow to 7-10 in (18-25 cm), and are good for bedding and for window boxes. They bear flowers 1- 2 in (2.5-5 cm) wide. These blooms range in color from mahogany red through orange and yellow, and may be single, semidouble, or double; many are "crested," with a central, raised knot of tightly rolled petals. Hybrids are the 'Boy' series (fully double; yellow, orange, and red); 'Queen Sophia' (semidouble, russet-edged with gold); and the 'Disco' series (single; yellow, red, and bicolored).

Mule (Triploid) marigolds are crosses of African and French marigolds and are compact plants, 12-14 in (30-35 cm) tall, that may flower in as few as 5 weeks from seed. They are sterile and cannot set seed, and bear exceptionally heavy crops of large double flowers, in hues from red to yellow.

Signet marigolds *(T. tenuifolia)* are compact plants (to 8 in/20 cm) and have ferny, lemon-scented foliage and dainty, single yellow flowers. They make ideal edging plants.

Choosing a site

Marigolds flourish in full sun on well-drained, relatively nutrient-poor soils. It is better to avoid rich soil because it will encourage foliar growth instead of flowers.

▼ **Scattered** through the vegetable garden, marigolds can help cleanse soil of the root-knot nematode, a plant parasite. For a serious infestation, plant whole beds of marigolds in spring and rototill them into the soil in late fall.

MARIGOLDS FOR WINTER FLOWERS

1 Dwarf African marigolds, such as 'Discovery,' bloom indoors in January if started in early October — sow three to four seeds into a 6-in (15-cm) pot of sterilized, well-drained potting soil.

2 Set the pot in a sunny but cool windowsill and keep soil evenly moist. When seedlings have developed two or three pairs of leaves, carefully remove all but one plant.

3 Be careful not to overwater the new plants. Irrigate only when soil is dry (allow it to become dry). Feed with a liquid fertilizer every 2 weeks. Remove spent flowers before they go to seed.

4 As weather turns warm in spring, harden off plants by setting them outdoors for a few hours each day. Move them into the garden when danger of frost is past.

Starting from seed

Sow outdoors as soon as soil warms to 60°F (15°C), covering seeds with a sparse sifting of fine soil. Germination takes about 7 days; when seedlings have developed at least one pair of true leaves, transplant them to a fertilized bed. Space African marigolds 12-18 in (30-45 cm) apart; French marigolds, 8-12 in (20-30 cm) apart; and Signets, 12 in (30 cm) apart. For earlier bloom, sow indoors in flats of sterile seed-starting mix 6 to 7 weeks before date of last frost. Move the flats with germinated seedlings to a sunny but cool windowsill (50°F/10°C nights, 60°F/15°C days). Prick out to flats of potting soil, setting seedlings 2 in (5 cm) apart.

Cultural methods

Before sowing the seed, dress the soil with a low-nitrogen fertilizer. During dry spells, water the plants deeply but sparingly. Take care not to wet the foliage, as this invites Botrytis.

Pests and diseases

Cold, wet weather or a poorly drained, heavy soil may cause marigolds to fall prey to root, crown, and stem rots. Though they are generally pest-free, marigolds may be attacked by Japanese beetles, mites, and slugs.

CUTTING MARIGOLDS

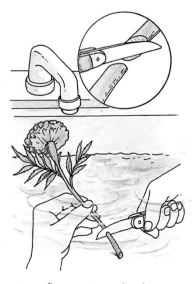

1 To make flowers last, cut in early morning with a sharp knife. Strip away lower leaves before setting flowers in a bucket of cool water.

2 Recut flowers at a node where a leaf joins a stem. Hold them under water as you make the cut and use a sharp knife (do not use scissors, as they will crush the hollow stems).

3 Stand the flowers in water enriched with sugar and bleach (1 T/15 ml each per qt /.95 liter of water). Leave for several hours in a cool, dark place before arranging.

VERSATILE ZINNIAS

Resistant to both heat and humidity, zinnias bloom throughout summer — furnishing brilliant color to everything from window boxes to borders.

The true workhorses of the garden, zinnias are easy to grow, quick to bloom, and gloriously colorful. Unusually tolerant of heat and humidity, they flower right through the dog days of summer and on into fall, continuing their show long after most other annuals have quit. The diversity of this plant — it ranges in height from 6 in (15 cm) to 3 ft (90 cm) and may bear a cloud of small daisylike blooms or giant blossoms as full as a dahlia's — offers the gardener a wide choice. Moreover, the color palette of its blooms is one of the most expansive of any plant, for it includes nearly every hue except blue.

Like marigolds, zinnias are used to fill the gaps left in perennial borders as the spring bloomers become dormant. And because zinnias display more varied colors, they blend into far more planting schemes than the uncompromising marigolds. Sturdy zinnias make superb material for beds, and by choosing types of varying heights and growth habits, you can fashion a fast-blooming border from zinnias alone. Cheerful and reliable in window boxes, tubs, and other containers, zinnias also star in the cutting garden. The chartreuse-green, long-stemmed zinnia 'Envy' is a special favorite of flower arrangers.

Choosing zinnias

There are about 20 species, all natives of the Americas. In fact, the ancestors of the common garden types came from Mexico.

Zinnia leaves are nearly stemless, undivided, and uncut; they sprout from opposite sides of the stems in opposing pairs. Their flowers may be single (as in the species or wild types), semidouble, or fully double globes of closely massed petals. In the single and semidouble forms, zinnia flowers resemble the daisy's pattern of disc and ray: a circle of variously colored petals surrounding a central button that is commonly yellow.

Zinnia elegans is the species that has sired most of the cultivated types. These have flowers

▲ **The dahlialike** scarlet 'Big Tetra' is the jewel in this crown of cosmos, zinnia, rudbeckia, and goldenrod. Zinnias are a flower-arranger's favorite — they are long-lasting as cut flowers and offer every color except blue.

▼ **'Ruffles' hybrid zinnias** and others provide the sparks of cherry red and pink that enliven this golden border of African marigolds, calendulas, and nasturtiums.

in many forms. While the typical zinnia makes a flattened rosette, some of the *elegans* cultivars produce pompon-type blooms, dahlia look-alikes, or even cactus-type blossoms in which the petals are rolled into quills.

Zinnia elegans cultivars include some notably compact plants such as the 'Thumbelina' strain, which is 6 in (15 cm) tall. Despite its diminutive size, this annual bears showy 1¼-in (3-cm) semidouble blossoms of pink, red, yellow, and lavender. The long-popular 'Peter Pan' strain produces plants that begin flowering at a height of 6 to 8 in (15-20 cm) but that continue to grow, topping out at 14 in (35 cm). So-called "border zinnias" grow even taller: The 'Border Beauty Hybrids' stand 22 in (55 cm) tall at maturity, bearing dahlia-type double flowers of pink, red, or yellow. Rising to 2½ ft (75 cm) or more are the giant-flowered cultivars, such as the 'Zenith' hybrids. Planted in the back of a bed, they offer cactus-type 6-in (15-cm) blooms in shades of red, salmon-pink, orange, and yellow.

Z. haageana is a bushy annual that makes a mound 2 ft (60 cm) tall, with its pinwheel-shaped flowers that are 1½ in (5 cm) wide. 'Old Mexico' and 'Chippendale Daisy' bear reddish petals tipped with gold; 'Persian Carpet' has maroon, brown, pink, and cream as well.

Z. angustifolia may overwinter in mild-weather regions; it forms compact plants of narrow leaves and 1-in (2.5-cm) flowers. This species' sprawling growth makes it suitable for hanging baskets.

Choosing a site

Zinnias flourish in spots that receive full sunlight throughout the day. They also prefer an airy situation (humid, still air promotes the mildew that can blight leaves and blossoms). Where the aeration is less than ideal, plant the disease-resistant *Z. haageana* cultivars. Well-drained but fertile soils produce the healthiest growth.

Starting from seed

The easiest method of starting zinnias is to sow seeds where the plants are to bloom. Wait until the soil has dried and warmed in the spring. Thin seedlings to a distance of 6 to 12 in (15-30 cm) apart — the spacing varies with the size of the cultivar.

For earlier bloom, start seedlings indoors 6 weeks before the last expected frost. Zinnias have sensitive roots and do not like to be transplanted. Sow seeds into peat pots filled with sterile seed-starting mix. Later you will be able to set them out into the garden with little disturbance.

Aftercare

Do not overwater seedlings when you are transplanting them. Moisten the soil thoroughly but do not soak it. Once established, plants will benefit from deep watering during hot, dry weather. Try not to wet the leaves because moisture invites mildew. To maintain vigorous growth and flowering, fertilize once a month with a complete fertilizer.

If bushy, bloom-laden plants are desired (as for bedding displays), pinch back the topmost buds when the seedlings have produced three or four pairs of leaves. If you want cut flowers, leave plants unpinched to develop longer stems and larger blossoms. However, you will have to stake the taller cultivars.

◄ **Merging the cutting garden** and vegetable patch can turn these utilitarian beds into a garden ornament. Here, the lush leaves of carrots and greens serve as a foil to zinnias 'Canary Bird' (yellow), 'Oriole' (orange), 'Illumination' (white), and 'Will Rogers' (red).

BOUNTIFUL BEGONIAS

**Although begonias cannot survive frost, both
the showy tuberous types and the fibrous-rooted wax
ones make lush summer plants.**

Several thousand named cultivars have been bred from the tuberous-rooted begonias. The members of this group — known as *Begonia × tuberhybrida* — are of complex parentage and are variable in growth habit, flower shape, and flower color. All can be grown outdoors — displayed in annual beds, tubs, window boxes, or hanging baskets. However, you must plant them after all danger of frost has passed and lift and bring them under cover in the fall.

Most cultivars have green leaves that resemble the ears of an African elephant — somewhat heart-shaped but with irregularly sized lobes. There are some pink and red varieties that have purplish-tinted leaves.

All begonia leaves have hairy undersides and hairy, fleshy stems that are brittle and easily damaged.

The second group of begonia cultivars that is popular for flower beds is *Begonia semperflorens,* or wax begonias. These are also of mixed parentage, but have a fibrous root system and are more uniform in growth habit than the tuberous species. They form compact, low-growing plants that produce plentiful, small flowers in shades of red, pink, or white. Their small, glossy leaves may be green or bronze.

Choosing tuberous begonias

Growth habit is the first characteristic to consider when choosing a tuberous begonia. Plants may be bushy and upright or have pendulous stems. The former are excellent for flower beds as well as for containers, while the latter are more suitable for hanging baskets or around the edge of tubs and urns, where the flowering stems can hang freely.

There are several main groups of tuberous begonias; these are distinguished by flower features. Most have double flowers, though singles and semidoubles are available. On any one plant, regardless of the group, there may be a few relatively insignificant, single female flowers. However, these blooms are generally overshadowed by the larger male flowers, which can vary from 2 in (5 cm) to 6 in (15 cm) wide.

Large-flowered double types are sometimes known as camellia-flowered begonias. They have the biggest blooms of all, usually 4-6 in (10-15 cm) wide. The fully double male flowers are most prominent, but are intermingled

▼ **Multiflora and pendulous begonias**
Excellent plants for pots and containers, tuberous begonias provide brilliant splashes of color on a patio, porch, or deck throughout the summer.

TUBEROUS BEGONIA TYPES

large-flowered double

large-flowered double

multiflora

rosebud

multiflora

picotee

marginata

fimbriata

pendula

marmorata

bertinii compacta

with a few single female flowers, which bear a twisted yellow stigma and are backed by a large-winged ovary.

These plants grow to about 1-2 ft (30-60 cm) in height, with a corresponding spread, and may bear up to a dozen large camellia- or rose-like flowers at any one time. The blooms appear in succession throughout summer and early fall and come in most colors, including intense and pastel shades, except blues or mauves.

Multiflora types are similar in habit and flower shape to the large-flowered doubles, but bear many more, though much smaller, flowers per plant. Sometimes listed as *B.* × *multiflora-maxima* cultivars, these plants are found in a wide range of bright colors and may have bronze foliage. They are attractive in flower beds because of their compact size of about 6-8 in (15-20 cm).

Rosebud types have double flowers up to 5 in (12 cm) wide, with raised centers that resemble partially opened rosebuds.

Picotee types have moderately sized double flowers with pale petals edged in a darker shade, generally rose-red.

Marginata types, often sold as *B. crispa marginata* cultivars, have single or semidouble flowers edged with a contrasting color. The petals have frilly edges.

Fimbriata types are similar to the large-flowered doubles, but their brightly colored flowers, which are 4-5 in (10-12 cm) wide, have ruffled or fringed petals and resemble very large carnations.

Pendula types, including *B.* × *lloydii* and *Boliviensis* cultivars, have trailing or pendent stems, smallish, rather narrow, pointed leaves, and prolific clusters of single or semidouble pointed flowers up to 2½ in (6 cm) wide. They are ideal for window boxes, and, unlike other begonias, some of these cultivars have a mild fragrance. Colors vary, but red, rose-pink, and bright yellow are the most familiar.

Marmorata cultivars are distinguished from the large-flowered doubles by the color of their blooms. These are always rose-pink with white spots or blotches. The plants rarely exceed 9 in (23 cm) in height.

Bertinii compacta begonias form very neat, compact, bushy plants, which are no more than

RAISING TUBEROUS BEGONIAS

1 Begin growing dormant tubers in early spring or midspring by embedding them in a flat or bowl filled with a moist blend of peat and sand. Ensure that the tubers lie flush with the surface, with their hollow tops turned uppermost.

2 When strong leafy shoots develop, replant each tuber into a 4-5-in (10-12-cm) pot filled with potting soil. Keep the soil moist at all times. If you are growing several different varieties, label each plant clearly.

3 If grown for indoor display, plants must be replanted a second time into 6-8-in (15-20-cm) pots. For very large flowers, restrict plants to one strong shoot and two to three side shoots by pinching back.

4 Harden off young bedding plants in late spring. As soon as all danger of frost is past, set them out 12-15 in (30-38 cm) apart in well-drained, humus-rich soil in a sunny or semi-shaded, sheltered position.

STAKING TUBEROUS BEGONIAS

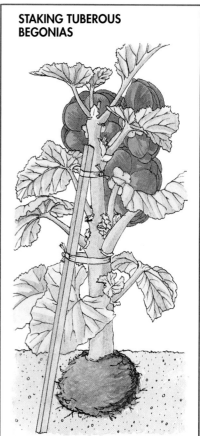

Most tuberous begonias do not need support, provided they are planted in a reasonably sheltered spot. The large-flowered doubles, however, can become top-heavy when in full bloom, and thus should be staked to prevent damage. The stems and flower stalks are fragile, so staking and tying must be done with care.

Insert a short, sturdy stake at the back of the plant, far enough away from the stem at the base to avoid puncturing the tuber. Lean the stake toward the stem and tie them together with soft string.

---

6 in (15 cm) tall. Their masses of small, single flowers come in a range of bright colors. These begonias are recommended for the edges of a border or bed, or to fill pockets in a rock garden.

Growing tuberous begonias
Dormant begonia tubers are available at nurseries and through mail-order catalogs in early spring. The tubers that are widely available in retail outlets are of a modest size, capable of producing good-sized bedding plants. Larger tubers must be obtained from specialty nurseries.

If they have been correctly stored, the tubers should feel firm and may have tiny growth shoots — pink or greenish nodules — in their hollowed-out tops (the tubers resemble a shallow bird's nest). Handle them carefully to avoid damaging these new shoots.

Start growing the tubers in early spring or midspring. You will need a heated greenhouse or sunny windowsill indoors, although an unheated greenhouse can be used if you wait until midspring before planting. The temperature must be about 64°F (18°C), with a minimum night temperature of 50°F (10°C).

The tubers must be planted the correct way up, with the hollow tops uppermost. Place them in a moist peat-and-sand mixture (half and half) in a 3-in (7.5-cm) deep flat or bowl, making sure that their tops lie flush with the surface. Do not bury the hollow tops because they may fill up with water and rot. (For the same reason, avoid wetting the hollow tops when watering begonia tubers.) Space the tubers a few inches (centimeters) apart.

As soon as strong leafy shoots develop, replant each tuber into a 4-5-in (10-12-cm) pot filled with potting soil. Keep the soil constantly moist, but not too wet. When you are growing large exhibition-quality flowers, pinch back all but one strong shoot, then restrict this shoot to two or three side shoots. When a begonia is to be a bedding plant, allow all the shoots to develop. When grown indoors, a begonia will outgrow its original pot and need to be transferred to a pot 6-8 in (15-20 cm) deep.

In late spring, harden off bedding plants in a cold frame. When all danger of frost has passed, plant them out 12-15 in (30-38 cm) apart in any good, well-drained garden soil, enriched with composted organic material. In the North, the site should receive several hours of sunlight daily — early morning or late afternoon sun is ideal. In the South, where midday sun can scorch the soft flower petals and leaves, filtered shade is preferable. Plant the begonias under an overhanging shrub or perennial, for instance. Also, avoid exposed sites where the brittle stems and flowers can break during high winds or driving rain.

Little routine care is needed for outdoor begonias, except to ensure that the soil remains moist at all times. Erratic periods of wetness and drought result in flower and bud drop. Sometimes the blooms are hidden beneath large leaves, but you can ease the blooms out by hand or cut off a few leaves with a sharp knife.

Large-flowered doubles, or any types that have been restricted to one main stem, need support. Insert a sturdy bamboo or metal stake beside the tuber, angled to meet the top of the stem. If this support is put at the back of the plant — all flowers and leaves tend to face one way — it will be almost invisible. Tie the stem in a few places, using soft twine that won't cut the delicate tissues.

While they are flowering, give tuberous begonias grown in containers a liquid fertilizer approximately every 3 weeks.

Lifting and storing Before the first hard frost occurs, lift tubers from the ground and take them indoors. If the foliage has not yet begun to die down, replant the tubers in boxes of moist potting soil and let them grow until the leaves fall naturally.

Once the leaves turn yellow, dry off the plants by gradually withholding water. Cut down the stems, lift the tubers, and remove all dead and dying shoots close to them; then brush off loose roots. Examine each tuber for signs of rot — if present, cut it away with a sharp knife and dust the wound with sulfur. If tubers have tun-

nels caused by vine weevils, treat them similarly, but discard any with serious damage.

Bury the tubers in dry, sterilized soil in a deep flat or box. Overwinter them in a frost-free place at a temperature of about 45°F (7°C). Water the tubers occasionally during winter.

Growing wax begonias
Begonia semperflorens, or wax begonias, do not have tubers; they produce a fibrous root system and are generally grown from seed each year. Mixed-color strains are common, but named varieties with pink, red, or white flowers, and glossy green or bronze foliage, are also available. F1 hybrids give the best results.

In late winter or early spring, sow seeds in a flat filled with a sterilized commercial seed-starting mixture at 61-75°F (16-24°C). Begonia seeds are tiny and should be simply scattered on the surface of the leveled, gently firmed, moistened mixture; do not cover up the seeds.

Germination takes 2 to 4 weeks, according to the temperature. Prick off seedlings when the first true leaf is visible and continue to grow them at a temperature of about 61°F (16°C) in relatively humid conditions.

The gardener without a greenhouse or special propagation box

▲ **Wax begonias** Raised in quantity from seed, bedding begonias spread a carpet of color throughout summer and early fall. Compact and sturdy, pink, red, white, or mixed F1 hybrids are available.

may find it difficult to keep seed flats sufficiently warm or to provide seedlings with enough light during the growing season. A garden center may be a more practical source of transplants — most offer these popular plants in the spring. Starting begonias from seed, while not as easy, will greatly increase the selection of cultivars and hybrids available to you.

To encourage bushiness, pinch back the growing tips of plants when they are 4 in (10 cm) tall, though most F1 hybrids will become fairly bushy without help.

Harden off the young plants in a cold frame and then plant them out in their flowering sites when all danger of frost is past. Choose a sunny or partially shaded spot where the soil is rich and moist but well-drained. Space the plants 8-10 in (20-25 cm) apart and water them well.

Wax begonias flower all summer and continue until the first hard frost. At this time, they can be discarded or put in pots and brought indoors to a cool room or porch, where they will continue to flower for several more weeks.

A RIOT OF DAHLIAS

**Their brightness and complex flower shapes,
as well as their handsome foliage, add an exotic
touch to the garden in late summer.**

The dahlia, which originated in subtropical Mexico, has tuberous roots, hollow stems, and dark green or purplish leaves. These lush leaves make a striking background for the exotic shades and shapes of the blooms. This plant requires rich soil, constant watering, and regular feeding.

Dahlia classification

There are two groups of dahlias — bedding dahlias, which are grown annually from seed, and half-hardy tuberous border perennials, which are described here. Although suitable for mixed beds, the latter are generally grown on their own.

Tuberous dahlias are further classified into groups according to the form of their flowers. The most popular are the decorative, cactus, ball, and pompon types. As with the daisy family to which they belong, the blossoms of dahlias consist of a ring of sterile florets around a disc of fertile true flowers; this structure gives the appearance of a single flower.

Single-flowered dahlias have blooms comprised of a single outer ring of florets, which may overlap each other, and a central disc of stamens. The flowers grow up to 4 in (10 cm) wide.

Anemone-flowered dahlias are the same size, but have double flowers with flat, outer florets around a densely packed group of shorter florets, often of contrasting colors.

Collarettes have flowers 4 in (10 cm) wide, with yellow centers made up of stamens and a single row of florets around the edge. An inner collar of smaller florets surrounds the stamens, lying between them and the petals.

Peony-flowered dahlias may reach a diameter of 4-5 in (10-12.5 cm). Each bloom has two or more rings of flat ray florets and a central disc.

Pompon dahlias have globular blooms that do not exceed 2 in (5 cm) in diameter. The florets are rolled for their entire length.

Ball dahlias are similar to pompons, with ball-like blooms, though these are sometimes flattened on top. The florets are blunt or rounded at the tip, and are arranged spirally. Each floret is rolled for more than half its length. Ball blooms are generally 4-6 in (10-15 cm) wide.

Decoratives have a formal shape and fully double flowers, with no central disc. The ray florets are broad, flat, and bluntly pointed at the tips; they are usually slightly twisted.

Cactus dahlias also have fully double flowers, but they have narrow, pointed florets that are rolled back, or *quilled,* for more than half their length.

Semicactus dahlias are similar to the cactus type, but the florets

---

▼ **Dahlia blooms** Available in a vast range of pure and mixed colors, dahlia flowers also come in a variety of shapes and forms. Ideal for garden display and for cutting, they bloom with abandon until the first frosts.

are broader. These are quilled for half or less of their length.

Decoratives, cactus, and semi-cactus types are grouped by flower size — giant (more than 10 in/25 cm in diameter), large (8-10 in/20-25 cm in diameter), medium (6-8 in/15-20 cm in diameter), small (4-6 in/10-15 cm in diameter), and miniature (under 4 in/10 cm in diameter).

Plant height varies according to group; giant decoratives reach up to 4-5 ft (120-150 cm), but single-flowered types are rarely more than 2 ft (60 cm) tall.

Preparing the site

Although dahlias will thrive in any good garden soil that is neither too alkaline or acidic, they prefer a slightly acid, well-drained loam.

These plants are greedy feeders, so be sure to dig a heavy dressing of compost or other organic matter into the soil in the fall. In addition, add 4 heaped teaspoons (about 20 ml) per sq yd/sq m of sterilized bone meal dressing. Leave the surface rough so that frost and winter

PLANTING TUBERS

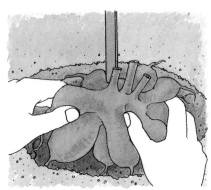

1 When danger of frost is past, place the dormant tuber horizontally in a hole, 6 in (15 cm) deep, with the base of the old stem close to a strong wooden stake.

2 Cover with a planting mixture of loam and nitrogen-rich organic fertilizer, filling the spaces between the tubers. Press in the tuber with your fingers.

TYPES OF DAHLIA FLOWERS

single-flowered

anemone-flowered

collarette

peony-flowered

pompon

decorative

ball

cactus

semicactus

weather can break it down well.

Then select a planting position in a warm, sunny, and wind-sheltered site where there is plenty of air circulation; in hot climates, choose a spot that receives light afternoon shade.

Planting the tubers

Plant dahlia tubers — the dormant, fleshy rootstocks — in midspring to late spring, when the danger of frost has passed. New growth arises not from tuberous roots but from the crown, which is the base of the old stem. Examine each tuber and make sure that each tuber includes at least one piece of old stem with an undamaged bud point, or *eye*.

Space tall varieties (those up to 4-5 ft/120-150 cm high) about 2-3 ft (60-90 cm) apart, medium types (those reaching 3-4 ft/90-120 cm high) 2 ft (60 cm) apart, and short, or bedding, types 15 in (38 cm) apart.

Insert wooden stakes, 1-in (2.5-cm) square, in the bed where the tubers are to be planted — bamboo canes are too fragile to serve as support. The stakes should be slightly shorter than the eventual height of the plants.

Dig a hole, 6 in (15 cm) deep, in front of the stake so that the eye on the base of the old stem can be planted against the stake. Half-fill the hole with a planting mixture of 1 bucketful of good

AFTERCARE

1 About 2 or 3 weeks after planting, tie the plants to the stakes with string. In midsummer, mulch with bark chips, dry straw, grass clippings, or composted manure. Water the mulch thoroughly.

loam or potting soil and 4 tablespoons (60 ml) of nitrogen-rich organic fertilizer, such as blood meal. Place the tuber on this mixture, with the crown about 2 in (5 cm) below the surface.

Cover the tuber with more soil and planting mixture. If there are several tuberous roots on the stem, see that the mixture fills the spaces between them to keep out slugs. After filling the hole, press the soil in with your fingers. Don't water in the tubers.

Pot-grown plants

Young dahlia plants can be bought from garden centers, already growing in pots. Once you

2 As the plants grow, add more ties. Check that the lower ties are not too tight. Support side shoots with string looped around a triangle of canes. Remove weeds by shallow hoeing.

have prepared the site as outlined above, plant them out in late spring or very early summer, after danger of frost is past.

Watering

When tubers or potted plants are first set out, they may be harmed by overwatering. In fact, it is fine for the roots to search for moisture. Once dahlias begin to flower, however, they need a lot of moisture. In dry spells, the plants should be watered well.

Use an automatic sprinkler or soaker hose to ensure that the whole area around the dahlias receives a thorough soaking. Alternatively, if plants are spaced

2-3 ft (60-90 cm) apart, a watering can will be effective. Give each dahlia about 3 gallons (15 liters) of water — less, if the plants are set closer together.

In hot, sunny weather, water plants on heavy, clay soils about every 5 days; water those on lighter soils about every 3 days.

Mulching

When a plant is about 1 ft (30 cm) high, put a 1-in (2.5-cm) layer of bark chips, grass clippings, or other organic mulch around the base, but not against the stem. Then water the area well. The mulch helps to control weeds and conserve moisture.

Providing support

All but the bedding dahlias need support to prevent damage from winds and heavy rains. Two or three weeks after planting, tie in the stems. Loop string around the stake about 4-8 in (10-20 cm) above the ground, then bring the string around the flower stem in a figure-eight pattern. Fasten the knot against the stake, not against the plant's stem.

As the plant grows, tie it again higher up the stems. Check that the lower ties have not become too tight around the main stem. To contain and protect the side growths, insert three thin stakes firmly in the ground in a triangle around the main stake. Each should be about 9 in (23 cm) from it, sloping outward. Loop garden string around the three, enclosing the side growths.

Pinching and disbudding

Most large-flowered dahlias send

PINCHING DAHLIAS

1 Two or three weeks after planting, pinch back the growing point of the stem. For overwintered tubers, this job is done in late spring or early summer. For plants grown from cuttings and divisions, wait until a few weeks later.

2 Two weeks later, about six new growing points (shoots lighter than the older leaves) will appear in the leaf axils. Remove the uppermost pair of shoots to promote vigorous growth in the lower side shoots.

3 These side shoots will each produce a terminal flower bud, with wing buds just below it. For large blooms, pinch back the wing buds when they are big enough to be removed without injuring the stem of the terminal bud.

up strong center growths, but exhibit little side growth until the center shoots develop flower buds. You can induce bushy growth by pinching back the leading shoot some weeks after planting. If you want very large flowers, remove the small flower buds that develop at the base of each main flower stem.

To promote longer-stemmed side shoots and encourage top growth, cut off leaves growing on the main stem within a few inches of the ground.

Fertilizing

Plants in soil that has been well prepared will not need much extra food. Mulching with well-composted manure will help growth if the soil is sandy.

An additional feed can be given after the second pinching. Scatter a handful of a balanced commercial flower fertilizer around the base of each plant. Do not allow it to come into contact with any of the leaves, as they can scorch very easily. Avoid high-nitrogen feeds at this time of year; they will encourage leaf growth and lower the quality of the tubers for winter storage.

Water well after feeding with a dry fertilizer. Stop normal feeding at the end of summer, but give a topdressing of superphosphate and sulfate of potash (in equal parts by weight) in late summer or early fall.

Winter storage

At the end of the growing season, dahlias should be lifted and stored during the winter in a frost-free place. The following spring they can be used to produce cuttings, or they can be replanted in the ground.

Immediately after the first frost in the fall has blackened the foliage, cut the stems back to about 6 in (15 cm) above the ground. Lift the roots before the onset of severe frosts.

When it is time to do so, use a garden fork to loosen the soil around the tubers without damaging them. Then lift them by pressing back on the fork handle. With a blunt-ended stick, carefully remove surplus soil from between the tuberous roots. Avoid breaking the old stems. Label the stumps, then place the tubers upside down in an airy, dry place for 2 weeks to allow

STORING DAHLIA TUBERS

1 After the first frost has blackened the foliage, cut back all the stems to about 6 in (15 cm) from ground level. Tubers can be left in the ground for a few more weeks, but they must be lifted before the first hard frost.

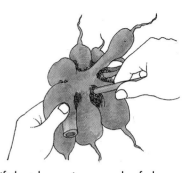

2 Lift the tubers using a garden fork. Carefully ease out all loose soil from between the tubers, taking care not to break off the old stems. Fasten labels to the stumps so they can be easily identified the following spring.

3 Dry off the tubers thoroughly by placing them upside down in an airy, dry place for about 2 weeks. Set the dry tubers on a 6-in (15-cm) layer of dry potting soil or sand in a deep box and dust them with sulfur.

4 After making sure that none of the tubers is touching the sides of the box, cover them all with another layer of soil or sand. Then cover with a piece of old carpeting or felt to absorb condensation. Store in a frost-free garage or shed.

moisture to drain from the stems.

Dust the tubers with sulfur to prevent fungus infections and store them in a cool, dry place, such as a cold frame or a frost-free garage.

Preserving tubers intact over the winter is a somewhat tricky proposition. It is essential to prevent them from withering, yet they must not be kept too moist. Commonly, tubers are stored in boxes of dry sand or potting soil.

Another method is to pour a pound of melted paraffin wax into a bucket of warm water, slipping the cleaned tubers into the water, then slowly lifting them out. Let the wax coat them thoroughly. After the wax hardens, the tubers can be packed into a box of peat moss or sawdust and stored as shown above.

Propagation of dahlias

New dahlia plants can be raised from cuttings or by division of the tubers. In late winter or early spring, put the tubers in flats of

damp potting soil, covering them to just below the crowns. When new shoots are 3-4 in (7.5-10 cm) long, sever them above the base with a sharp knife. Trim the shoots to below the lowest leaf joint and remove the lower leaves.

Dip the cuttings in a hormone rooting powder, then insert them in pots of equal parts peat and sand. Place the pots in an unheated propagation box and keep them shaded and moderately moist.

After 2 or 3 weeks, move each rooted cutting into a 3-in (7.5-cm) pot filled with equal parts sharp builder's sand, loam, and peat moss. Keep them in a well-ventilated greenhouse or warm sunroom or porch, providing shade for the first 2 days. Harden off plants in midspring and set them out when all frost is past.

Alternatively, divide the tubers with a sharp knife, ensuring that each piece contains a piece of old stem and a growth bud. Keep the divisions in individual pots in a cold frame until planting time.

POTTED PELARGONIUMS

**Cheerful and free-flowering, pelargoniums
are perfect for colorful outdoor containers and summer
bedding, as well as for indoor or greenhouse display.**

The term "pelargonium" may sound exotic, but it is the correct name for the flower that many of us use to fill pots and window boxes — the geranium. In fact, true geraniums belong to a genus of hardy perennials that is distinct from the popular summer bedding plant, though both belong to the same plant family (the Geraniaceae).

The botanical name *Pelargonium* derives from the Greek word *pelargos*, meaning "stork." Its ripe seed heads resemble the head and beak of that bird, and thus a pelargonium is sometimes referred to as a storksbill. A true geranium, on the other hand, is commonly known as a cranesbill.

Native to South Africa, the pelargoniums found in most gardens are hybrids and cultivars, often of complex parentage. These tender, somewhat woody subshrubs are actually perennial, but are usually treated as annuals and are grown yearly from cuttings or seed.

Today, gardeners have hundreds of beautiful named varieties of pelargoniums from which to choose. Most flower beginning in late spring and continue until the first fall frost. Indoors, pot-grown plants will bloom year round under the right conditions.

The two larger upper petals of the five-petaled flowers are often veined or suffused with a color that is darker than the bottom three. Semidouble and double blooms with extra petals are typical. Flowers are borne in rounded clusters, forming a dense or open head, in colors ranging from white through shades of pink, red, orange, and mauve to wine-purple. Cream-colored pelargoniums are rare, however, and yellows and blues are never seen.

Several species are valued for their shapely or colorful leaves, or for their aromatic foliage. The common types, however, have unpleasantly scented foliage. In all cases, the aroma is released only when leaves are bruised.

Classification

Four main groups of pelargoniums are recognized: zonal, regal, ivy-leaved, and scented-leaved.

Zonal pelargoniums are the most popular types grown outdoors for beds and container displays. They form a large group of hybrids and varieties, listed as *Pelargonium × hortorum.* Plants are bushy, growing up to 1-2 ft (30-60 cm) in height. The main stems become woody with age, but side growths are more fleshy.

The term "zonal" refers to the leaves, which are rounded or kidney-shaped, 3-5 in (7.5-12 cm) wide, and generally scalloped edged, with a prominent outer bronze or darker zone.

Individual flowers are up to 1 in (2.5 cm) wide, forming a dense head up to 6 in (15 cm) wide. Semidoubles and doubles are common; those with very double flowers are known as rosebud types. The Stellar hybrids have starry, rather ragged flowers and incut leaves.

F1 and F2 seed strains can bloom within 4 months of sowing. Other varieties are usually grown from cuttings.

Miniature zonal varieties, which reach only 6 in (15 cm) in height, make good houseplants and may also be used for edging in outdoor displays.

Fancy-leaved zonal varieties have distinctly colored leaves. They range from the yellow-marked 'Happy Thought' to the multicolored 'Mrs. Cox.'

Regal pelargoniums, often called "Lady Washington geraniums," resemble zonal types in size and habit, but have toothed, fluted leaves with uniform coloring. They are classified as *Pelargonium × domesticum.* The term "regal" derives from the fact that many varieties were developed in the late 1800's in the greenhouses of the British royal family.

◀ **Zonal pelargoniums** Universally popular, brightly colored zonals can be displayed in beds, tubs, window boxes, and other containers. If they are given good soil and full sun, they will flower profusely from late spring until the first fall frost.

zonal
single flowers

zonal
double flowers

zonal
semidouble flowers

Regal flower heads are up to 6 in (15 cm) wide (similar in size to the zonals), but the individual blooms are much larger — up to 2 in (5 cm) wide. Regal flowers are mostly single, often with frilly petals, and come in many rich and unusual shades. Bicolored flowers are frequent and attractive veining patterns may be prominent.

The flowering period of this type is more limited than is that of the zonal pelargoniums — regals mainly bloom in late spring and early summer, though if you deadhead the flowers, the plants may bloom again in late summer. Regal pelargoniums are grown from cuttings and are more suited to a greenhouse.

Ivy-leaved pelargoniums, belonging to the species *P. peltatum,* have a trailing habit and look best in hanging baskets or around the edges of tubs. Some are referred to as cascade types. Their rather fleshy, glossy, and lobed leaves resemble ivy. Up to 3 in (7.5 cm) wide, they are generally smaller than those of either zonals or regals.

Flowers, which may be up to 1 in (2.5 cm) wide are single, semidouble, or double. Their color range is more limited than other species — reds and purples, for example, are not widely seen. The blooms are borne in small, open clusters; the brittle stems, however, may trail to 3 ft (90 cm). Branching only occurs if the growing tips are pinched back.

As with zonal types, ivy-leaved pelargoniums sometimes have attractively variegated foliage.

Scented-leaved pelargoniums are grown chiefly for their foliage; their flowers are borne in small clusters, or are sometimes absent. They make excellent pot plants for a greenhouse or sunny windowsill.

The aromatic scents are often very powerful and include peppermint, chocolate-peppermint, rose, lemon, orange, and nutmeg. Other fragrant-leaved species have the scent of apple, eucalyptus, or pine. The oak-leaved pelargonium *(P. quercifolium)* is among this group, but its large leaves are not pleasantly scented.

Choosing the site

Pelargoniums can be grown all year indoors, and are great for planting outdoors during summer, either in open ground or in containers. They need as much sunlight as possible to promote strong, compact, and bushy growth. Sparse light produces a lanky appearance.

Indoors, choose a sunny windowsill to display pelargoniums, and turn their pots regularly to avoid lopsided growth. During the hottest summer sun, move plants outdoors to more airy conditions to prevent leaf scorch.

Pelargoniums thrive in temperatures ranging from 50°F (10°C) to 75°F (24°C). The higher temperatures that are common in the Southern states discourage good growth. In regions with lower temperatures, plants do better when grown indoors. However, it is preferable to keep them in a spot where the temperature drops significantly at night.

Although any ordinary, well-drained soil is suitable for plants grown in open ground, pelargoniums prefer neutral to slightly acid conditions. Commercial potting soils or a mix of 3 parts soil to 1 part composted manure are ideal for container-grown plants.

Buying young plants

Garden centers and nurseries offer a wide choice of young pelargoniums in late spring and early summer, for planting either

zonal starry
single flowers

zonal rosebud
double flowers

fancy-leaved zonal
single flowers

outdoors or in pots indoors. Although these plants are moderately expensive to buy, you will save time and space by not propagating them from seed.

Select only compact, healthy plants. Avoid those with straggly stems or yellowing lower leaves. Plants with lots of flower buds but few open blooms will provide the best display in the weeks to come. Regal pelargoniums, for example, produce their flowers in one main flush in early summer.

Growing from seed

F1 and F2 hybrid zonal and ivy-leaved pelargoniums may be grown from seed. Sow in late winter in pots or flats of sterilized seed-starting mix at a constant temperature of 61-64°F (16-18°C). The seeds will germinate in about 3 weeks. Low or fluctuating temperatures cause erratic sprouting.

When the seedlings are large enough to handle, transfer each one into a 3-in (7.5-cm) pot of sterilized potting soil. Or, if space is limited, set out the seedlings in flats before potting them up.

Harden them off and plant out in late spring or early summer. Alternatively, transplant them into larger pots filled with the manure-enriched soil described previously, and grow on indoors.

Growing from cuttings

All pelargoniums can be grown from softwood cuttings. This method of propagation is the only successful way of keeping a favorite named variety from one year to the next. With care, mature plants can be grown on indoors in pots for several years, but they tend to become very leggy. It is advisable to renew them annually.

Cuttings root best in early spring and late summer, when both leaf and stem growth are at their optimum. Those rooted in spring, taken from overwintered stock plants, produce small flowering plants for the summer of the same year. The ones that are rooted in late summer must be overwintered indoors and will produce larger plants for flowering the following summer.

Choose a healthy shoot, preferably without flowers. With a sharp knife, cut off a shoot tip, about 3 in (7.5 cm) long, just above a leaf node. (If all shoots have flowers, trim the buds and flowers.) Gently pull away the lower leaves and any stipules, or "whiskers." Trim the base of the cutting just below a node.

Do not use hormone rooting powder for pelargoniums; it can cause swelling and cracking of the stem, and then rotting. Insert each cutting into a pot, 2½-3-in (6-7.5-cm) deep, containing moistened builder's sand or put several cuttings in a larger pot.

Keep the cuttings in a humid, warm place, shaded from direct sun. They should be put in a propagation box or covered with

Pelargonium crispum lemon-scented leaves

ivy-leaved semidouble flowers

regal

ivy-leaved double flowers

fancy-leaved zonal double flowers

regal

regal

TAKING SOFTWOOD CUTTINGS

1 Using a sharp knife, cut terminal, nonflowering shoots, 3 in (7.5 cm) long, from overwintered plants in early spring or from any mature plant in late summer. If the parent plant is to be grown on, too, slice cuttings just above a leaf node, trimming the cutting below another node later.

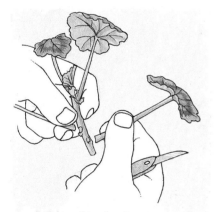

2 Carefully pull the leaves away from the lower part of the cutting. Each cutting needs only a couple of young, fully expanded leaves.

3 Gently tear away all the stipules — tiny leaflike structures at the base of the leaf stalk. If left, these can rot in the rooting medium and impair rooting.

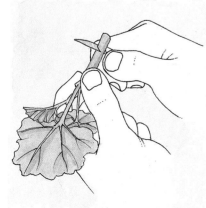

4 Trim the cutting right below a leaf node, making a very clean cut with a sharp knife or razor blade — ragged cuts can also cause rotting.

5 Press the cuttings gently into the rooting medium to just below the lowest leaf. Cover the pot with a plastic bag or put it in a propagation box.

a plastic bag. Bottom heat will promote rooting; a temperature of 64°F (18°C) is ideal. Mist-spray with tepid water and occasionally turn the plastic bag inside out.

The formation of new top growth is a sign of rooting; it takes about 3 weeks, or slightly longer for regal types. Young plants should then be potted on into a well-drained, manure-enriched potting soil.

Routine care

Regular pruning is not needed, but some zonal and ivy-leaved types produce one unbranched stem unless pinched back early. Deadhead regularly and snap off all yellowing or brown leaves.

During the growing season, let the soil dry out between thorough waterings.

Fertilizer requirements vary according to plant and soil type. Feed regals and fancy-leaved zonals weekly with a commercial tomato fertilizer. Also, spray occasionally with a solution of 8 tablespoons (200 ml) of Epsom salts to 2½ gallons (9.5 liters) of water to prevent magnesium deficiency, which causes yellowing between leaf veins. Zonal and ivy-leaved types require a liquid fertilizer with extra nitrogen — that is, a 2–1–1 ratio. Begin feeding actively growing plants about 10 weeks after potting up and every 10 to 14 days thereafter.

Lifting and overwintering

Either take cuttings in late summer and discard the parent plants in fall, or lift and store the plants for the winter and take cuttings from them in spring.

Lift bedding plants in midfall and put them in individual pots or several to a flat, packed with moist potting soil. Trim off the upper two-thirds of all shoots.

The safest place to overwinter the plants is in a greenhouse or frost-free sun-room, with a minimum temperature of 45°F (7°C).

Alternatively, trim each plant to a height of 6 in (15 cm) and strip off all the leaves. Shake the soil from the roots and bury the whole plant on its side, 6 in (15 cm) deep, in slightly moist potting soil. Store the plants this way in the corner of a cool, frost-free basement, shed, or garage. In early spring, put them in pots or use the new shoots as propagation material.

PANSIES AND VIOLAS

**Wherever you garden, be it a tub, a bed, or an edging,
grow several varieties to have a show of cheerful
pansies and violas for months on end.**

A gardener's favorite, the genus *Viola* consists of some 500 species of herbaceous perennials and annuals. All the cultivated species are perennial, though many pansies are short-lived and are treated as hardy or half-hardy annuals or biennials.

The flowers of both pansies and violas have a pair of upper petals, a pair of side petals, and one lower petal that extends backward as a hollow tube, or spur, in which nectar is secreted.

This sweet liquid is available only to insects with long tongues, such as bees and butterflies. In their efforts to reach the end of the spur, they pollinate the flower.

The lower and side petals of most species are streaked with dark lines that lead to the nectar source. Known as honey guides, these markings reflect the ultraviolet spectrum of sunlight, a sign to many pollinating insects.

Pansy, viola, and violet are the three common names for *Viola*.

Pansies are the large group of garden varieties and hybrids classified under the name *Viola × wittrockiana*. These have large flowers and are available in a wide color range — including shades of cream, yellow, orange, red, mauve, purple, or white.

Up to 4 in (10 cm) wide, pansy flowers are distinguished by prominent markings on their side and lower petals that suggest a small "face" — some look as though they are smiling at you, but others seem to scowl. The petals are rounded and overlap each other, forming an almost circular and rather flat flower that tends to face the sun. The nectar spur is short.

Borne on long stalks, pansy leaves are oval, with rounded marginal serrations. In addition to the true leaves, there are some lance-shaped, leaflike appendages, or *stipules*, at the base of each leaf stalk. These may be divided into several narrow lobes.

Pansies are most often grown for bedding displays. Seed-propagated plants are raised annually and are discarded after several months of flowering.

Violas are like small pansies, with flattish flowers consisting of rounded petals. Measuring about 1-2 in (2.5-5 cm) wide, viola flowers do not have bold face markings, but honey guides are present. Although their color range is as wide as that of the pansies, they tend to have softer shades. The smallest violas — with flowers about 1 in (2.5 cm) wide — are called violettas.

A loosely defined group, violas include varieties and hybrids chiefly of the species *V. cornuta* and *V. tricolor*. Many are hardy perennials that will persist for years, often building up large, thriving colonies. Because violas do not breed true from seed,

◄ **Large-flowered pansies** Available in single colors or mixed selections, pansies flower over a long period and are among the brightest additions to flower beds and containers.

Viola × wittrockiana
pansies

hybrid viola

Viola cornuta 'Alba'
horned violet

propagate them from cuttings.

Some pansies have been bred for pure flower color and so lack the typical face markings. As a result, there is confusion as to the distinction between a pansy and a viola. Purists favor violas because of their subtle coloring and compact habit. Lovers of bold colors prefer pansies, and there is no doubt that these showy plants belong in flower beds and container plantings.

Violets have quite a distinct, pleasing appearance. They produce smaller flowers than either pansies or violas — usually no more than 1 in (2.5 cm) wide. These have narrow petals that overlap only at their base. The nectar spur is well developed, forming a backward projection. Thus, violets have more three-dimensional blooms than the other two groups, and they tend to be nodding rather than upright.

The heart-shaped leaves of this attractive flower are borne on long stalks. Many species form a dense ground cover, spreading by prostrate stems, or *stolons,* and some even become uncontrollable — though pretty — weeds.

Scent is traditionally associated with violets, but it is only the sweet violet *(Viola odorata)* and its varieties that have a powerful fragrance. For centuries, an oil extracted from the flowers of the sweet violet has played an important role in scent making and food flavoring. The double-flowered varieties — Parma violets — are crystallized and used for food decoration. Many hybrid violas and pansies have a mild scent.

Choosing plants

For an annual flower bed, tub, or window box, the hybrid annual or biennial pansies *(Viola × wittrockiana)* are a handsome choice. Since these plants prefer cool, moist weather, they flower primarily in late spring and early summer in the North, though some new heat-tolerant strains, such as 'Water Colors' and 'Majestic Giants,' will provide color throughout the summer and into the fall. In the South, pansies may be set out in the fall to bloom in periods of milder weather during the winter.

There are many mixed-color pansy-seed strains that can be selected for the following characteristics: vigor, large flowers, prominence or absence of face markings, resistance to cold or heat, or tolerance of wet weather. Single-color selections are also available. F1 hybrids are the most uniform in height and growth habit; these factors make them the best (and the most expensive) choice for formal beds.

For edging a perennial bed or for pockets in a rock garden, choose any of the perennial viola hybrids, such as 'Arkwright Ruby,' 'Chantryland,' 'Irish Molly,' and 'Jersey Gem,' or any of the larger-flowered species, including *V. cornuta.*

The delightful, small wild pansy *V. tricolor* is also at home in a rock garden or amidst paving stones. It is one of the parents of the large-flowered modern pansy hybrids, with its tricolored flowers, ½-1 in (1-2.5 cm) wide, in shades of cream, yellow, reddish-purple, or blue. These blossoms bloom profusely from late spring until early fall. Though only annual in most gardens, this plant self-seeds readily. *V. tricolor* has acquired many common names, mostly derived from its value in old-fashioned love charms — heartsease, Johnny-jump-up, and love-in-idleness.

Several prostrate (creeping) violets make excellent ground cover. They include the marsh violet *(V. cucullata)*, with its small white-based violet flowers; the

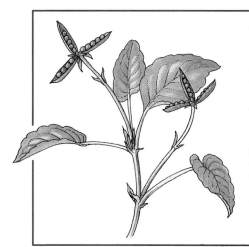

COLLECTING SEEDS

Pansies, violas, and violets can be grown from seeds that are collected from mature plants, but cultivars won't breed true. Each seed capsule consists of three boat-shaped pods. As the pods ripen they dry and shrink, squeezing the seeds. When the tension becomes too great, the pods split lengthwise and eject their contents. The seeds may be thrown up to 6 ft (1.8 m) from the plant. If you want to collect the seeds, harvest the capsules before they explode.

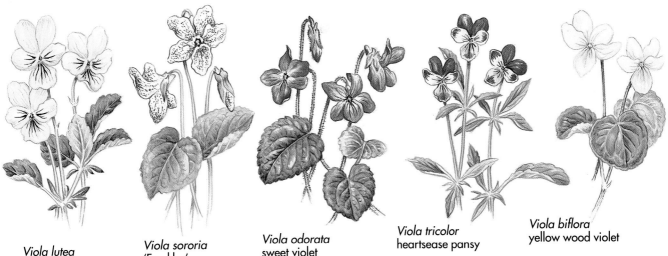

Viola lutea
mountain pansy

Viola sororia
'Freckles'
violet

Viola odorata
sweet violet

Viola tricolor
heartsease pansy

Viola biflora
yellow wood violet

violet-blue Australian violet *(V. hederacea);* the mauve-flowered *V. labradorica* 'Purple Leaf'; and *V. pedata,* the bird's-foot violet.

One of the daintiest violets of all is *V. sororia* 'Freckles' (sometimes listed under *V. septentrionalis).* Its very pale blue flowers are heavily spotted with purple.

Selecting the site

Most violas, violets, and pansies thrive in a sunny position, but they will generally tolerate semi-shade. Moist, well-drained soils are best for all but *V. labradorica,* which does well in dryish, shady sites. *V. cucullata,* on the other hand, likes wetter soil.

Violas can also be grown in an unheated greenhouse. Plant them in pans or troughs filled with a well-drained potting soil that has been enriched with organic material.

Growing from seed

Viola × wittrockiana and *V. tricolor* pansies are usually grown from seed each year. You can treat them as half-hardy annuals, hardy annuals, or hardy biennials, according to the time of year that you wish them to flower and therefore the time you sow them.

For winter flowers from zone 8 southward, sow pansy seeds during early summer to midsummer of the previous year. Use a sterilized seed-starting mix in a flat or shallow pot for germinating the seeds. At an ideal temperature of 65-75°F (18-24°C) germination takes 2 to 3 weeks, but higher temperatures may slow down the process in a cold frame.

Prick out the seedlings when they are big enough to handle. Space them 4 in (10 cm) apart in a shaded nursery bed, or put them into 3-in (7.5-cm) pots in a cold frame, then transplant them to their final site in early fall.

For summer-flowering pansies in the North, overwinter the young potted seedlings in a cold frame and plant them out in the flowering site in midspring to late spring. They can also be sown, as already described, in late winter or early spring indoors in moderate heat. Prick out the seedlings into flats of potting soil as soon as they are large enough to handle. Harden them off before transferring them to their flowering sites, where they will bloom the same year.

You can also sow seeds of *V. tricolor* and its varieties directly in their flowering site in early spring to midspring. Thin out seedlings as necessary; the plants will bloom the following year.

Taking cuttings

All *Viola* species can be propagated from cuttings. In midsummer, take cuttings, 1-2 in (2.5-5 cm) long, from nonflowering basal shoots. Insert them in flats of sterilized rooting medium and place in a cold frame or cool, sheltered spot. Keep them moist and shaded.

Transplant rooted cuttings to individual 3-in (7.5-cm) pots of potting soil. Plant them out in their flowering site between early fall and early spring.

Aftercare

Pansies, violas, and violets need little routine care and attention. Just water them well during dry

TAKING VIOLA CUTTINGS

1 With a sharp knife or razor blade, take cuttings, 1-2 in (2.5-5 cm) long, of strong, nonflowering basal shoots in midsummer.

2 Trim the bottom of each cutting below a node and strip off the lowest leaves. Dip the end of each cutting in a hormone rooting powder.

3 Insert the cuttings into the rooting medium in a flat or pots. Place in a sheltered, shaded spot. Once rooted, transplant to larger pots.

27

periods and deadhead frequently to extend the flowering season.

Pests and diseases

The plants may be infested with aphids, whose sticky honeydew secretions soil the leaves below the point of infestation, causing a black mold to develop. In dry weather, red spider mites may also become a problem. To control these two pests, spray plants with an insecticide containing malathion.

In moist conditions, slugs and snails may eat the foliage and must be deterred (p.60).

Fungal diseases, known as root and crown rot, may become endemic in soils where pansies have grown for several years. Typically, fungi enter the plants through their roots, causing the leaves to turn yellow and wilt, then the roots and stem bases to rot. Finally, the top growth collapses. While you can drench the soil with a recommended fungicide, an easier solution is to plant your pansies in a different site each year.

▲ **Perennial violas** The dainty, pure colors of these violas make them ideal for colonizing at the front of flower beds, along the edges of paths, and in pockets in a rock garden.

▼ **Violet ground cover** Clumps of heart-shaped leaves, a free-flowering habit, and the ability to spread rapidly make violets a great ground cover for moist, semishaded, or sunny spots.

POPULAR IMPATIENS

Although their ability to bloom in the shade has made impatiens America's favorite annual, many cultivars succeed just as splendidly in a sunny spot.

While other flowers compete for a place in the sun, impatiens is content to fill shady spots with color. (Given adequate irrigation, it also performs well in areas of medium sun.) Its popularity stems from the fact that many strains thrive at the base of a shade tree or on the north side of a house. The blossoms, which come in soft pastels or vibrant tropical hues, are the perfect choice for brightening up a planting of hostas or ferns. The New Guinea types also produce brilliantly variegated foliage that contributes color to the garden even when they are not in bloom.

Choosing cultivars

Although many species are perennial, impatiens are extremely sensitive to frost, and so are usually grown as annuals. These succulent-stemmed, branching plants bear broad, pointed leaves and spurred single or double flowers that are up to 3 in (7.5 cm) wide. There are about 850 species of impatiens worldwide, but the cultivated types belong to three groups.

Impatiens wallerana, called "patience plant," or "sultana," ranges in height from 6-24 in (15-60 cm) and forms a compact or spreading mound of leaves and flowers, 1-2 in (2.5-5 cm) wide. The latter may be single or fully double, as in the aptly named 'Rosebud' strain; sultanas serve equally well as bedding plants or as fillers for hanging baskets.

New Guinea impatiens produces very showy flowers (white, and shades of pink, red, and lavender) as well as bold foliage of bronze or green striped with cream or red. Too bright for mass plantings, these impatiens work best as accent points or container plantings and appreciate several hours of direct sunlight.

I. balsamina, or "garden balsam," is an upright plant, suitable for bedding or for a mixed shady border. The stems reach a height of 24-30 in (60-85 cm), with flowers 1-2 in (2.5-5 cm) wide at the bases of the uppermost leaves.

Starting from seed

Start *I. wallerana* seeds 8 to 10 weeks and *I. balsamina* 6 weeks before the last expected frost. Sow them into a flat of sterile seed-starting mix, then cover seeds with a thin layer of vermiculite. Water and set in a propagation box, or cover the flat with a clear plastic top or bag. Maintaining even moisture is crucial for germination. Put the flat in a spot that receives indirect light on a heating cable or mat that

◄ **Hybrids** of the species *Impatiens wallerana,* or "patience plant," flourish in spots where no other bedding plant would, and provide a lively alternative to pachysandra, ivies, and other shade-tolerant ground covers.

will keep the soil between 70-75°F (21-24°C). Once seedlings begin to appear, remove the cover and place them in an area of strong but filtered light. A fluorescent-lit plant-growth unit is ideal, since it provides warmth and aeration. Most New Guinea impatiens are propagated by cuttings, but a few recent cultivars such as 'Tango' and 'Spectra' may be grown from seed.

Aftercare

Plant the seedlings in a compost-enriched, well-drained soil, spacing them 9-12 in (22-30 cm) apart, depending on the vigor of the cultivar. Protect roots with a layer of organic mulch. Proper watering is critical to impatiens. Water them deeply and regularly in hot weather. Impatiens signal their thirst with flagging leaves.

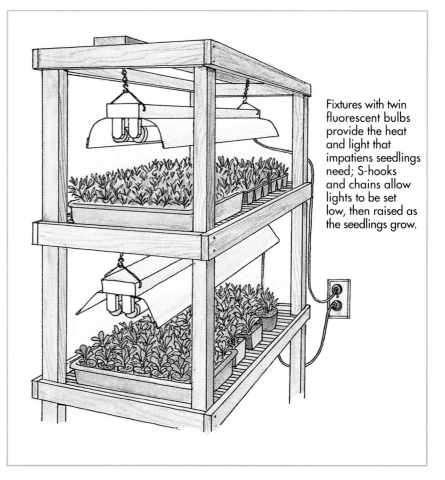

Fixtures with twin fluorescent bulbs provide the heat and light that impatiens seedlings need; S-hooks and chains allow lights to be set low, then raised as the seedlings grow.

▼ **Compact 'Super Elfin' hybrids** reach a height of just 10 in (25 cm) but cover themselves with flowers throughout the summer. Here, the blossoms in many different shades turn a shaded garden into a soft patchwork quilt.

LIVELY PETUNIAS

With their bold trumpet-shaped blooms in a rainbow of colors, petunias star in hanging baskets and beds, and provide good ground cover.

▲ **'Cascade' petunias** spill over the border of a path, softening the masonry's hard edge. The sprawling growth of this series of grandiflora hybrids also makes it an excellent ground cover for steep banks.

▼ **In summer's heat,** most flowers do poorly in a hanging basket. Petunias have a high tolerance for drought, which makes them an outstanding choice for this type of display.

There is no better advertisement for the plant breeder's art than the modern petunia. Its ancestors are a pair of Argentinean wildflowers, two modest plants not much more glamorous than their relative the potato. A century and a half of crossbreeding has produced a summer-garden favorite.

Hundreds of cultivars offer a rainbow of color — in every hue except bright yellow and orange — and a variety of flower forms. Their versatility makes them ideal for every type of planting from a cottage garden to a formal bed. There are also trailing petunias that are perfect for hanging baskets and sturdy, weather-resistant multifloras that are great as ground cover for steep banks. In the desert Southwest, petunias may be planted in the fall to provide color in the winter. Though petunias' fragrance is faint during the day, it gains strength at twilight and fills the summer night with perfume. (Some are more fragrant than others.) As a group, petunias retain much of their wild ancestors' vigor and adaptability. Although some overbred types are slightly temperamental, in general, petunias are among the easiest and most resilient of flowers to grow.

Petunia hybrida, the cultivated form of the flower, is a freely branching, weak-stemmed plant covered with fine, sticky hairs. Usually grown as an annual, it is a perennial in the extreme southern part of the United States, where a single plant may flourish for years. Blossoms, developed one to a stem from leaf axils (the points where the leaves join the stalks), are typically trumpet-shaped, though there are double forms with carnationlike blooms as well as ruffle-edged flowers. Their pattern of coloration varies dramatically, from solid to striped and streaked flowers, to trumpets of red, rose, blue, or purple edged in white (picotees).

Petunia classification

Nurserymen use the size of the flower to divide petunias into two broad classes.

Grandifloras, as the name suggests, have the largest blossoms, up to 4½ in (11.5 cm) wide. Their stems are lax and have a sprawling habit of growth, which is particularly marked in the 'Cascade' series of hybrids. When grandifloras are in full bloom, the flowers present a waterfall of color. Grandifloras are the petunias of choice for hanging baskets and look particularly fine when planted alongside the border of a walk or a flight of steps where the blossoms can spill over the edge of the masonry.

The second major group of

petunias, multifloras, produces flowers that are more abundant and smaller (about 2 in/5 cm wide) than grandifloras. Multifloras tend to be bushier, more compact plants and are better suited for use in bedding and other mass plantings. They are also more resistant to damage from rain and Botrytis disease, which wet weather can bring, and will continue to bloom well in conditions that flatten the grandifloras' larger and more delicate flowers.

Choosing the site

Because petunias are so adaptable, they will grow almost wherever you set them. But unless your choice of sites meets a couple of requirements, the plants will not bloom satisfactorily. Any fertile garden soil is fine for petunias, as long as it is reasonably loose and well drained. The plants will not perform well in heavy, wet soils. In addition, avoid excessively rich soils, as they will foster foliar growth at the expense of flowering. In the North, set the plants in a site that receives direct sunlight throughout most of the day; in the South, select a spot that is lightly shaded.

Starting from seed

Growing petunias from seed requires extra patience and attention to detail. As a result, many gardeners prefer to purchase their petunias as ready-to-plant seedlings at a garden center. Still, starting from seed greatly increases the choice of cultivars, since a garden center rarely offers more than a handful of the most popular selections. If you want to grow any of the many interesting but less common cultivars, you will have to start your own plants.

If you start petunias from seed, you must plan ahead. It takes 8 to 10 weeks to bring petunias from seed to the stage where they are ready for transplanting outdoors. So if you want to begin planting in the middle of May, you must sow the seeds in late January or early February.

Petunia seeds are very tiny — about 285,000 make up an ounce (gram) — and so are difficult to handle. To make sowing easier, mix the seed with fine sand that is dry and clean. Then, sprinkle

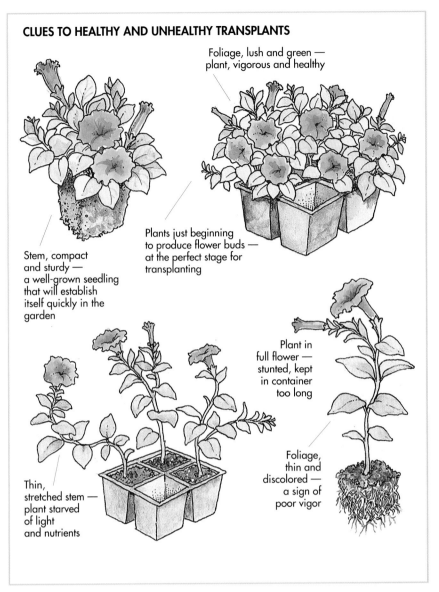

CLUES TO HEALTHY AND UNHEALTHY TRANSPLANTS

Foliage, lush and green — plant, vigorous and healthy

Plants just beginning to produce flower buds — at the perfect stage for transplanting

Stem, compact and sturdy — a well-grown seedling that will establish itself quickly in the garden

Plant in full flower — stunted, kept in container too long

Thin, stretched stem — plant starved of light and nutrients

Foliage, thin and discolored — a sign of poor vigor

it over the surface of a flat filled with finely sifted, sterilized seed-starting mix, or with sterilized potting soil topped with a layer of milled sphagnum moss. Do not bury the seed; just press it gently into the seed-sowing medium. After sowing, set the flat in a shallow pan of water, letting the moisture rise up through the soil by means of capillary action. (Do not, however, use a hose or a watering can, as either is liable to wash the seed away.) Cover the flat with a clear top (a pane of glass or plastic bag or wrap) and set it in a warm place (such as on the top of the kitchen refrigerator) where the soil will remain at a temperature of about 70-80°F (20-27°C). The seedlings should appear within 8 to 10 days, at which time you should uncover the flat and move it to a well-lit, warm windowsill where temperatures are 60-65°F/16-18°C during the day and 50-55°F/10-13°C at night. Be sure to keep the soil

evenly moist, but not too wet.

Aftercare

Plant out petunias after all danger of frost is past, setting them 7-10 in (18-25 cm) apart. At this time, pinch back the tips of the seedlings' stems to encourage branching and compact growth. Feed monthly with a complete fertilizer at the rate recommended on the product label. Water deeply and as often as once a week in hot, dry weather. Deadhead the plants to prolong and increase blooming. If the plants flag and lose vigor after the first flush of flowers fades, cut them back to force new growth.

Pests and diseases

Petunias are susceptible to several viral diseases, which are often spread by aphids. To avoid the tobacco mosaic virus, refrain from smoking around the plants. If you smoke, wash your hands before touching the plants or beds.

Herbaceous perennials

For many gardeners, the most satisfying way of adding color and variety to the garden is to create a mixed border. This type of planting scheme, which includes permanent shrubs as well as plants that die back every winter, has taken over from the old-fashioned herbaceous (purely flower) bed.

The mixed border almost always contains certain perennials whose popularity never fades. Year after year, they appear on catalog covers, remain best sellers in garden centers, and grace gardens everywhere. Among the best-loved examples are tall blue and white delphiniums, exquisite bowl-shaped maroon peonies — which can have a life-span of 50 years or more — and pastel-colored pinks, with their cottage-garden charm.

Whether these perennials produce stunning blooms, inferior ones, or none at all frequently depends upon the gardener's knowledge. Do certain plants prefer sun or shade, for example, or damp or dry soil? When perfect plants develop in your garden, it is often the result of just a few minutes' well-timed work.

In order to show the vibrant colors and individual shapes of flowering perennials to their best advantage, however, it is important to provide a relaxing green background of carefully chosen foliage perennials. They are as versatile as flowering plants, and they come in almost as wide a selection. The elegant hosta, for example, takes an infinite variety of forms, with luxuriant, often variegated foliage. And ferns have almost as many enthusiastic supporters now as in their Victorian heyday; keep them in mind, especially for shady areas. To lend airy touches to compact plant groupings, consider using the graceful ornamental grasses that florists have long found invaluable for their arrangements.

Fall glory Popular late-flowering border perennials include the double-spray chrysanthemums.

GARDEN CHRYSANTHEMUMS

**Chrysanthemums owe their popularity
to the tremendous diversity of size, form, and color they
bring to the late-summer and fall garden.**

In recent years botanists have reclassified many plants traditionally regarded as chrysanthemums — thus, they now may appear with unfamiliar names, such as *Dendranthemas* or *Leucanthemums*. For the gardener's purposes, however, the plants haven't changed, and they will be treated together here in their traditional grouping, though identified according to the new system.

Annual chrysanthemums, which produce single, semidouble, or double flowers, often with beautiful rings or zones of color, are all grown from seed. They include tricolor chrysanthemums *(Ismelia carinatum)*, garland chrysanthemums *(C. coronarium)*, and feverfew *(Tanacetum parthenium)*.

Among the hardy perennials are the white-flowered Shasta daisy *(Leucanthemum × superbum)* and pyrethrums *(Tanacetum coccineum)*, which have pink, red, or white daisylike flowers.

Korean hybrid chrysanthemums *(Dendranthema)* are half-hardy perennials with single or semidouble flowers, usually grown as dwarf bushes that reach about 2 ft (60 cm) tall. They can overwinter outdoors as far north as zone 4.

Florist's chrysanthemums *(Dendranthema × grandiflora)* are grown principally for cut flowers and for exhibition. Pinch back their tips and buds to increase bushiness and blossoms. Varieties that flower in the open before midfall are known as "early flowering." Those that bloom after the frosts have begun are "late flowering." In cold-weather areas, these should be moved indoors in the fall.

"Cushion" chrysanthemums are bushy plants covered with masses of starlike flowers. They are commonly treated as annuals, grown in pots or in a nursery bed during summer, then transplanted to flower beds in early fall for an instant display.

Garden preparations

Rich soil is essential for chrysanthemums — separate beds make it easier to prepare the soil and carry out seasonal jobs.

Choose a site that is well drained, sunny, and sheltered from strong winds. Dig the plot thoroughly in the fall, incorporating a bucketful of well-composted manure or garden compost together with a handful of bone meal per sq yd/sq m. Allow winter frosts to break down the soil.

In midspring, spread a dressing of general-purpose fertilizer, such as 5–10–5, at a rate of one handful per sq yd/sq m and fork it into the top 3 in (7.5 cm) of soil.

Buying young plants

Plants delivered from a mail-order nursery usually arrive in early spring to midspring, though late-spring delivery is acceptable. Generally, these are individually wrapped in plastic to prevent loss of moisture. However, if the roots are dry, stand the chrysanthemums in water overnight.

Plant them in flats or individually in 3-in (7.5-cm) pots partially filled with equal parts loam, peat, and builder's sand. Space the plants 3 in (7.5 cm) apart and spread out the roots. Cover with more soil, press the soil around the plant, then water gently.

If you have a greenhouse, keep the potted plants on the floor,

◀ **Spray chrysanthemums** In late summer and early fall, the group known as florist's chrysanthemums produces lovely sprays of single or semidouble flowers in warm shades of white, cream, yellow, orange, bronze, red, pink, and purple.

dampening the floor in hot weather to increase humidity. After a few days, move the chrysanthemums onto benches and shade them from strong sun. Harden the plants off in a cold frame before planting them out.

Alternatively, put the flats or pots in a cold frame or sun-room. For the first few days, spray them periodically with water if the weather is warm, and protect them from bright sun.

After a week, you may allow the plants full light. Open a window or lift the top of the cold frame slightly on warm days to give the plants fresh air, but close the window or frame cover at night. Keep plants just moist — do not overwater them.

By late spring, open the window or frame fully, shutting it only when a frost is forecast. Unfortunately, birds may nip the growing tips of plants set in an outdoor frame. You can deter them by suspending a tent of plastic garden netting over the frame. If planting has to be delayed due to bad weather, apply a weak liquid fertilizer to the actively growing plants.

Planting out
In late spring, the chrysanthemums will be ready for planting out. Insert stakes, about 4-5 ft (1.2-1.5 m) long, at each planting position, allowing 15-18 in (38-45 cm) between plants.

With a trowel, make a hole

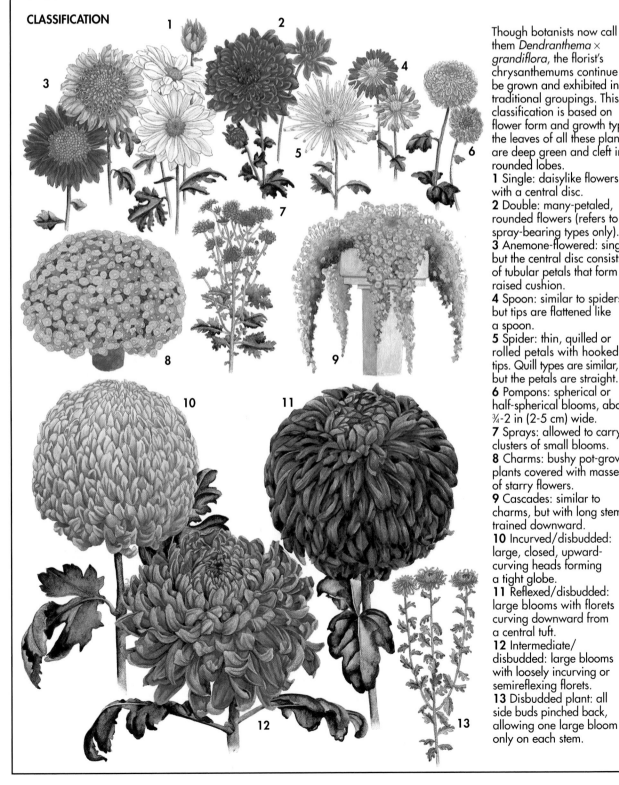

CLASSIFICATION

Though botanists now call them *Dendranthema × grandiflora*, the florist's chrysanthemums continue to be grown and exhibited in traditional groupings. This classification is based on flower form and growth type; the leaves of all these plants are deep green and cleft into rounded lobes.

1 Single: daisylike flowers with a central disc.

2 Double: many-petaled, rounded flowers (refers to spray-bearing types only).

3 Anemone-flowered: single, but the central disc consists of tubular petals that form a raised cushion.

4 Spoon: similar to spiders, but tips are flattened like a spoon.

5 Spider: thin, quilled or rolled petals with hooked tips. Quill types are similar, but the petals are straight.

6 Pompons: spherical or half-spherical blooms, about ¾-2 in (2-5 cm) wide.

7 Sprays: allowed to carry clusters of small blooms.

8 Charms: bushy pot-grown plants covered with masses of starry flowers.

9 Cascades: similar to charms, but with long stems trained downward.

10 Incurved/disbudded: large, closed, upward-curving heads forming a tight globe.

11 Reflexed/disbudded: large blooms with florets curving downward from a central tuft.

12 Intermediate/disbudded: large blooms with loosely incurving or semireflexing florets.

13 Disbudded plant: all side buds pinched back, allowing one large bloom only on each stem.

close to the stake that is slightly larger than the root ball. Place the plant in the hole with as much of its root ball intact as possible, then press in and cover with 1 in (2.5 cm) of soil.

Tie the stems loosely to the stakes with string or paper- or plastic-covered wire ties. Water only if the soil is dry. Watch out for slugs and protect young plants against cutworms by encircling the base of the stems with cardboard or foil collars.

Aftercare

As the chrysanthemums grow, continue to tie them to their stakes. Starting in early summer, fertilize them every 10 days until the first flower buds develop. Use a liquid fertilizer in dry weather.

Water plants thoroughly once a week in dry weather. Overhead sprinkling is fine during the summer, but do not wet the chrysanthemums' foliage in the fall, as that can cause mildew.

Pinching In late spring or very early summer, pinch back the growing tip of the main stem just above the first pair of fully developed leaves. Side shoots will appear from the main stem at the leaf axils. It is on these shoots, known as *breaks*, that the flowers will develop. Pinching is a means of increasing the speed with which the plant produces flower-bearing side shoots.

As the breaks grow, pinch back those that are not required, one at a time, over a few days, until only the desired number remain. Six to eight breaks are sufficient for cut flowers, and two to three for exhibition-quality blossoms.

Retain those breaks that are neither excessively weak nor too thin. These will then be of equal thickness and length. During the summer, the remaining breaks will themselves form side shoots. Remove these shoots from the leaf axils without damaging the rest of the plant.

Do not pinch back spray-type chrysanthemums a second time. Most early-flowering types give good results if the growing tips are pinched back just once, when the plants are 9 in (23 cm) high.

Disbudding A flower bud forms at the tip of each shoot soon after midsummer. Known as the crown bud, it is surrounded by smaller buds or shoots. To avoid the creation of a cluster of small,

PLANTING YOUNG CHRYSANTHEMUMS

1 Half-fill flats, 3 in (7.5 cm) deep, with potting soil. Spread out each plant's roots, then fill in with more soil. Or, plant individually in small pots.

2 Keep plants indoors in a sunny, cool location and spray with water in warm weather. Guard against insect pests that can spread viral diseases.

3 Replant outdoors in late spring. In early summer, encourage flowering side shoots by pinching back each plant's growing tip just above the first pair of fully developed leaves.

4 Tie each plant loosely to a wooden stake with garden string or ties. Label each variety clearly. Protect against slugs; also apply a granular or liquid fertilizer every 10 days.

inferior blooms, you must pinch back all of the smaller buds, one at a time, over several days. The buds should show color by late summer.

Cutting the blooms

If you intend to cut blooms for indoor display, give the plants a good watering. Cut them the following morning while the stems still contain a lot of moisture.

With pruning shears, cut about 2 ft (60 cm) below the bloom. Strip the leaves from the bottom half of the stem. Stand the flowers immediately in a deep vase of water and leave for 24 hours in a cool, shady place.

Lifting for winter

To preserve plants through cold winters, and to guarantee a good source of cuttings for the spring,

store roots and stem bases under cover in a cool, frost-free place. First, leave the chrysanthemums in their beds until midfall and then cut the stems down to 9 in (23 cm). Lift the plants with a garden fork, cut away all the new basal growth, and remove the top layer of soil. Place these clumps in labeled boxes.

Cover these clumps — roots and stems — with potting soil. Lightly water them before moving them to a greenhouse, cold frame, or sun porch. Keep it cool, but not freezing. Water the soil only when it dries out.

In late winter, raise the temperature to about 45°F (7°C) and increase watering slightly to rouse plants from dormancy and encourage the growth of new shoots. These will become the perfect material for cuttings.

LIFTING AND OVERWINTERING

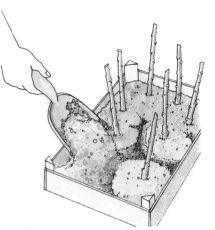

1 About a week after blooms have faded, cut down stems to 9 in (23 cm). Using a garden fork, loosen the soil around the roots, then lift the bases of the plants along with their root balls.

2 With pruning shears, cut off all new basal growth at ground level. (It will wither as the plant enters dormancy.) Remove the top layer of soil, easing it out from the roots with your fingers.

3 Put the plants in labeled boxes, pack with potting soil, and lightly water to settle the soil. Store in a cool, frost-free spot, such as a cold frame or sun porch.

Taking cuttings

If you have a heated propagation box, take cuttings in very late winter; in an unheated cold frame or sun porch, take cuttings about a month later.

Fill a seed flat or 3-in (7.5-cm) pots with a rooting medium composed of equal parts peat moss and sharp builder's sand. Sprinkle a layer of fine sand on top, then press down gently.

Remove basal shoots from the sprouting clumps — ideally when the shoots are 2½-3 in (6-7.5 cm) long — but cuttings from longer growth will also work. If there is no basal growth, you can take cuttings from the main stem, but these tend to bud prematurely.

Trim the cuttings carefully, then dip the bases in hormone rooting powder before pushing them into the rooting medium to a depth of 1 in (2.5 cm). Space them 1½-2 in (3.5-5 cm) apart, or four to a pot. Top with a layer of clean builder's sand. Settle in with a fine spray of water, which will wash the sand down.

Place the cuttings in the propagation box (or return to the cold frame or sun porch). Water again only if the rooting medium dries out and be sure to provide shading from strong spring sun. If cuttings droop in warm weather, spray gently with water.

Rooting takes about 10 days in a heated propagation box, or 4 to 5 weeks in a cold frame. When rooted, lift the plants and move them into larger pots or deeper boxes. Plant them out as you would nursery plants.

TAKING CUTTINGS

1 In early spring, remove new basal shoots, which should be 2½-3 in (6-7.5 cm) long, from overwintered plants (above). If there are no basal shoots, take cuttings from the main stem.

2 Trim off the lower leaves very carefully, without tearing the skin on the stem. Damaged tissues are more susceptible to attack by fatal damping-off disease.

3 With a sharp blade, cut straight across the stem immediately below one of the nodes from which a leaf has been removed. The cutting should now be 1½-2 in (3.5-5 cm) long.

4 Dip the bases in rooting powder, then insert the cuttings in a flat of rooting medium and cover with builder's sand. Water, then place in a spot with bright, but indirect light. Mist periodically.

PRIMULAS AND POLYANTHUS

Gems of spring, primulas offer sparkling color for every shaded situation, from borders and rock gardens to waterside and windowsill.

More than 500 species of *Primula* are known; these are mostly native to temperate regions in the Northern Hemisphere. A large number of primulas are suitable for gardens, while a few perform well as houseplants, too.

The hardy garden primulas consist of alpine species, ideal for rock gardens, and border types, which are better adapted to bedding or planting among other flowers, especially in a woodland setting. Both the alpine and border types require a humus-rich, well-drained but moist soil. There are also several species, sometimes called "waterside primulas," that have a special need for moisture. These perform best when planted at the edge of a pond or stream, in a bog garden, or at some other site where the soil remains continually moist.

None of these primula types can tolerate the heat of full sun in summer. Nor can they bear dry soil or the extreme fluctuations of soil moisture during the growing season. As a result, only a few species (notably *P. obconica* and *P. sinensis*) succeed in areas of hot and humid summers.

Primulas do best in regions of mild, moist summers, such as the Pacific Northwest, the coastal Northeast, or the upper Midwest, though with attentive irrigation they may flourish in such high-elevation areas as Denver.

Primulas are, however, quite cold hardy. The polyanthus types are generally winter hardy through zone 3.

Planted in a hospitable site, primulas tend to be reliable, relatively carefree sources of spring color. With the onset of summer, they become semidormant. They resume growth with the return of moist, cool weather in the fall, when they cover the soil with an attractive carpet of crinkled, dark green leaves before their winter sleep. The genus includes the primrose and the cowslip, from which the polyanthus is bred.

Classification

The botanical classification of the genus *Primula* is rather complex. Some 30 categories (or sections) are recognized. Each one is made up of primulas with similar physical and genetic features, although the distinctions are not always immediately obvious to the casual observer. However, each section has similar requirements for soil type, planting position, and routine maintenance.

Most primulas are small perennials with a tufted clump or rosette of fresh green leaves and five-petaled flowers in clusters or on single stalks. The arrangement of the flowers is an important characteristic in the classification, as is the presence of a whitish powdery coating on the leaves and stalks, known as

▼ **Polyanthus primulas** Offsprings of the wild primrose and cowslip, polyanthus primulas are happy in moist soil and dappled shade.

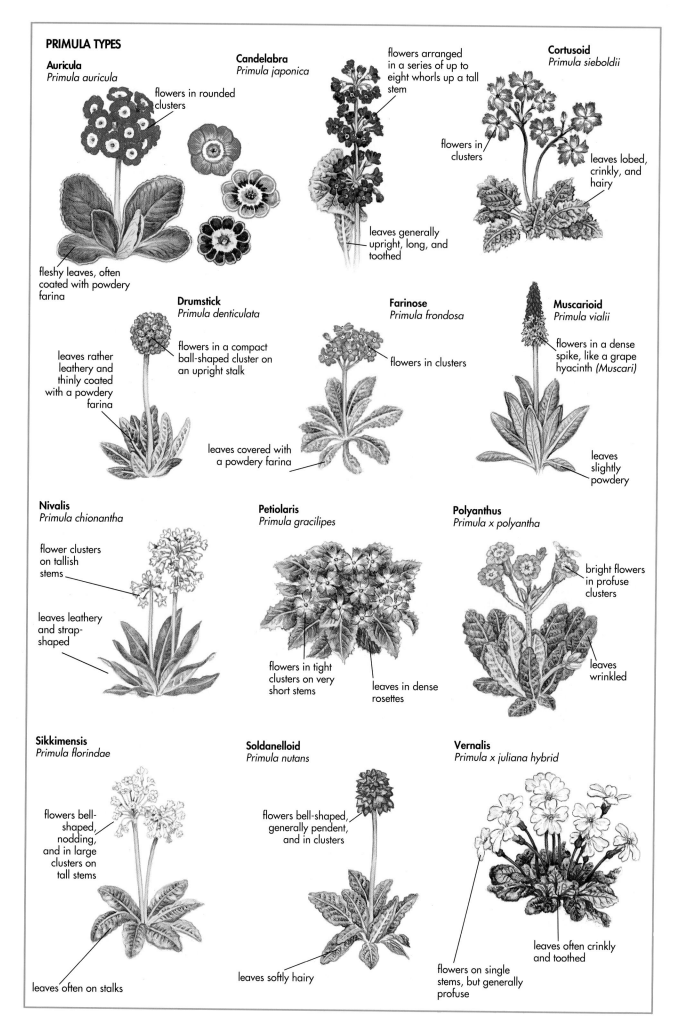

PRIMULA TYPES

Auricula
Primula auricula

flowers in rounded clusters

fleshy leaves, often coated with powdery farina

Candelabra
Primula japonica

flowers arranged in a series of up to eight whorls up a tall stem

leaves generally upright, long, and toothed

Cortusoid
Primula sieboldii

flowers in clusters

leaves lobed, crinkly, and hairy

Drumstick
Primula denticulata

leaves rather leathery and thinly coated with a powdery farina

flowers in a compact ball-shaped cluster on an upright stalk

Farinose
Primula frondosa

flowers in clusters

leaves covered with a powdery farina

Muscarioid
Primula vialii

flowers in a dense spike, like a grape hyacinth (*Muscari*)

leaves slightly powdery

Nivalis
Primula chionantha

flower clusters on tallish stems

leaves leathery and strap-shaped

Petiolaris
Primula gracilipes

flowers in tight clusters on very short stems

leaves in dense rosettes

Polyanthus
Primula x polyantha

bright flowers in profuse clusters

leaves wrinkled

Sikkimensis
Primula florindae

flowers bell-shaped, nodding, and in large clusters on tall stems

leaves often on stalks

Soldanelloid
Primula nutans

flowers bell-shaped, generally pendent, and in clusters

leaves softly hairy

Vernalis
Primula x juliana hybrid

leaves often crinkly and toothed

flowers on single stems, but generally profuse

farina (the Latin word for flour). The primulas that carry this coating are described as *farinose.*

Growing border primulas

Popular border and bog primulas belong mostly to the Candelabra, Drumstick, and Sikkimensis groups. These are the tallest garden primula species, thriving in suitable climates in any fertile soil that does not dry out in spring or summer.

Candelabra primulas include *Primula beesiana, P. bulleyana, P. japonica,* and *P. pulverulenta.* They are distinguished by flowers that are borne in up to eight rings, or whorls, up the stem. These, along with the drumstick primula *P. denticulata,* are best grown in a shady spot or a woodland setting, especially by a pool or stream.

Sikkimensis primulas have showy bell-shaped flowers that tend to nod or hang downward in large clusters at the top of a single sturdy stalk. They include the giant cowslip *(P. florindae)* and the Himalayan cowslip *(P. sikkimensis).* Both have yellow flowers and make good ground cover on moist, or even wet, soils.

Plant border primulas in midfall or early spring. Break up the soil thoroughly before planting, using a garden fork, and work in plenty of leaf mold and well-decayed manure, with a dressing of organic fertilizer.

Keep the soil moist in dry weather. Apply a mulch each spring to retain as much soil moisture as possible. Plants need little routine care, other than to deadhead them. This removal may encourage a second flush of flowers, and will prevent self-seeding and cross-pollination, which is of particular concern with invasive primulas.

If you provide primulas with an environment that they like, though, the plants may surround themselves with offsets (smaller plantlets) by their second spring. This competition will detract from the parent's bloom. To prevent this situation, lift the whole clump once the flowers have faded and separate the plants. Then return the parent to its original site and use the offsets to colonize new areas.

Growing alpine primulas

In general, the alpine primulas do best in a rock garden or in a similar place with well-drained gritty soil that has plenty of humus. Plant the alpines in fall or early spring, in partial shade or full sun. Each of the major types of alpine primulas has slightly different preferences.

Auricula primroses, such as *P. marginata* and *P. × pubescens,* typically have meal-coated leaves and rounded flower clusters; they prefer rich, moist but very well drained soil in light shade. The species-type, yellow-flowered *P. auricula* is usually grown outdoors. However, there are a number of named selections and cultivars that succeed as windowsill plants, if given a cool but brightly lit spot and a well-drained, peat- or compost-enriched, sandy potting soil.

Cortusoid primulas, such as *P. sieboldii,* have crinkly lobed leaves and need a light, humus-rich, permanently moist soil in a lightly shaded site. Similarly, the farinose types, such as *P. frondosa* and *P. rosea,* also enjoy a cool, moist position in light shade or sun; the latter even thrives in boggy soils.

Soldanelloid primulas, such as *P. nutans,* with clusters of bell-shaped flowers, are harder to cultivate since they like moist, peaty soils with a gritty texture and prefer a cool, semishaded site. Alternatively, grow them indoors or in a shaded cold frame.

Vernalis primulas (better known as primroses), such as *P. × juliana* hybrids, *P. veris,* and *P. vulgaris,* and Muscarioid primulas, such as the summer-flowering *P. vialii,* also favor cool, light shade and do well in light, humus-rich soils.

Vernalis types are best divided regularly to avoid overcrowding. For very well drained soils in cool semishade, Nivalis primulas, including *P. chionantha,* and the Petiolaris primulas, such as *P. gracilipes* and *P. whitei,* are ideal choices, provided the soil is given plenty of humus.

Propagation

Most garden primulas can be propagated by division after they have flowered. Plant the divisions directly into their flowering positions. Division is suitable for *P. denticulata, P. × juliana, P. rosea, P. florindae,* and *P. japonica.*

Primulas, especially the named

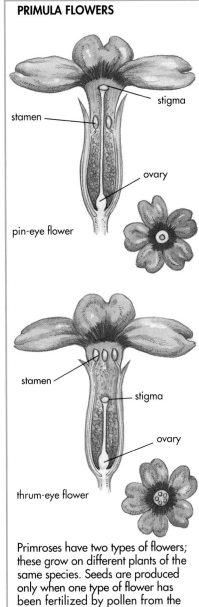

PRIMULA FLOWERS

stigma

stamen

ovary

pin-eye flower

stamen

stigma

ovary

thrum-eye flower

Primroses have two types of flowers; these grow on different plants of the same species. Seeds are produced only when one type of flower has been fertilized by pollen from the other type of flower. The structure of the two flowers is neatly arranged so that foraging long-tongued bees and other insects will transfer pollen from the correct stamens to the correct stigma.

cultivars, can also be propagated from cuttings taken during summer. Take cuttings, 1-2 in (2.5-5 cm) long, of dwarf, mat-forming, or tufted species, such as *P. marginata, P. minima,* and *P. auricula,* from early summer to late summer. Put them in a pot or flat of well-drained, organic-enriched potting soil, and place in a cold frame, or cover them with a clear plastic bag supported on a wire frame and keep in a cool, shaded spot. When rooted, transplant individually into 3-in (7.5-cm) pots containing the same type of potting mix. Plant out in permanent flowering positions the following spring or fall.

▲ **Candelabra primulas** These tall, vibrantly colored primulas flower in early summer. They thrive in moist soils, spreading by self-sown seedlings.

Close examination of a tufted or mat-forming primula usually reveals small shoots that can be detached with a few of their own roots. Potted up and grown like cuttings, they will develop into flowering-size plants quickly.

The remaining species can be increased successfully from seeds, although named cultivars will not breed true. However, the seeds must be sown as soon as they are ripe, usually from late spring to early fall, or when they are purchased. Sow them in flats or pots of moistened seed-starting mix in a cold frame or in a cool but frost-free spot indoors or in the garden. If you rinse the seeds in cold water before sowing them, it may improve germination, since they are often coated with a natural germination inhibitor. Old seeds are very difficult to germinate.

Do not cover the seeds with soil; just press them into the surface. Then cover each flat with a sheet of glass or plastic to conserve humidity — a step that is particularly important for the moisture-loving border primulas.

Don't worry if the seeds haven't germinated by fall. Leave the pots or flats uncovered in the garden over the winter, and the effects of cold weather will probably stimulate germination the following spring. Some primula species may take 2 years to germinate. After germination, remove the cover. Keep the soil moist and the seedlings lightly shaded, as one day of hot sun will kill them.

When the seedlings are large enough to handle, prick them out into flats of sterilized, organic-enriched, well-drained potting soil. Once the plants outgrow the flats, set the border and large-growing species in nursery rows outdoors, and pot up the dwarf species singly into pots, 2-3½ in (5-9 cm) deep, of the same type of potting soil and then plunge them up to their rims in a moist bed outdoors. This will prevent the primulas from drying out. Set the plants in their permanent positions in early fall or the following spring.

Bedding polyanthuses
Polyanthuses (polyanthus primroses) are a group of garden hybrids derived from several primula species, principally *Primula vulgaris* (primrose) and *P. veris* (cowslip). Mixed-color strains in-variably include almost every color, even blue, a rarity among garden plants. They may be pastels or vivid shades, and bicolors or tricolors, with a bright yellow eye (occasionally there is no eye). Polyanthus flowers differ from those of the true primrose as they grow in bold, tight clusters on a strong single stem, rather than singly on individual stems.

Polyanthuses are short-lived semievergreen perennials that are suited to planting along a woodland path. They combine nicely with hostas, but also show off in borders with other spring bloomers, such as bleeding hearts, grape hyacinths, forget-me-nots, and trilliums. Many strains are also lovely for pots.

Unlike most primulas, polyanthuses thrive in heavy soils, provided they don't get waterlogged in winter. They flourish in a humus-rich, woodland-type soil. For best results, fork in generous amounts of leaf mold and composted manure, as much as half a wheelbarrow-load for every square yard (meter) of bed.

Plants can be bought already started in containers from a nursery or can be raised from seed. Sow seeds shallowly in flats of seed-starting mix (just press them into the surface) in a cold frame or cool but frost-free windowsill from early spring to midsummer. Shade them from direct sun; if the soil dries out or gets too hot, germinating seedlings will die. The temperature should not exceed 55-60°F (13-15°C).

Prick out seedlings into flats when they are large enough to handle and grow them on in a cool, shaded location, giving them plenty of ventilation during warm weather. Transplant to a flowering site in early fall to midfall. Water them well and watch out for slugs and snails, which can devour polyanthus plants.

Don't allow fallen leaves to smother the plants in fall. To improve the flower color and quality, spread potash-rich wood ash (from the fireplace) over polyanthus and primula beds.

Slugs are the primulas' greatest enemy. If not controlled with baits or traps, they will eat the foliage and disfigure the flowers. Red spider mites also infest primula foliage but may be washed off with a stream of water. Deer also like to graze on primula foliage.

DELPHINIUMS

The stately delphiniums, the rear guard of the herbaceous border, respond to loving care with a magnificent show.

The dense flower spikes of delphiniums, typically blue but also pure white or shades of mauve, pink, red, or yellow, rise like sentinels at the back of flower beds — if you cosset the plants with good cultivation. These herbaceous perennials are not long lasting; they steadily decrease in height and flower production unless renewed regularly. Luckily, you can easily raise them from seeds or from basal cuttings of existing stock.

Most perennial delphiniums are hybrid varieties bred from the species *D. elatum*. They include the large-flowered *(Elatum)* types, the Pacific hybrids, and the *Belladonna* varieties. The *Elatum* group is divided into tall types, which reach up to 6½ ft (2 m), and dwarf varieties, which grow to 3-4 ft (90-120 cm). Both of these have huge flower spikes, in shades of blue, pink, and white, usually with a contrasting eye. The *Belladonna* varieties are shorter and more graceful, with looser flower spikes in the same color range.

▼ **Hybrid delphiniums** In addition to the traditional blue delphiniums, the color range now includes red, pink, yellow, and cream.

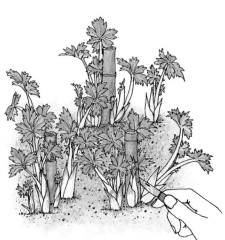

TAKING CUTTINGS

1 Gently ease away the soil from the crown to expose the base of young shoots — which are brittle. With a sharp knife, slice off these shoots very close to the woody crown. Discard any with blackened cut ends — they are diseased.

2 Cuttings will root in jars set on a windowsill. Put a 1-in (2.5-cm) layer of sand in each jar and add water to just above the sand. Insert the cuttings in the sand. Maintain the water at this level.

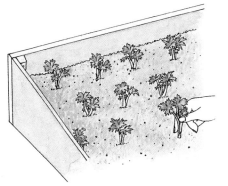

3 Cuttings also root well in a cold frame. Insert them in a 1-in (2.5-cm) layer of moist builder's sand. Shade from strong sun and keep cool. Water only if sand is very dry; slight limpness is not harmful. Keep the leaves dry.

Delphinium seeds are short-lived — and poisonous. Sow collected seeds as soon as they are mature (black) in flats of sterilized seed-starting mix or in an outdoor bed. Cultivars do not breed true, and so are best raised from cuttings taken in spring for flowering the following year.

Cultivation

Delphiniums dislike acid soils — pH 7 to 7.5 is best. They are shallow-rooted, so deep cultivation is unnecessary. Choose a sunny, sheltered position. Begin cultivating the soil 2 to 3 months before planting. Clear all weeds from the site. Delphiniums do not like to be disturbed, so weeding may prove difficult later.

Dig out the top 9 in (23 cm) of soil from the bed. Mix it with composted manure at the rate of 1 spadeful to every 4 spadefuls of soil, together with some lime if the soil is acid. Replace the planting mix and allow it to settle.

Before planting, for each sq yd/sq m of soil, rake in a handful of bone meal (to supply phosphorus for the roots) and a handful of nitrogen-rich cottonseed meal.

Planting

Set out young plants in early fall or midspring in the North, and at any time during winter in the South. Cuttings taken early in the year should be hardened off by midspring and ready for planting in late spring.

Plant when the soil isn't too wet. Space the delphiniums 2-3 ft (60-90 cm) apart in slightly deeper planting holes than those the plants originally occupied. Press the plants in well — loose roots don't take up water quickly. To avoid later root disturbance, insert strong stakes at the same time; tie the growing stems to the stakes with soft twine.

A few weeks later, small flower spikes will appear. Prevent these from growing by pinching them back. New, vigorous shoots will emerge from below soil level, building up a good crown. Allow only these shoots to flower the first year.

Maintenance and care

Each plant will produce several shoots from ground level in early spring. Let only the strongest five develop; use the others as cuttings or discard them.

PLANTING OUT

1 Rooted cuttings can be transplanted directly from a jar or cold frame. Soon young plants will establish themselves. Protect them with overturned glass jars for the first few weeks.

2 Alternatively, harden off the cuttings in a cold frame before planting out. Set them in the ground, slightly lower than the surrounding soil, and press in well using your shoe. Water thoroughly.

STAKING AND TYING

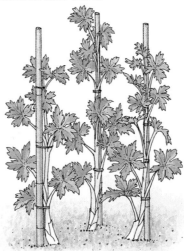

1 Stake in midspring to late spring. If growing just a few shoots, stake and tie each plant to a 3-ft (90-cm) bamboo stake. Tie securely up the stem but more loosely below the tip.

2 If there are several shoots per plant, insert three stakes around the crown and bind with soft twine. Secure stem bases, but allow flowers to sway gently. Otherwise, they may snap off.

Hoe the surrounding soil to permit maximum penetration of rainwater around the roots, or apply a mulch to conserve water.

Never dig around delphiniums, or you will damage the roots. Apply high-nitrogen fertilizer, such as blood meal, when the plants are growing actively.

Once each main flower spike has faded, cut it out to encourage the lateral shoots to produce a second flush. Also, deadhead lateral blooms. If new shoots have appeared at ground level by this time, cut the old stems to the ground and allow a couple of these new ones to grow on to flower. Pinch back the blooms of others, leaving foliage to build up the crown's strength.

In late fall, cut all the stems down to about 4 in (10 cm).

Exhibition-quality blooms

Delphiniums grown for exhibition need particular attention.
❏ Space plants far apart — 30 in (75 cm) between each one.
❏ Allow only four or five spikes to develop, but don't thin them all at once. Pinch them back over a few weeks.
❏ Apply nitrogen-rich fertilizer in early spring, then potash about 6 weeks before flowering.
❏ Stake the plants firmly and water well during the summer.

GLORIOUS PEONIES

**Incredibly hardy and long-lived, peonies
have elegant foliage and beautiful bowl-shaped flowers,
making them one of the most highly prized perennials.**

Peonies fall into two main categories — herbaceous perennials and deciduous shrubs, or "tree peonies." The former type is the best known, and has been the subject of much hybrid breeding. Hundreds of cultivars are now available with single or double flowers in all shades of pink, red, and white, many of which also have a delicious fragrance.

The Chinese peony *(Paeonia lactiflora)* is the parent of the widest range of hybrids and cultivars, though semidouble and double-flowered varieties of the wild European peony *(Paeonia officinalis)* are also popular. Other outstanding (though difficult-to-find) peonies include the single, pure white *P. emodi,* the crimson *P. anomala,* the silky pink *P. arietina,* as well as the

showy *P. mlokosewitschii,* whose magnificent lemon-yellow flower bowls, which contain dense clusters of golden stamens, can appear as early as April.

Herbaceous peonies generally form bushy clumps 2-3½ ft (60-100 cm) high, which is a perfect size for use in mixed or perennial beds. In addition, they can be grown in a bed on their own for cut flowers and exhibition. Since most bloom in very late spring to early summer, they make excellent partners for bearded irises and other old-fashioned garden favorites. The foliage may be deeply divided or almost fernlike; often it takes on coppery or reddish-purple autumnal tints.

In the fall, many herbaceous peonies provide a third decorative feature — bright red seed

pods that split open to reveal glossy blue-black seeds. These pods may be collected and used in dried flower arrangements.

Newly planted peonies can take several years to establish, but once settled in, they will provide a reliable show for some 50 years. Though they will grow satisfactorily with very little routine care, you can protect them from weather damage and ensure that they produce the best-quality blooms by staking the stems and thinning out any prolific growth.

▼ **Double-flowered peonies** The spectacular, many-petaled wine-red blooms of *Paeonia lactiflora* 'Karl Rosenfeld' are as much as 6 in (15 cm) wide. They are so heavy that a shower of rain makes them droop unless the plants are supported.

PEONY FLOWER TYPES

single

semidouble

Japanese

double

anemone

Peonies are able to withstand winter temperatures as low as -40°F (-40°C), and to enjoy long periods of summer heat. It is not surprising therefore to find these perennials thriving under a wide variety of climatic conditions.

Peony classification
Peonies are classified according to the formation and number of petals in their flowers.
❏ Single types have five or more petals arranged in a ring, with a central boss, or cluster, of golden yellow pollen-bearing stamens.
❏ Semidouble types have five or more outer petals and a center filled with a mixture of golden or yellow stamens and broad petals.
❏ Japanese types are similar to the singles, but the central cluster of pollen-bearing stamens is missing. Instead, the center of the flower consists of a large cluster of stamens that resemble shredded petals, or *staminodes*.
❏ Double types have few or no

stamens; the flowers are composed almost entirely of a tight cluster of many broad petals.
❏ Anemone types have at least five outer petals, usually in two or more rings. The stamens are transformed into narrow petal-like growths, known as *petalodes*. These may be the same color as the true outer petals, or yellow.

Planting
In the North, peonies should be planted while dormant in the fall; in the South, before growth starts in the spring. Although they do best in a sunny position, these plants will bloom in lightly shaded or open woodland spots in areas with hot summers. At the southern end of the peonies' range (zone 8), an airy situation will protect the flower buds against fungi that may destroy them in humid conditions.

These plants will prosper in any well-drained garden soil — lime-rich, neutral, or slightly acid

— but they prefer a rather heavy soil to a light, sandy one. Once established, they won't tolerate root disturbance, so it is important to give them a good start by thoroughly preparing the soil.

Allow more space for peonies than for most other herbaceous perennials, as they form large, rounded clumps. A minimum spacing of 2 ft (60 cm) between plants is essential, and, for a life-long planting, 3-ft (90-cm) spacing in all directions is preferable. Fill the gaps between peonies for the first few years by planting some annuals, biennials, or short-lived perennials.

Dig a hole about 1½-2 ft (45-60 cm) deep. Break up the soil at the bottom with a garden fork. If the soil is heavy and drains poorly, add several handfuls of sharp builder's sand or grit.

Before you refill the hole, mix in a generous amount of composted manure, leaf mold, or garden compost with the soil,

HERBACEOUS AND TREE PEONIES

Herbaceous peonies die down to ground level every fall, and new succulent stems arise each spring. Their foliage is dark green or bronze, but their shape is variable. Flower buds are globular. Most commonly found in red, pink, and white, the blooms may be any one of five distinct types: single, semidouble, double, Japanese, or anemone.

Tree peonies have woody, rough-barked, branching stems that do not die down in the fall. Foliage is deciduous and generally pale. Their flower buds are flatter than herbaceous types, with a raised center point. Flowers may be single, semidouble, or double, in shades of red, pink, yellow, and white, often with a dark eye. Sizes vary greatly.

especially if it is heavy and sticky. In a pinch, even straw will do. Then refill the hole until it is 8-10 in (20-25 cm) deep.

Hold the peony root in place in the hole, with the crown growth buds uppermost, so that the crown is 1-2 in (2.5-5 cm) below the surface. (Crowns planted too deeply will not flower.) Fill around the root with good garden soil, but do not add fertilizer. Press in well with your fingers as you work, but take care not to break the fleshy, brittle root.

Once the planting hole has been filled completely, press in the soil around the crown with your feet — without standing on the crown. Scatter a small handful of bone meal around the planting site, forking it in lightly with a hand fork. Label the plant clearly and water it well.

Routine care

As long as the planting area is correctly prepared, the peonies will not need any more fertilizer for several years. About 4 years after planting, sprinkle a handful of bone meal around each peony in spring and fall, and fork it in lightly with a hand fork. Treat the area within a 1½-ft (45-cm) radius of the crown, but stay at least 6 in (15 cm) away from the main stems. If the soil is light and sandy, start applying fertilizer after 2 or 3 years, since this soil type does not easily retain essential nutrients.

A topdressing of composted manure applied in spring may improve the vigor of peonies, especially on light, quick-draining soils. Avoid putting it immediately above the crowns, as it may encourage disease. Do not overfeed the plants, or you will promote soft stem and leaf growth, as well as poor-quality flowers. Water well during very dry spells, especially in spring. At other times, rainfall should provide adequate moisture.

Weeding around peonies must be done with care. It is best to pull weeds by hand or paint them with a systemic herbicide. If you use a hoe, do not dig deeper than 2 in (5 cm) within 6 in (15 cm) of the crown.

PLANTING PEONIES

Label each plant clearly. Position the next peony at least 3 ft (90 cm) away.

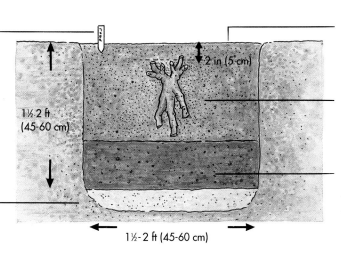

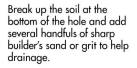

1½-2 ft (45-60 cm)

2 in (5 cm)

Break up the soil at the bottom of the hole and add several handfuls of sharp builder's sand or grit to help drainage.

1½-2 ft (45-60 cm)

Press in, scatter a little bone meal around the planting area, forking it in lightly with a hand fork. Water well.

Hold the peony root gently in position so that the crown will be about 1-2 in (2.5-5 cm) below the surface. Refill with good garden soil.

Part-fill with a layer of good garden soil mixed with composted manure or garden compost.

One method of reducing weed growth involves laying a mulch around the root area of the plants in spring, but do not cover the crowns themselves.

Support Herbaceous peonies have large, heavy flowers that tend to break their stems, especially in exposed sites. Some form of support is necessary.

The most effective way to hold peonies up is with commercially produced wire-ring supports attached to bamboo or metal-

ENCOURAGING LARGE BLOOMS

1 Provide adequate support for all herbaceous peonies. When the plants are half-grown, insert either wire-ring supports attached to metal-linking stakes or use conventional stakes and soft string.

2 Cut out the weakest stems before they show flower buds in order to divert the plant's maximum energy to strong flowering stems.

3 Disbud flower stems, pinching back all side buds as soon as they appear. Leave just the topmost flower bud on each main stem to develop.

linking stakes. Slip them over the plants in midspring when shoots are half grown. Besides providing support, they also let the stems splay out, thus creating a natural, rounded bush.

If available, twiggy sticks can be used for support. They should be about 3 ft (90 cm) long, which allows for 6-12 in (15-30 cm) to be placed in the ground. Insert the sticks around the crown when the stems are about 1 ft (30 cm) tall, then mesh the twigs together across the crown. Heavy blooms grown for exhibition can be individually supported on bamboo or wooden stakes, tied loosely but firmly with soft garden string at two or three places on the stem.

Disbud peonies to produce fewer but larger blooms. Pinch back all the side buds as soon as they appear, leaving just the main terminal bud on each stem.

Another method for encouraging larger blooms is to cut out some of the shoots entirely at ground level. Remove only the weakest ones when they are approximately one-third grown.

For a good display of flowers in the garden, no disbudding or shoot thinning is necessary.

Deadhead herbaceous peonies once the flowers fade. It is the leaves that will build up energy in the crown for the next year.

A few peonies, especially *Paeonia mlokosewitschii*, develop showy seed pods in late summer and fall that eventually split open to reveal a brilliant red lining and rows of pea-sized, glossy blue-black seeds. Plants that have these spectacular seed pods should not be deadheaded.

Cut down all the stems to within about 1-2 in (2.5-5 cm) of the ground in the fall. Bag and dispose of the debris — do not use it for compost, as the dead leaves may be infested with Botrytis disease. Clear away all other leaf litter and debris from around the crown.

Cut flowers

Peonies make gorgeous cut flowers for indoor decoration. To prevent them from dropping their petals, cut the blooms as they begin to open. Then lay them flat in a cool, dry place indoors for 24 hours. Trim ½ in (1.5 cm) from the stems and stand them in deep water.

Propagation

Herbaceous peonies can be raised from seed, but it may take a while before you see results. Hybrids and cultivars do not breed true, so division is the only really successful means of propagation. However, this method should not be carried out as a routine operation, as with most other perennials, because peonies resent root disturbance and take several years to recover, if at all. It may be safer to buy new stock.

If you do wish to try dividing peonies, lift the plants in early fall after first trimming down the top growth. Next, cut the tough crowns with a sharp knife, ensuring that each section has some roots and three to five dormant growth buds. Shorten the longest roots until they measure about 4-6 in (10-15 cm) in length. Divisions from the outer edges of the clump usually produce the best results.

Replant each division as you would for mature plants. Blooms may not appear in the first summer, and in the second summer they may be rather small and sparse. By the third year, however, you may have a good show of flowers with exactly the same color and form as that of the parent plant.

DEPENDABLE DAYLILIES

**Among the longest-lived perennials, daylilies are
also persistent bloomers. Mix hybrids of different seasons
to prolong the flowering display.**

If you've ever admired the "ditch lilies" that line so many of rural America's highways, you know how self-reliant daylilies can be. Those orange trumpets are the descendants of an Asian wildflower, *Hemerocallis fulva,* that came into our country with the first European settlers and eventually escaped from home gardens to flourish on its own in meadows and along roadsides. A couple of centuries hasn't diminished its freshness at all. And when you first see a display of the modern hybrid daylilies, you will realize just how beautiful toughness can be.

The hybrids range in size from dwarfs, such as 'Elfin,' which rise to just 10-11 in (25-28 cm), to stalwart border types, such as 'Hyperion,' whose stems may reach 40 in (1 m) high. The flowers are found in every conceivable shade of red, orange, yellow, pink, purple, and white, with individual blossoms measuring up to 7-8 in (18-20 cm) wide. These

may be lily-shaped, ruffle-edged, or doubled into a puff. Some have petals attenuated into a star or a "spider" form. Although each flower opens for only one day, a succession of blossoms on each plant gives it a blooming season that lasts several weeks. Many species are sweetly scented.

Depending on the size of the plant and flower, daylilies are frequently used in mixed flower beds, or as edging alongside paths, or woven through a foundation planting. They also make outstanding ground covers — the clumps of arching leaves are handsome by themselves.

Anatomy of a daylily
Unlike the true lilies *(Lilium),* which develop from a bulb, daylilies *(Hemerocallis)* sprout from a cluster of fleshy roots. Their clump of sword-shaped, grasslike leaves may be either deciduous or evergreen, depending on the cultivar (those with evergreen foliage tend to be less cold

hardy and are grown mainly in the South). Flower buds form on branched stalks, or *scapes,* that rise from the center of the leaves, and each scape commonly bears a number of buds. Blossoms appear to have six petals (known to botanists as *tepals),* six pollen-bearing stamens, and a long, central pistil. Many hybrids have double blossoms — flowers with two times (or more) the natural number of petals. Breeders have also produced strains of *tetraploids,* daylilies with double the usual number of chromosomes; these make outsized flowers and huskier plants.

Choosing daylilies
These perennials are grouped by flower size: miniatures produce

---

▼ **The "ditch lily"** of rural America, *Hemerocallis fulva* (also called the tawny daylily) makes a tenacious and floriferous ground cover for a sunny or semishaded bank.

▲ **Each daylily flower** lasts just one day. But each plant bears several buds that will open as other blossoms wither, thus providing a continuous display. A border such as this one may flower from late spring into late fall.

blossoms less than 3 in (7.5 cm) wide; small-flowered daylilies measure 3-4½ in (7.5-11.5 cm) wide; and large-flowered daylilies exhibit blooms more than 4½ in (11.5 cm) wide. In addition, daylilies are classed by the height of their scapes: *dwarfs* have scapes less than 12 in (30 cm) tall; *low* cultivars have scapes that measure 12-24 in (30-60 cm); *mediums* have scapes 24-36 in (60-90 cm); and *talls* have scapes more than 36 in (90 cm).

Nursery catalogs frequently specify the blooming season of each cultivar: extra-early, early, early-midseason, midseason, late-midseason, late, or very late. The timing of these seasons varies from climate to climate. For example, extra-earlies may begin flowering in March in zones 9 and 10, and as late as the end of June in zone 3. This information allows gardeners to plant cultivars of different seasons, thus extending the flowering time.

Another important factor to consider before buying daylilies is their root structure. Some types produce dense root masses that confine themselves to slowly expanding clumps, while others send out *rhizomes,* or underground stems, 1 ft (30 cm) long, that sprout new plants at their tips. Plantings of rhizomatous daylilies, such as the species *H. fulva* or the cultivars 'Nashville Star' (deciduous) and 'Irish Elf' (evergreen), quickly knit themselves into a single sheet

▶ **One of the first daylilies to bloom** in the spring, 'Stella de Oro' also reblooms periodically into fall. Though delicate in appearance, this miniature hybrid is vigorous enough to hold its own among other perennials or even shrubbery.

and so make the most effective ground covers.

One species that was crossed with *H. fulva* to produce modern hybrids is the lemon lily, *H. lilio-asphodelus* (syn. *H. flava).* The lemon lily is known as an extended bloomer because, unlike most daylilies, which open their flowers in the morning, it blooms in the late afternoon; the flowers remain open through the night. This unusual trait has been passed to many of its offspring. And now that many home gardeners find their daytime hours increasingly harried, there is a greater interest in the extended types. Some popular hybrids among this group are 'Bitsy' (yellow; low-growing; miniature; extra-early), 'Eenie Weenie' (light yellow, with a green throat; dwarf; miniature; early season to midseason), 'Green Ice' (pale yellow, with a green throat; medium-tall; mid-season to late season), 'Lusty Lealand' (fire-engine red, with yellow throat; medium-tall; large-flowered; midseason), and 'Stella de Oro' (ca-

nary yellow; low-growing; miniature; early season).

It is impractical to recommend particular daylilies because there are more than 35,000 cultivars, and that number increases dramatically each year. Daylilies are among the easiest flowers to hybridize (see p.52), and amateur breeders are constantly bringing out new types, many of considerable merit. The safest way to select daylilies is to order from a catalog that specifies which cultivars have been awarded the American Hemerocallis Society's Award of Merit. Just 10 plants are so honored each year, and the award is given only after at least 4 years of nationwide testing.

Cultivation

Daylilies are among the hardiest perennials; they will bloom for years, even on dry, rocky soil and in moderate shade. Nevertheless, they respond well to good care, rewarding the gardener with lush growth and more generous blossoms. In the North, plant daylilies in a spot that receives full

▲ A fine example of a large-flowered bicolor daylily, hybrid 'Frans Hals' bears red-petaled flowers 5 in (12.5 cm) wide, with orange throats, in late midseason.

sun all day; in the South, set them in a position that has some light shade in the afternoon. Prepare the soil by digging to a depth of 18 in (45 cm), incorporating generous amounts of compost, leaf mold, or peat moss, and adding 5-10-5 fertilizer at the

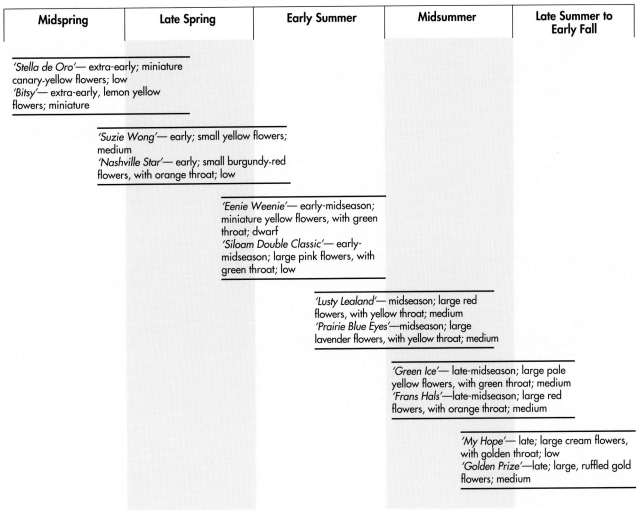

MIXING DAYLILIES FOR EXTENDED BLOOM

Midspring	Late Spring	Early Summer	Midsummer	Late Summer to Early Fall
'Stella de Oro'— extra-early; miniature canary-yellow flowers; low 'Bitsy'— extra-early, lemon yellow flowers; miniature				
	'Suzie Wong'— early; small yellow flowers; medium 'Nashville Star'— early; small burgundy-red flowers, with orange throat; low			
		'Eenie Weenie'— early-midseason; miniature yellow flowers, with green throat; dwarf 'Siloam Double Classic'— early-midseason; large pink flowers, with green throat; low		
			'Lusty Lealand'— midseason; large red flowers, with yellow throat; medium 'Prairie Blue Eyes'—midseason; large lavender flowers, with yellow throat; medium	
			'Green Ice'— late-midseason; large pale yellow flowers, with green throat; medium 'Frans Hals'—late-midseason; large red flowers, with orange throat; medium	
				'My Hope'— late; large cream flowers, with golden throat; low 'Golden Prize'—late; large, ruffled gold flowers; medium

rate of 2 lbs (.90 kg) per 100 sq ft/9 sq m.

Daylilies may be planted at any time from spring until a month before the first expected hard frost in fall. Water new plantings regularly during periods of hot, dry weather, applying as much as 1 in (3 cm) of water once a week.

Propagation

Daylilies do not breed true from seed, and therefore named cultivars are usually propagated by division. Since well-tended plants increase rapidly in size, you may want to divide them in the spring of the fourth or fifth year. Lift and divide each clump with a pair of spading forks. A large clump may yield as many as a half-dozen offspring.

The common wild daylily *Hemerocallis fulva* (sometimes called the tawny daylily) is sterile — its flowers do not yield any seeds— and can be propagated only by division or by lifting and transplanting the plantlets produced at its rhizomes' ends. Most daylily hybrids, however, do set seed, but the plants produced are not identical to the parent. That can be an advantage in terms of hybridization, which relies on controlled crosses of different plants.

Begin hybridization by choosing two cultivars whose qualities you wish to mix — perhaps one is a particularly vigorous plant and the other bears outstanding flowers. Then take the pollen-covered anther of the "father" (see illustration above) and stroke it across the stigma (the tip of the pistil) of the other flower, the "mother." With most daylilies, early morning — when the flowers are freshest— is the best time to pollinate. Evening-blooming types should be pollinated at dusk, as they open. The maturity of both anther and stigma is also an important consideration. The anther should be at the stage where it has just split open and its pollen is powdery and yellow; the tip of the stigma should be glistening and sticky.

After you have helped transfer the pollen to the stigma of the mother flower, snip off its anthers so they cannot pollinate and defeat your effort at a controlled cross. Record the names of the parents on a weatherproof label and attach it to the base of the pollinated mother flower.

HYBRIDIZING DAYLILIES

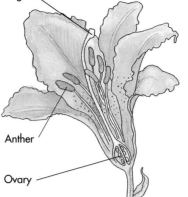

Stigma

Anther

Ovary

1 Choose two hybrids with complementary strengths, such as an unruly plant with outstanding blooms and a compact but common dwarf. Then identify the sexual organs: a male anther in one plant, a female stigma in the other.

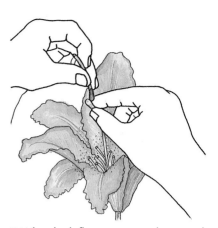

2 When both flowers are newly opened, select a pollen-coated anther from the father and brush its tip across a stigma of the mother flower. Clip off all the anthers in the mother flower to prevent them from pollinating, too.

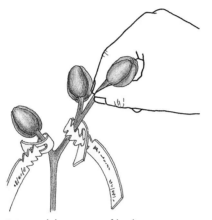

3 Record the names of both parents on a weatherproof label and attach it to the base of the pollinated mother flower. If pollination has been successful, the ovary will swell and a seedpod should form. When it turns brown and begins to split along its seams, harvest the seeds.

4 Store the seeds in plastic bags (one per pod) of moist sphagnum moss. Chill for 4 to 8 weeks. Then sow them into flats of sterilized, soilless growing medium. Moisten, cover, and keep warm (70-75°F/21-24°C); germination can occur within days but may take weeks.

If the pollination is successful, a seedpod should start to form after each mother flower fades. Once it turns brown, swells, and cracks (generally after about 45 to 60 days), the seed is mature. Pick the pods and shell the seeds of each pod into separate plastic sandwich bags and label them. Add a handful of moist (not wet) sphagnum moss to each bag, seal them, and chill in the refrigerator for a period of 4 to 8 weeks.

Afterward, sow the seeds in flats (a separate, labeled flat for the seeds of each pod) filled with some sterile, soilless growing medium. Set seeds ½ in (1.25 cm) apart in rows spaced 1 in (2.5 cm) apart. Cover them with ¼ in (6 mm) of more soilless mix. Water

the flats, cover them with a clear propagation top or a plastic bag supported on a wire frame, and set them on a heating cable or in some warm spot so that the soil stays at a temperature between 70-75° F (21-24° C).

Uncover the flats as soon as the seedlings appear and move them to a sunny windowsill. Keep them indoors over the winter. When the seedlings reach a height of 1 in (2.5 cm), transplant them into peat pots filled with more soilless growing medium. In the spring, once the danger of frost has passed, transplant the seedlings out into a nursery bed. Growth will be slow at first; it will take at least 2 years for the new plants to flower.

PINKS AND CARNATIONS

Delicately colored pinks add cottage-style charm to any garden; the classic beauty of carnations makes them a border star.

Perennial pinks, along with border and florist's carnations, biennial sweet Williams, and annual bedding pinks, belong to the genus *Dianthus.* It's difficult to distinguish a pink from a carnation; in fact, in French and German, the word for pink means "little carnation." A pink is a light, dainty plant, with flowers carried on slender stems. Although it may have almost perfect form, it is never as solid and sculptured as a carnation. However, its scent is often more pronounced. The carnation is larger and more formal in appearance as a result of centuries of selection and breeding. An excellent cut flower, it is used extensively in floral arrangements, corsages, and boutonnieres for special occasions. The carnation also adds a special elegance to garden displays.

Choosing pinks

This group of flowers divides into two broad groups: the old-fashioned perennial pinks and the modern pinks. The former types, derived from the species *Dianthus plumarius,* produce one central stem the first year and flowering side growth a year later. Unfortunately, this delay in blooming makes them less popular than the modern ones, though the old-fashioned cultivar 'Mrs. Sinkins' is still widely grown.

Modern pinks *(Dianthus × allwoodii)* are obtained by crossing an old-fashioned pink with a florist's carnation. They grow faster and yield many more blooms than their old-fashioned relatives, flowering mainly during early summer and midsummer, and again in early fall and midfall. However, they must be regrown from cuttings or layers more often than old-fashioned pinks, usually every 2 or 3 years.

In addition to the named forms of old-fashioned and modern hybrids, there are numerous species of pinks that have never lost their popularity. They include the short-lived but strongly fragrant *D. alpinus.* It is 4 in (10 cm) tall and has pale pink to purple blossoms, with a white eye and purple spots. The little maiden pink, *(D. deltoides),* 6 in (15 cm) high, is perfect for growing in paving crevices, where it will flower profusely throughout summer. The native Cheddar pink *(D. gratianopolitanus,* or *D. caesius)* lasts longer than most other pinks and forms low, wide gray-green mats of foliage with a wealth of fringed, scented pink flowers.

Border carnations

These plants are also divided into two basic groups: the border, or outdoor, types, which were common in European gardens as long ago as the sixteenth century, and the perpetual-flowering, or florist's, carnations, which were first bred in greenhouses in the United States during the late nineteenth century.

The relatively short-lived border carnations flourish outdoors and are frost hardy (to zone 4). They bloom from midsummer to late summer, producing just one flush of heavy, large blossoms each year. Although borne on sturdy stems, they must be staked. The edges of their petals are smooth and flat, unlike the serrated ones that distinguish the florist's carnations. Border carnations are often scented.

▶ **Modern pinks** Provided pinks are given full sun, they will flower for months, covering foliage with a mass of blooms that never need staking. The single-flowered 'Daphne' bears bicolored flowers of the palest pink, with crimson eyes; it is short-lived and must be propagated by cuttings, usually every 2 years.

PLANTING PINKS AND CARNATIONS

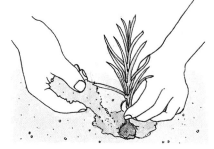

1 Do not plant too deeply — only ¼ in (6 mm) of stem should be covered, with lower leaves clear of the ground.

2 Press in the plant by hand, making sure not to push the roots and stem any lower into the soil.

Color classification

The palette of available pinks and carnations runs from pure white to yellow, salmon, lilac, rose, and crimson-purple. It is the pattern of coloration, however, that is of importance because it is used to classify them.

❑ Self types have flowers of one solid color.

❑ Bicolored types have flowers whose central eye is in a contrasting color. The variety 'Doris,' probably the most widely grown modern pink, is typical of this category, with its red-centered salmon-pink flowers.

❑ Fancy types have flowers with a single-colored background that is flecked, striped, streaked, or lined in a contrasting color.

❑ Laced-type pinks have a dark zone, or eye, at the base of each petal, which is extended in a band around the petal edge. The remainder of the petal — the ground color — is white, cream, or pink.

❑ Picotee carnations have a ground color of white or yellow and a red or purple margin. Another category of dianthus, the clove type, is distinguished by its scent, not color. The fragrance of its flowers resembles that of the aromatic spice.

Choosing the site

Most old-fashioned and modern pinks grow about 15 in (38 cm) high; they look attractive when grouped in the front of sunny borders. Dwarf hybrids and species types are ideal for rock gardens, walls, raised beds, and cracks among paving stones. Pinks prefer slightly alkaline soils, but they grow well in a wide range of soils, provided they are not too acid. They are also tolerant of urban pollution and salt spray in seaside gardens. However, poor drainage, heavy shade, or water drips from overhanging trees or shrubs are usually fatal. Carnations require the same sunny growing conditions.

Planting

Prepare the planting hole by digging in fertilizer in late summer. Apply a light dressing of lime to acid soils. Wood ash has a similar effect and has the additional benefit of supplying potassium, which improves flower quality. Before planting, scatter 4 handfuls per sq yd/sq m over the site.

New stock can be set out in early fall to midfall or early spring. The advantage of fall planting is that the roots can become established before cold weather arrives and then begin to grow immediately in early spring. There may, however, be winter losses, and in cold-weather regions (zones 7 and farther north), early-spring to midspring planting may be preferable.

Plant the more compact species pinks, such as *D. deltoides* and *D. gratianopolitanus*, 1 ft (30 cm) apart, and set the delicate *D. plumarius* and *D. alpinus* even closer, about 8 in (20 cm) apart. Modern pinks are stronger growing and thus need to be spaced 1½ ft (45 cm) apart, while sweet Williams *(D. barbatus)* require a minimum of 2 ft (60 cm) between plants.

Set border carnations at least 9 in (23 cm) apart; however, 15 in (38 cm) apart is even better, as this distance allows for stronger growth. For reliable perennial performance, increase the space to 1½ ft (45 cm) apart. Bury the roots of pinks and carnations, covering no more than ¼ in (6 mm) of the stem. Press the soil

AFTERCARE

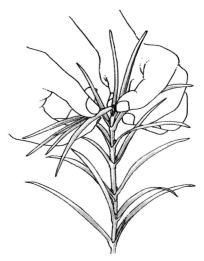

1 To encourage bushiness, pinch young modern pinks in their first season. Select the sixth to eighth node from the base; bend the stem sharply at that point.

2 Support tall varieties of old-fashioned pinks and border carnations with small pea sticks or tie the flower stems to thin stakes.

3 After blooming, remove all old flower stems completely. Plants may produce a second flush of flowers if given a high-potassium fertilizer.

'Orange Elf'
florist's
carnation
picotee type

▲ **Classic form and purity** of color
make carnations a favorite for both flower
arrangements and buttonholes; this
cultivar exhibits the picotee pattern
of coloration.

firmly around the plant, but
avoid pushing the stem and roots
any deeper. Water lightly.

Aftercare
Water plants well during dry
weather. Modern pinks do not
need any support, but old-fashioned pinks, with their taller and
weaker stems, look tidier if
grown through short, twiggy pea
sticks, or if each flower stem is
tied to a thin stake. Border carnations require support so that
flowers will not be knocked down
by rain or wind storms. Keep
them upright by securing stems
to a metal stake with soft garden
string. Remove the stems of fading blossoms and water the
plants thoroughly. Apply a high-
potassium fertilizer to encourage
future blooms.

Pinching modern pinks
Old-fashioned pinks produce only
one stem in the first year and
should be allowed to grow
unchecked. Modern pinks, on the
other hand, must be pinched
back in their first season to encourage breaks, or *side shoots,*
and to create strong, bushy
growth. Allow the plants to develop 9 or 10 fully grown pairs of
leaves before pinching. If they do
not reach this stage until fall,
postpone the job until the following spring. (Pinching might force
late growth that would be damaged by very cold weather.)

Pinching is best done in the
early morning in damp weather
when the stems are full of moisture and break more easily. Select
the sixth, seventh, or eighth node
from the base and hold it be-

tween your finger and thumb.
With the other hand, bend the
stem sharply down at the chosen
node. Usually it will snap cleanly, but if it does not, bend the
stem to the other side at a right
angle. If this method fails, do not
pull the stem; cut it with a sharp,
clean knife just above the node.

Do not pinch out the growing
tip; such pruning will result in
just one or two side shoots near
the top. After the initial pinching,
the side shoots will develop from
the leaf nodes. Modern pinks
need to be pinched only in their
first growing year.

▼ **Border elegance** With their gray-
green foliage and elegant coral-pink
blooms, these border carnations —
though short-lived — dominate a red-
and-pink planting scheme.

LAYERING BORDER CARNATIONS

1 The easiest method of propagating border carnations is by layering in mid-summer to late summer. Select vigorous shoots that have not borne flowers. Strip off some of the lower leaves.

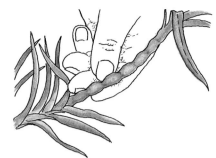

2 Leave four or five pairs of leaves at the tip. To counteract any stiffness in the stem that may make layering difficult, bruise it between each node with your thumbnail.

4 Carefully open out the cut. Make a shallow hole, then fill it with a moist rooting medium of equal parts peat and sand. Press the cut tongue portion of the stem into the mixture.

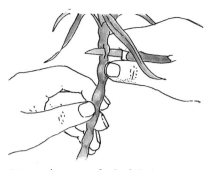

3 Insert the point of a knife below the first node beneath the top leaves. Cut down through the next node and, turning the blade, make an outward cut to form a tongue on the stem.

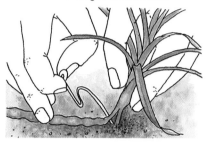

5 Anchor the stem with a piece of bent galvanized wire so that the cut is buried 1in (2.5 cm) below the surface. After 6 weeks, roots should have formed and the young plant can be severed.

Disbudding border carnations

In early summer, a crown bud forms at the top of the border carnation stem, and it usually provides the best and largest bloom. In addition, side shoots, each carrying one or more buds, grow from the stem. To ensure good-quality blooms, remove some of these shoots.

When the flower buds are about the size of a pea, pinch out the side shoots and buds below the crown bud, for a distance of about 3 in (7.5 cm). On the remaining side shoots, pinch out to leave only the terminal buds.

Taking cuttings

The primary method of increasing stocks of modern and old-fashioned pinks is by stem cuttings; it is the only reliable way of propagating cultivars — seeds do not breed true except from the species types. Take cuttings right after the main flush of flowers has finished, generally in early summer. Select vigorously growing, compact side shoots and, with a sharp knife, cut them off close to the main stem. Water the parent plants well the day before you take the cuttings to ensure that they will be full of sap. Using the same sharp knife, cut each shoot just below the node (count-ing downward from the shoot's tip) where the fourth or fifth pair of leaves joins the stem. Strip off the bottom pair of leaves and dust the base of the cuttings with hormone rooting powder.

If you intend to keep the parent plant after taking cuttings, do not remove too many shoots, or you will spoil its appearance.

Pinks and carnations are prone to a variety of fungal, bacterial, and viral diseases, and these may be spread from plant to plant by the knife with which you take the cuttings. To keep plants healthy, always sterilize the knife before using it. Dip the blade into alcohol, then place it in a hot flame. Loosely fill a 3½-in (9-cm) clay or plastic pot with sterilized potting soil to within 1½ in (4 cm) of the rim. Top the pot with a mixture of equal parts peat and coarse sand. Then insert six to nine cuttings, making sure that the bases of the lowest leaves are not covered. Tilt the cuttings inward slightly so that they are able to support each other until strong roots develop.

Water the planting mixture and label the cuttings with the cultivar name and the date of potting. Place the pot in a cold frame or cover it with a clear plastic bag that is supported on a wire frame and set it in a spot where it will receive full light but no direct sun. After a few days, open the frame or bag slightly to allow some air circulation. Spray the cuttings in warm weather to keep the atmosphere around them humid.

Rooting usually takes 18 to 30 days. Cuttings can be planted in their flowering sites 2 or 3 weeks later. Water them in dry weather until they are well rooted.

Propagation by layering

Pinks and border carnations can be increased by layering in mid-summer or late summer, once the plants have finished flowering (see p.56).

Propagation by seeds

Species pinks generally breed true from seeds, but cultivars will show great variation. However, propagating from seeds is an easy and inexpensive way to obtain large numbers of plants.

In midspring to midsummer (the earlier the better), sow the seeds in flats or pots filled with a seed-starting mix. Place them in a cold frame or on a cool windowsill. When the first true leaves appear, prick out the seedlings into flats and grow them until they have developed enough to be moved outdoors.

HOSTAS FOR FOLIAGE

**For adaptability and the sheer luxuriance of
their foliage, hostas are unrivaled — the leaves come
in a variety of colors, shapes, and textures.**

The genus *Hosta* comprises as many as 40 species of mostly very hardy, herbaceous perennials from Korea, China, and Japan. Sometimes known as plantain lilies, and previously listed under the alternative genus name *Funkia,* these decorative members of the lily family (Liliaceae) play a valuable role in the garden as abundant suppliers of varied foliage color, shape, and form.

Hostas are named in honor of an Austrian botanist, N.T. Host. Hundreds of cultivars have been bred, providing an almost endless selection of variegated and colored-leaved forms, suitable for partnering with a whole host of other perennials or shrubs. They are perfect for shady borders — though many tolerate sun — and like moist soil, particularly alongside a water garden. Hostas also offer excellent ground cover and, once they are established, can be left undisturbed for many years to come.

The leaves of hostas are attractive from the moment they emerge from the ground in spring until the fall, when they assume rich golden yellow and bronze tints. Their textures vary considerably: they may have many veins, or be puckered, crinkly, smooth, or undulating. As for color, the conspicuous foliage may be cream, yellow, golden green, midgreen, dark green, or blue-green. Most hostas also produce upright spikes of white or mauve flowers in summer. The trumpet-shaped blooms are pleasantly scented.

Choosing hostas

The hostas you choose will depend on the characteristics you desire — height and spread, leaf color, or leaf texture. In turn, leaf color affects a particular plant's suitability for sun or shade.

If you want all-green foliage, ranging from palest gray-green to somber dark, choose any of the

▲ **Hosta flowers** In summer, tall flower spikes add to the elegance of hostas. Although the flowers are usually in shades of lilac-mauve, some hostas bear white, scented blooms.

▼ **Ground cover contrasts** The large, quilted and glossy leaves of *H. sieboldiana* offer a dramatic contrast to the smaller, wavy-edged, and cream-centered foliage of *H. undulata.*

following true species: *Hosta elata, H. fortunei, H. lancifolia,* or *H. plantaginea.* Some hybrids also have rich, all-green foliage, including *H. rectifolia* 'Tall Boy,' *H.* 'Honeybells,' and *H.* 'Royal Standard.'

Blue-green or glaucous foliage provides a stunning contrast in a mixed planting. This coloring is a feature of *Hosta sieboldiana* (often known as *H. glauca*) — especially the variety 'Elegans' — the *tardiana* hybrid, 'Halcyon,' and *H. ventricosa.*

White-, cream-, and yellow-variegated hostas are also popular among gardeners, as they can brighten up a foliage planting. The variegation patterns are quite wide-ranging, with some etching the leaf margins, others marking between the leaf veins, and a number marbling or splashing the leaf with irregular patches of cream or white.

Species, variety, or hybrid names that include "marginata" imply that the leaves are edged with a contrasting color. The species *H. sieboldii* (syn. *H. albomarginata*), for example, has lance-shaped, narrow, glossy green leaves, edged with a thin margin of white. Varietal names with the prefix "albo" suggest that the variegation is white; "aureo" or "aurea" implies yellow variegations. Some examples include *H. ventricosa* 'Aureo-marginata' and *H. fortunei* 'Albo-marginata.'

Central variegations, stripes, or splashes are found in such varieties as *H. undulata* 'Medio-variegata' and also *H. ventricosa* 'Aureo-maculata.' A still greater choice is offered by the cultivars *H. sieboldiana* 'Frances Williams,' and *H.* 'Gold Standard,' both of which have golden-edged blue-green leaves, and *H.* 'Thomas Hogg,' with its cream-edged, glossy dark leaves.

Leaf shapes range from the very narrow *H. lancifolia* to the broad and rounded *H. sieboldiana.* Sizes vary from about 5 in (12.5 cm) long to as much as 15 in (38 cm). The leaf blades can be relatively flat, as in *H. ventricosa,* or distinctly wavy, as in *H. undulata.* Usually the veins are prominent, giving the leaves a striped appearance, but in some cases they are netted, as in *H. fortunei* and *H. sieboldiana* and their varieties.

Hosta foliage is variable in color, size, and texture:
1 *Hosta sieboldiana* 'Elegans'
2 *Hosta fortunei* 'Aurea'
3 *Hosta crispula*
4 *Hosta ventricosa* 'Aureo-maculata'
5 *Hosta fortunei* 'Albo-picta'
6 *Hosta undulata* 'Medio-variegata'
7 *Hosta* 'Gold Standard'
8 *Hosta rectifolia* 'Tall Boy'

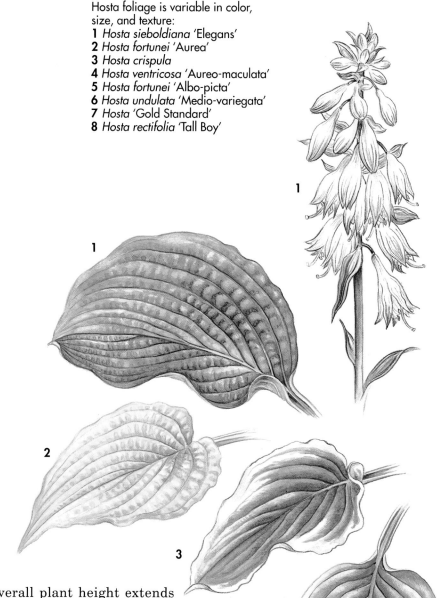

Overall plant height extends from the low-growing *Hosta minor,* which forms a carpet of leaves about 8 in (20 cm) high, to the tall-growing *H. elata,* which reaches as high as 3 ft (90 cm). Although the flowers of all hostas rise above the foliage, they are not dominant enough to be a factor when you are designing a planting scheme. Hosta sizes quoted in plant catalogs frequently include the height of the flower spikes; the leaf clumps themselves are often shorter.

Preparing the site

Hostas prefer well-drained but moisture-retentive soil that is rich in organic matter. Before planting, dig in plenty of leaf mold, well-rotted garden compost, or composted manure.

All-green varieties tolerate almost any situation, whether in full shade or full sun. However, heavy shade tends to reduce a plant's ability to flower well, and full sun can scorch the leaves. For ideal results, choose an intermediate position in light or semi-shade. In general, variegated, pale-leaved varieties produce the finest colors in shady conditions and are susceptible to scorching in a sunny spot.

Planting hostas

Hostas bought from a garden center or nursery are invariably pot-grown and can be planted in the garden at any time of year, as

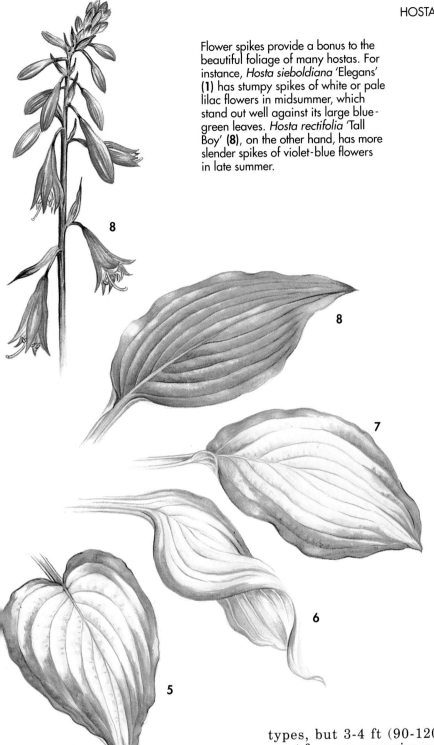

Flower spikes provide a bonus to the beautiful foliage of many hostas. For instance, *Hosta sieboldiana* 'Elegans' (**1**) has stumpy spikes of white or pale lilac flowers in midsummer, which stand out well against its large blue-green leaves. *Hosta rectifolia* 'Tall Boy' (**8**), on the other hand, has more slender spikes of violet-blue flowers in late summer.

dead and rotting leaves once the autumnal tints have faded. Young plants may benefit from a winter mulch of dry leaves to protect their crowns.

Unlike most other herbaceous perennials, hostas do not require regular division. Indeed, they are best left undisturbed throughout their life and allowed to build up a substantial colony. Plants will live for more than 30 years in a suitable site. Old plants develop a very tough, woody crown and are almost impossible to divide; they are even harder to reestablish.

Propagation
Despite the problems encountered with division, this method is the main one used for propagating hostas. However, it is best to divide fairly young plants that have not become too tough and woody. Lift the crowns in early spring and break them up into sections, each with two or three leaf shoots and a few strong roots. You may need a sharp knife or small pruning saw to split up mature crowns.

Alternatively, propagate hostas from seed. If you do not deadhead them, the flower heads will develop viable seeds, which you can collect and sow. Sometimes seed is available from mail-order seed suppliers, but it may be relatively expensive. Garden hybrids will not breed true from seed, but interesting new variegations or leaf shapes can be obtained.

Sow seeds as soon as they are mature or in spring in a moist seed-starting mix at a temperature of about 50°F (10°C). Allow 1 to 3 months for germination. When seedlings are large enough to handle, transplant them into individual small pots and grow them on in a cold frame. Young plants should be ready to set out in their permanent site the following spring. Harden them off gradually before planting them outdoors, and do not expect any flowers until the second year.

Pests and diseases
Slugs and snails are the major enemies of hostas — they often chew holes in young leaves, and sometimes eat them completely. You can easily recognize the slime trails they leave on and around the plants.

Fortunately, there are many nonchemical deterrents for slugs

types, but 3-4 ft (90-120 cm) apart for more expansive ones.

To move plants from one area of the garden to another, transplant in early spring when the crowns are just sprouting new leaves. Make the planting hole of a sufficient size so that the roots can be spread out well and the crown can lie flush with the soil surface. Press the plant in and water it thoroughly.

Aftercare
Hostas need little routine care. Staking and pruning are unnecessary. Water them well in periods of dry weather, especially when they are in a sunny site. After flowering, deadhead them.

In the fall, clear away all the

their roots will not be disturbed. They dislike irregularities in water supply, however, so they are more likely to grow successfully if you set them out in mid-fall or early spring when they have few or no leaves. Hostas planted in warmer periods of the year will need more frequent watering to prevent wilting and leaf scorch. Space the plants according to the size of the particular cultivar — as little as 1 ft (30 cm) apart for the smaller

and snails. For example, you can surround each plant or the entire bed with a strip of copper foil. Since slugs have soft bodies, a ring of some sharp or gritty material, such as coarse sand or diatomaceous earth, can also repel them. Ashes can burn slugs and snails, and a ring of it may prove similarly reliable. You must restock the barrier regularly, especially after heavy rain.

These pests are also attracted to yeast; try setting beer-filled traps around your hostas. Of course, the traps have to be refilled every few days.

Although chemical slug baits that contain metaldehyde or methiocarb give the most efficient control, they must be used with care. Follow the maker's instructions as to the suitable time and conditions for application. The effectiveness of slug baits varies according to temperature and humidity levels. Don't leave these chemicals outdoors if you allow pets in your garden.

Crown rot may also attack hostas during prolonged spells of wet weather. It causes sudden wilting and death. To offer the best protection, make sure that the plants are adequately spaced and that the soil is well drained.

◄ **Hosta albo-marginata** Now called *H. sieboldii,* the old species name more accurately describes the handsome foliage. Thin white margins outline the lance-shaped, glossy green leaves. Only 12-18 in (30-45 cm) high, the plant is topped in summer with violet-striped lilac flowers.

PREVENTING SLUG AND SNAIL DAMAGE

1 Metaldehyde or methiocarb pellets provide the most reliable means of control against slugs and snails. They remain effective for several days, but should be reapplied after heavy rain.

2 If infestation is not severe, sink beer-filled plastic containers around your hostas. Puncture holes just above soil level; attracted by the yeast, pests will crawl through the holes and drown.

3 In the interest of wildlife and pet safety, avoid chemicals. Instead, use circular barriers of copper foil, ashes, gritty sand, or diatomaceous earth to protect hostas from soft-bodied pests.

HARDY OUTDOOR FERNS

**Ferns, with their cool colors, are ideal for
those parts of the garden where little else will grow. They make
wonderful partners for other shade-loving plants.**

Ferns are among the most ancient plants on earth. Thousands of species grow naturally throughout the world; they can be found in habitats as diverse as tropical jungles, deserts, and even the Arctic Circle. Most, however, prefer moist soil in a partially shaded environment. Ferns can thus transform an area where few other plants will thrive into a wonderfully tranquil oasis of gentle foliage.

A fascinating property of hardy ferns is the ability to produce offspring with widely varying shapes of leaves (correctly known as fronds). A real enthusiast will grow nothing but ferns in a shady area, mixing species of different sizes, shapes of fronds, and shades of green. Other gardeners combine ferns with other striking foliage and flowering plants, such as primulas and hostas.

Ferns, however, do not need to be restricted to a shady corner — nearly all grow well in dappled shade beneath trees. Moreover, their serrated fronds make an effective contrast with the smooth bark on the trunks of trees, particularly the slender varieties of willow and beech.

Most ferns look best when set far enough apart from each other to prevent the fronds from intermingling. The spaces between the plants, or at the front of the border, can be filled with low-growing ground cover, such as bergenias, epimediums, and lilies of the valley *(Convallaria majalis)*, all of which do well in shady sites.

Many ferns are evergreen and enhance the garden in winter. The Christmas fern *(Polystichum acrostichoides)*, hart's-tongue fern *(Phyllitis scolopendrium)*, and the common polypody *(Polypodium virginianum)* are quite stunning, especially when their fronds are edged with sparkling frost. And for a rock garden, the small maidenhair spleenwort *(Asplenium trichomanes)* will remain bright when other plants have faded.

Planting ferns
Ferns will grow in all humus-rich soils except for those that are heavy and compacted. Many of these plants are not fussy about soil type, but they do require the right level of acidity or alkalinity (soil pH), depending on species. For example, beech *(Thelypteris* spp.), chain *(Woodwardia* spp.), and lady ferns *(Athyrium* spp.) need an acid soil, such as one that is enriched with oak leaves or sawdust. However, the maidenhair, spleenwort, and bulblet bladder fern *(Cystopteris bulbifera)* thrive only on alkaline sites, such as those that have been amended with ground limestone.

Most ferns should be protected from midday sun (especially in the South) and from strong winds. The north side of a house or fence is ideal because it shields the plants from strong sun but leaves them open to the sky. Another excellent planting position is in the shade cast by tall trees. Ferns grown in soil that remains moist throughout the summer, however, may tolerate more intense sunlight. The hay-scented fern *(Dennstaedtia punctilobula)* and the sensitive fern *(Onoclea sensibilis)* are especially hardy in this respect. And there are some ferns, such as the lordly ostrich fern *(Matteucia pensylvanica)*, that are

◄ Spring weather prompts the ostrich fern *(Matteuccia pensylvanica)* to unfurl its "fiddleheads." These open into plumelike fronds as much as 4 ft (120 cm) tall. This elegant fern thrives in moist, acid soils and is hardy to zone 2.

PLANTING FERNS

1 Carefully choose your planting site for ferns — most need shade and moisture. Dig the planting bed deeply in the fall or spring and sprinkle on sterilized bone meal at the rate of one good-sized handful per sq yd/sq m.

2 Add a 1-in (2.5-cm) layer of leaf mold or well-rotted garden compost on top of the bone meal, then fork both amendments into the soil to a depth of about 6-9 in (15-23 cm). Level the site before planting the ferns.

3 The exact planting method depends on the growth habit and root type of the particular fern. For crown-forming ferns, first manually remove all old, woody frond bases to allow the new roots to develop more quickly without hindrance.

4 Once trimmed, plant these ferns so that the crown is flush with the surface of the soil — the planting hole should be equal to the depth of the fern's entire root ball. Press the plant in carefully with your feet and water as necessary until growth is well established.

5 Rhizomatous-rooted ferns require a different method of planting. Using a sharp knife, trim a section of rhizome — lifted from the ground in early spring or bought from a nursery — so that each piece has at least one growing point from which new shoots will emerge.

6 With a hand fork or trowel, make shallow holes in the soil. Place each piece of rhizome in one of these holes. Cover with the planting mixture in step 2 and press down lightly with your fingers. Since the fern is now buried, label the planting site clearly.

7 Spleenworts are ideal for growing in rock gardens or naturalizing in drystone walls. First, remove one of the wall's stones, then place the fern on its side in the crevice. Cover the roots with a good layer of moist leaf mold before replacing the stone.

valued because they tolerate poorly drained, marshy soils that kill most other garden plants.

The best time for setting out ferns is in the early fall or spring. If they arrive from a nursery before they can be planted, do not allow the roots to dry out.

During moist weather, dig over the planting bed to a depth of 1 ft (30 cm) and break up the soil. Sprinkle sterilized bone meal over the surface at the rate of a good-sized handful per sq yd/sq m. Add a 1-in (2.5-cm) layer of leaf mold or garden compost on top of the bone meal, and then fork it all in.

For use in the garden, there are three types of ferns: crown-forming, rhizomatous-rooted (creeping types), and spleenworts.

Crown-forming ferns have fronds that emerge in a feathery crown from a stout root. Two of this type are the male fern *(Dryopteris filix-mas)* and the lady fern *(Athyrium filix-femina)*.

If planting these ferns in spring, first cut away the old woody frond bases so that new roots can develop more quickly. For fall planting, simply remove any damaged fronds. Then dig a hole to the depth of the fern's roots, place the fern in the hole, and fill with soil so that the crown is flush with the surface.

Rhizomatous-rooted ferns, such as the maidenhair ferns *(Adiantum* species) and the polypodies *(Polypodium)*, send up fronds along the rhizome without forming a crown. To plant them, make shallow depressions in the soil. Place each rhizome in an individual depression, then press the soil down lightly around it.

Spleenworts, a group of ferns

that belong to the genus *Asplenium,* grow best in vertical or sloping crevices. They are superb for rock gardens or drystone walls. Place the fern on its side in the crevice and cover the roots generously with leaf mold.

Aftercare

Once established, most ferns need watering only if the soil dries out during hot spells. After planting, cover the entire surface around the ferns with a mulch, 1 in (2.5 cm) deep, of shredded leaves.

Mulch with the same material in fall and again in spring. Before spreading the fall mulch on the bed, scatter bone meal around the plants at a rate of a generous handful per sq yd/sq m.

Weed ferns by hand — forking or hoeing can damage their root systems. In spring, encourage new shoots to form by removing dead fronds with a sharp knife or pruning shears, as near to the crown or base as possible.

Propagation by division

The easiest way to propagate crown-forming ferns, such as male or lady ferns, is by division of the crowns in early fall or spring.

Carefully dig up a clump of ferns with a fork, then use your fingers to ease the soil away from the rhizomes, or roots. With a sharp knife, cut the clump in half, taking care to do as little damage as possible to existing fronds and the buds of dormant "fiddleheads" — the new growth.

Subdivide the two new clumps by the same method, to produce several new plants, each with its own root system. Then replant the divisions in moist soil as shown on the facing page.

Rhizomatous ferns, those with a creeping growth habit, can also be propagated by division. In early fall or spring, dig up a clump and cut off any damaged fronds. With a sharp knife, cut the rhizomes into sections, each with at least one growing point — that is, the site on the rhizome from which new shoots are emerging. Then replant as shown on the facing page. Each division will form a new fern, reaching full size within a couple of growing seasons.

MULCHING FERNS

Mulch all ferns — except those growing among rocks or in a drystone wall — in spring and fall with a 1-in (2.5-cm) layer of shredded leaves. In fall, apply bone meal before the mulch.

Frond-base propagation

Because propagation by division is a slow process, hart's-tongue ferns are usually grown from the bases of existing fronds. Do this task during the spring or summer months, ideally in midspring to late spring.

Dig up a fern and wash the soil from its roots. Break the rootstock in half to get at the frond bases. With a sharp knife, remove a frond base, cutting as cleanly and as close to the rootstock as possible. Cut off as many frond bases as required.

Cut off the remains of the old fronds at each frond base. Then remove the old roots from the other ends. Place a layer of peat moss, ½ in (15 mm) deep, at the bottom of a clean plastic flat. Add ½ in (15 mm) of builder's sand that you have sterilized (do this by putting the sand in a fine-mesh sieve and pouring boiling water over it).

Lay the trimmed frond bases on the sand — a standard flat will take about 50-60 bases. Place a plastic propagation top (or plastic bag on a frame) over the flat and put it in a shady place. No ventilation is needed.

By the following spring, young

◀ **Hart's-tongue fern** The bright green *Asplenium (Phyllitis) scolopendrium* naturalizes easily in shady woodland settings. Dwarf forms of the variety 'Cristatum,' with crested tips, are suitable for the rock garden.

plants should have grown from the bases. Transplant each to a 2½-in (6-cm) pot filled with a mix of equal parts screened compost, sharp builder's sand, and finely ground sphagnum moss. As the plantlets develop, pot them on into the next-sized pot until a strong root system has been established. Finally, set them out in the garden in spring or fall.

Bulblet propagation

Some ferns, such as the bulblet bladder fern *(Cystopteris bulb-ifera)*, produce pealike bulblets along the midrib of each frond in late summer. New plants can be grown from these bulblets.

Place a ½-in (15-mm) layer of rooting medium over the bottom of a plastic flat. Add a ½-in (15-mm) layer of sterilized builder's sand. Detach healthy fronds from the fern and lay them flat on the sand, with the bulblets facing upward; secure with a bent piece of galvanized wire. Place a plastic propagation top (or plastic bag supported on a frame) over the flat and put it in a shady place.

The following spring, young plants should be growing from the bulblets along the midrib of each frond. When these are large enough to handle, carefully remove the old fronds from the flat. Be careful not to tear the root systems of the new ferns.

Detach the new plants from the old fronds and place them individually in 2½-in (6-cm) pots of the compost/sand/sphagnum mix. As they develop, transplant them to the next-sized pot until a strong root system has been established. Then set them out in the garden.

PROPAGATING HART'S-TONGUE FERNS

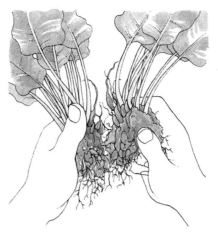

1 In midspring to late spring, just as new growth is beginning, dig up a mature fern and gently wash the soil from the roots. Carefully break or cut the root ball in half to expose the stalk bases of the fronds.

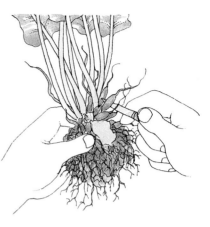

2 Using a sharp knife, cut away each of the frond bases, as close to the fern's rootstock as possible — the frond bases, if suitably healthy for propagation purposes, are swollen and somewhat tuberous in appearance.

3 Trim the cut frond bases at both ends. Fill a plastic flat with a layer of peat moss and then a layer of sterilized sharp sand. Lay the frond bases on the sand and cover with a propagation top. Keep the sand moist at all times.

4 A year later, young ferns should have grown from the bases. They are now ready to be transplanted to individual small pots filled with a mix of equal parts screened compost, sharp builder's sand, and finely ground sphagnum moss.

PROPAGATING FROM BULBLETS

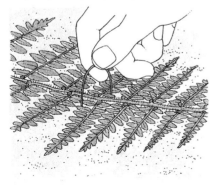

1 In late summer, lay a cut frond in a flat of sterilized sand, with the pealike bulblets facing upward. Secure the frond to the sand with a bent piece of wire. Cover with plastic.

2 Put the flat in a shady place in the garden or overwinter it in a cold frame. By the following spring, young ferns should be growing from the bulblets along the midrib of the old frond.

3 When the young ferns are large enough to handle, carefully detach them from the old frond and plant them individually in small pots of a compost/ sand/sphagnum mixture.

ORNAMENTAL GRASSES

Dainty hare's-tails, imposing pampas grasses, and impenetrable bamboos lend elegance and informality to a garden scene.

The huge family of grasses, the Gramineae, contains several thousand narrow-leaved flowering plants that are distributed throughout the world, from the Antarctic to the Arctic. Among them are the essential food plants — cereals — as well as numerous ornamental species, ranging from the ground-hugging green lawn grasses, to the colored-leaved and variegated border types, to the tall pampas grasses and towering bamboos. Members of the sedge family (Cyperaceae), cattail family (Typhaceae), and rush family (Juncaceae) are often grouped with grasses because they have a similar growth habit and leaf shape.

There are grasses suitable for all soil types and climates. They include evergreen, semievergreen, and herbaceous perennials, as well as several annual types. (Bamboos are often regarded as shrubs, however, because they have tough, woody stems — which are actually stiffened with silica.) Most grasses are able to tolerate air pollution, so they do well even in urban gardens.

Although ornamental grasses are flowering plants, many are grown specifically for their foliage. Individual flowers are small and generally not very showy, but when seen *en masse* in feathery sprays or in upright or arching spikes, they look quite elegant.

Classification

The botanical classification of the grass family has undergone several reorganizations and is still in a state of flux, but the basic form remains constant. Seven subdivisions are recognized, though not all of these are popular in home gardens. The varying structure of the floral cluster plays a major part in this categorization.

Group 1 includes the bamboos, such as *Arundinaria, Sasa, Chusquea,* and *Phyllostachys*. Originating in the Far East, these upright plants often grow to great heights. Bamboos have hollow, usually jointed stems and lance-shaped leaves. Some take many years to reach maturity, when they flower and then die.

Group 2 is similar in habit, but is not common in home gardens.

▼ **Fountain grass** Stirred by the softest breeze, *Pennisetum villosum* ripples its creamy white flower spikes over sea-green tufts of grass. A half-hardy perennial, it needs winter protection north of zone 9 and a site in full sun. The flower spikes are attractive when dried.

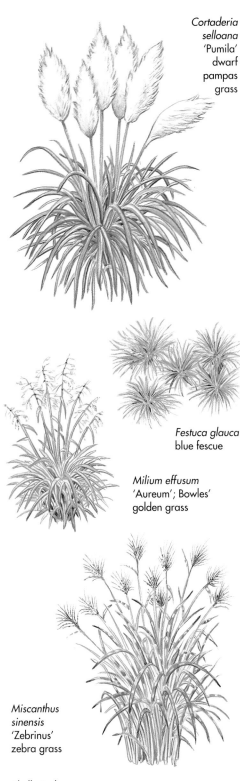

*Cortaderia
selloana
'Pumila'
dwarf
pampas
grass*

Festuca glauca
blue fescue

Milium effusum
'Aureum'; Bowles'
golden grass

*Miscanthus
sinensis
'Zebrinus'
zebra grass*

*Phyllostachys
aurea
golden
bamboo*

Group 3 is an unspecialized category of robust grasses, mostly with flowers in panicles, or branched clusters. It includes pampas grass *(Cortaderia selloana), Arundo,* and moor grass *(Molinia caerulea).*

Group 4 consists of grasses that are adapted to the intense sunlight found in savanna and tropical grasslands. Of interest are the gramma grasses *(Bouteloua* spp.) and cord grass *(Spartina).* Both have flower spikelets in racemes (unbranched spikes or sprays).

Group 5 is defined by grasses with a particular leaf anatomy and two-flowered spikelets — characteristics of little significance to the home gardener. Among the genera in this category are *Pennisetum, Panicum, Coix, Miscanthus,* and *Zea.*

Group 6 also has special botanical features that are of little significance to the home gardener. However, a wide range of garden grasses are found in this category, notably *Agrostis, Alopercurus, Arrhenatherum, Avena, Calamagrostis, Deschampsia, Festuca, Glyceria, Helictotrichon, Hordeum* (ornamental barley), *Phalaris,* and *Poa.*

Group 7 comprises tussocky or reedlike grasses, including feather or needle grass *(Stipa).*

The sedge family is also subdivided according to special botanical features mainly associated with flower structure, but these details are not of interest to the home gardener. The base of their leaves differentiate them from true grasses — sedges lack a joint where the leaf sheath meets the blade, so there are no swollen nodes. The stems are solid and often triangular in cross-section.

Sedges include *Carex, Cyperus,* and *Scirpus.* They are mostly rhizome-rooted perennials with narrow upright leaves, and grow in marshes or beside water.

The rush family is mostly marsh or waterside plants that have slender, tapering, pith-filled, stemlike leaves. Only two genera are grown in home gardens — *Juncus* and *Luzula.* These are distinguished from true grasses by their flowers, which are arranged in cymes — domed, flattened, or rounded clusters that have airy branchlets radiating outward.

Members of the cattail family, also known as bulrushes, are rhizome-rooted perennial marsh-

*Arundinaria
viridistriata*
variegated
dwarf bamboo

*Phalaris
arundinacea
'Picta';
gardener's
garters*

land plants that have upright stems topped by a spongy, cylindrical, densely compacted flower head, which resembles a poker. Cattail leaves are grasslike and flat. This family is represented by a single genus — *Typha.*

Choosing grasses

You can select grasses for your landscaping scheme based on size, foliage color, hardiness, and soil requirements. The shape and color of any flower heads may also influence your choice.

Most decorative grasses are suited to open, sunny positions in the garden. They give an informal, delicate, and graceful look to any group of plants, whether in a mixed border or a perennial or annual bed, and contrast well with colorful flowering plants.

Among the tall grasses are pampas grass *(Cortaderia selloana),* silver grass *(Miscanthus sinensis),* and giant feather grass *(Stipa gigantea),* all of which grow to 10 ft (3 m). Pampas grass produces plumes of feathery, silver-cream flowers; and there are pink-flowered varieties, such as 'Rosea,' and golden-variegated forms, such as 'Gold Band.' Silver grass has a variegated form striped with golden crossbands called zebra grass.

There are more moderately proportioned grasses for the mixed or perennial bed that offer a wider selection than the tall grasses. In flower, these may reach 2-4 ft (60-120 cm) in height. If you want green foliage, there are grasses with upright and compact flower spikes, or with feathery sprays, or with open, branched panicles that

Briza media
quaking grass

wave gently in the slightest breeze. Some genera are *Briza, Deschampsia,* and *Pennisetum.*

For bluish or gray foliage of moderate height, you may wish to choose *Helictotrichon semper-virens.* If you are looking for yellow foliage, consider golden foxtail grass *(Alopecurus pratensis* 'Aureus'). For cream-variegated foliage, you can try oat grass *(Arrhenatherum elatius bulbosum* 'Variegatum') or perhaps gardener's garters *(Phalaris arundinacea* 'Picta').

The front of a bed is the perfect place for shorter grasses — those that grow no higher than about 1½ ft (45 cm). These grasses can be planted in orderly rows as edging, informal drifts, or individual accents. Of interest are the blue-green or blue-gray fescues *(Festuca)* that thrive on poor soils and the white-edged creeping soft grass *(Holcus mollis* 'Albo-variegatus'), which is only 5 in (12.5 cm) tall.

Annual grasses can also be used to fill gaps between perennials or shrubs in a sunny bed. Many of them also make attractive partners for other annuals in a formal bedding scheme. They range in size from the extremely tall ornamental maizes *(Zea mays* cultivars), which are 3-5 ft (1-1.5 m) high, to the quaking grass *(Briza maxima),* Job's tears *(Coix lacryma-jobi),* the animated oat *(Avena sterilis),* and squirreltail grass *(Hordeum jubatum),* to the short and dainty love grasses *(Eragrostis)* and hare's-tail grass. For a partially shaded spot, choose perennials such as Bowles' golden

grass *(Millium effusum* 'Aureum'), *Hakonechloa,* or hair grass *(Deschampsia caespitosa).*

Several true grasses prefer moist soils or even truly wet conditions. Two of these are the variegated moor grass *(Molinia caerulea* 'Variegata') — which is 2 ft (60 cm) high and has a neat, tufted habit and cream-striped leaves — and the variegated cord grass *(Spartina pectinata* 'Aureo-marginata'), a 6-ft (1.8-m)-tall giant with yellow-edged leaves.

Bamboos also favor moist soils and tolerate sun or light shade. Their heights vary enormously, from the 15-ft (4.5-m)-tall *Pseudosasa japonica* to the 2-ft (60-cm)-tall *Pleioblastus humilis.* Foliage color may be all-green or decoratively marked with yellow (as in *Pleioblastus auricoma)* or white *(Sasa veitchii).*

The wet soil beside a pond or stream, or man-made pockets around a lined or concrete pool, are ideal for marshland grasses, sedges, rushes, and cattails. Most thrive in sun, but will tolerate some shade. Of the true grasses, variegated manna grass *(Glyceria maxima* 'Variegata') is the most popular. It grows to 2-3 ft (60-90 cm) and has handsome green, yellow, and cream-striped leaves.

Among the water-loving sedges are spike rush *(Eleocharis montevidensis* — zones 6-9) and, in the South, Egyptian papyrus *(Cyperus papyrus* — zones 9-10) and umbrella palm *(Cyperus alternifolius* — zones 9-10). On poor, moist soil, try growing corkscrew rush *(Juncus effusus* 'Spiralis'). These sedges and rushes, together with cattails, such as the 6-ft (1.8-m)- tall *Typha angustifolia* or the much shorter *T. minima,* can be planted with their crowns up to 6 in (15 cm) completely submerged underwater.

Planting grasses

You can buy perennial grasses from garden centers and nurseries in containers similar to those of other plants. The best time to plant these grasses is early spring, for then they will have plenty of time to settle down and become established during their first growing season. Bare-rooted clumps lifted from open ground should also be planted in spring.

Most ornamental grasses do best in an open-textured soil that is not too fertile — rich soil

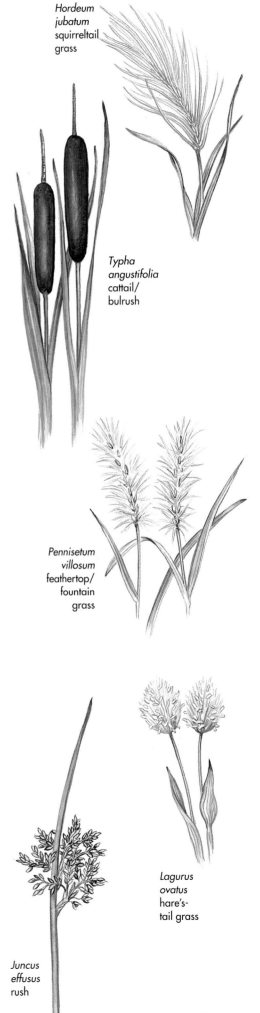

Hordeum jubatum
squirreltail grass

Typha angustifolia
cattail/
bulrush

Pennisetum villosum
feathertop/
fountain
grass

Lagurus ovatus
hare's-tail grass

Juncus effusus
rush

encourages leaf growth at the expense of flowers. If your soil is not well-drained, incorporate plenty of builder's sand or organic matter before planting grasses. By amending with organic matter, there is no need for you to add extra fertilizer.

Though grasses originate from both acid and alkaline soils, in cultivation they are mostly tolerant of either type, provided it is sufficiently moist.

Set young grasses in the ground at the same depth as they were grown at the nursery or garden center. Build a slight ridge of soil around each one to ensure that water drains into the root ball, rather than away from it. Thoroughly water the grasses.

The spacing between plants should be equal to the ultimate height of the foliage tuft, ignoring the flowers. In time, you will have a uniform carpet of foliage. However, if you want the outline of each tuft to remain visible, double the amount of spacing.

Many grasses spread by creeping stems or stolons, which often become extremely invasive in a mixed planting. For this reason, they should be planted within some kind of container. For instance, you can cut off the bottom of an old bucket or large pot and bury the remaining cylinder up to its rim in the ground. Then set the grass plant in the center of the enclosure, making sure to trim off any stolons that subsequently cross the barrier above the ground.

Restrict the spread of invasive bog-garden grasses and water-lovers by planting them in containers. Set them in the bog or at the pond edge, rather than in open mud.

Aftercare
To prevent undue drying out of the soil around grass roots on exposed sites, spread a liberal mulch of leaf mold or shredded bark and renew it every year. Water grasses frequently during very dry spells, especially the annual species.

After flowering, little routine care is necessary for most grasses. Use hedge or pruning shears to cut off all dead flower heads, stalks, and withered foliage. The timing of this trimming depends on the climate and the hardiness of the plants. When slightly ten-

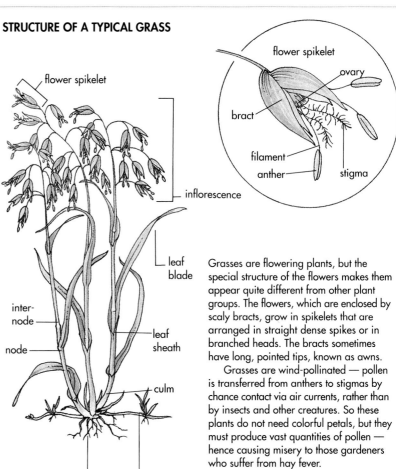

STRUCTURE OF A TYPICAL GRASS

flower spikelet

flower spikelet

ovary

bract

filament

anther

stigma

inflorescence

leaf blade

inter-node

leaf sheath

node

culm

root

stolon

Grasses are flowering plants, but the special structure of the flowers makes them appear quite different from other plant groups. The flowers, which are enclosed by scaly bracts, grow in spikelets that are arranged in straight dense spikes or in branched heads. The bracts sometimes have long, pointed tips, known as awns.

Grasses are wind-pollinated — pollen is transferred from anthers to stigmas by chance contact via air currents, rather than by insects and other creatures. So these plants do not need colorful petals, but they must produce vast quantities of pollen — hence causing misery to those gardeners who suffer from hay fever.

der species are grown in cold areas, it is advantageous to leave dead top growth intact until early spring — this step affords some protection for the rootstocks. Trim hardier types in late fall.

If self-seeding is not desired, deadhead grasses (especially annuals) as soon as the flowers fade, before seeds begin to swell.

Be very careful when trimming pampas grass — its saw-toothed leaves can cause gashes if your hands and arms are not protected. Many other grass leaves can also slice your hands if handled carelessly, so be sure to wear thick gloves when working with them.

If you want to encourage lush, more attractive foliage on perennial tufted grasses, cut the plants back to within 2 in (5 cm) of the ground in midwinter. Each year new growth originates from ground level, so removal of the previous year's growth not only improves the appearance of the plant, but also gives young shoots room to develop.

It is important to weed between grasses frequently because the wild grasses — some of which are similar in appearance to the culti-

vated types — may establish quickly and then be difficult to separate.

Propagation
Grasses grow readily from seed, which can be collected from naturally pollinated garden plants. There are very few hybrid grasses, and seed usually breeds true. Seed companies also supply a good range of ornamental grass seeds, especially of the annual types.

Sow annual grasses shallowly, directly into their flowering sites in early spring to midspring, at the same time as your lawn begins to grow. These plants prefer a hot, sunny site. Broadcast the seed or sow it in rows, then barely cover it with soil. As when sowing a lawn, cover the area with wire mesh or crisscrossed black thread to discourage birds from eating the seeds. Thin the seedlings to spacings about 6-12 in (15-30 cm) apart.

Alternatively, sow seeds indoors in pots or flats in very early spring. Increase rushes, clump-forming perennial grasses, and cattails by dividing their fibrous roots or rhizomes in spring.

Bulbs, corms, and tubers

Bulbs, corms, and tubers are widely used by many gardeners, particularly as several of these plants flourish indoors as well as outside. Their versatility alone makes them attractive choices — they can be used as permanent plantings that return year after year, as bedding plants (particularly tulips), as cut flowers to brighten the home, or as cheerful houseplants. Many varieties, especially narcissi and crocus, are ideal for naturalizing grassy areas and for forming colorful clumps beneath light shade trees.

Most bulbs, corms, and tubers require little attention yet provide long-lasting displays of flowers throughout the year. Imagine swaths of miniature irises and colonies of white snowdrops in the late winter; nodding daffodils and vibrant tulips opening their buds to the spring sun; stately irises, aristocratic lilies, and tall-stemmed globular alliums spanning spring and summer until the fall appearance of hardy cyclamens, spider lilies, and autumn crocuses.

Lilies have an exotic look, swaying in colorful splendor, and are surprisingly simple to cultivate. Gladioli can often seem too grand and intimidating to include in a flower bed, but even though they are cold-sensitive, they are easy to grow and produce an enormous mass of flowers for cutting and indoor display. Moreover, the corms are so inexpensive that they can be left to rot in the soil, and next season be replaced with new stock. Although tuberous begonias require more care than other plants, their vivid blooms throughout the summer are worth the extra effort you put into cultivating them.

Turk's-cap lilies These exquisite lilies are favorites among summer-flowering bulbs.

STATELY LILIES

The magnificent trumpet and Turk's-cap lilies are at home in flower beds or in planters on the front porch.

▲ **Regal lilies** The fragrant pure white trumpets of *Lilium regale* 'Album' are borne in huge clusters of over two dozen blooms in midsummer.

▼ **'Enchantment'** One of the most popular of the Asiatic Mid-Century hybrids, it bears vivid orange-red flowers, each up to 6 in (15 cm) wide.

Lilies belong to the genus *Lilium*, which includes about 80 species and thousands of hybrids, and are members of the botanical family Liliaceae. Many other plants, often associated with different genera or families, have acquired the word lily in their common name because of the shape of their flowers, but these may need different cultivation. Do not confuse true lilies with arum or calla lilies — those tropical blossoms florists sometimes sell as "lilies."

One of the oldest cultivated flowers, the lily has been cherished for some 3,000 years. The gleaming white Madonna lily *(Lilium candidum)*, for instance, has become a traditional symbol of purity. All lilies are perennial, bulbous-rooted plants, and most are hardy. They vary widely in size, flower color, flowering time, and cultural needs.

In the past, lilies were considered flowers that required great skill to grow. While this reputation holds true for some species, including the Madonna, many hybrids have been developed that are robust and disease-free. In fact, newer varieties frequently outshine their parents in vigor and range of color.

Flower types

Lilies can be divided into two main flower shapes — trumpet and Turk's-cap. Very wide trumpets are often called bowl-shaped, and some trumpet and Turk's-cap types have flowers facing upward, rather than the more typical downward or outward direction.

Trumpet lilies have large flowers and range in shape from the slender white trumpets of *L. formosanum* to the elongated and wide-flaring, purple-striped white trumpets of the towering *L. giganteum*, correctly listed as *Cardiocrinum giganteum*.

Turk's-cap lilies, such as *L. martagon*, have smaller, pendent flowers, with petals normally curving backward at the tips (strongly reflexed).

An outstanding example of the bowl-shaped type is the golden-banded lily of Japan, *L. auratum*. It has white flowers, 10 in (25 cm) wide, with a bright yellow central band on each petal, and is covered with crimson spots. These upward-facing lilies have flowers clustered in loose heads, such as the red star lily *(L. concolor)* from China.

There are lilies of almost every color and shade, except blue, and many are streaked or spotted. Most have prominent stamens. The flowering season outdoors ranges from early summer to early fall. One of the first species

Lilium regale
regal/royal lily
Division 9
species

'Connecticut King'
Asiatic hybrid
Division 1a
upward-facing flowers

'Discovery'
Asiatic hybrid
Division 1c
Turk's-cap flowers

Lilium auratum
golden-banded lily
Division 9
species

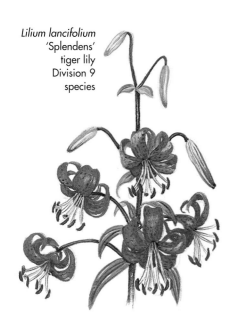

Lilium lancifolium
'Splendens'
tiger lily
Division 9
species

to appear is *L. pyrenaicum,* a native of the Pyrenees. It is a hardy yellow or orange-red Turk's-cap lily, with purple spots. Among the latest to bloom is the tiger lily (*L. lancifolium*) from Japan, with its vivid orange, black-flecked Turk's-cap flowers.

Many lily flowers are scented, but those with the heaviest fragrance, such as *L. pyrenaicum* and *L. martagon,* may be somewhat overpowering. They are best grown away from paths, house windows, or doors. On the other hand, the regal lily *(L. regale), L. longiflorum,* and many others are pleasantly scented.

There is an official classification of lilies that encompasses nine divisions based on origin and flower form. These may be subdivided according to specific flower shape or flower habit.

Asiatic hybrids — Division 1 — are mostly compact plants that grow up to 4 ft (1.2 m) tall. This group is further subdivided into those with upward-facing flowers (1a), those with outward-facing flowers (1b), and those with Turk's-cap flowers (1c).

Martagon hybrids — Division 2 — are hardy and easy to grow; they may reach up to 5 ft (1.5 m) in height, carrying spires of 20 to 30 Turk's-cap flowers.

Candidum hybrids — Division 3 — are mainly listed under the name *L. × testaceum.* They grow up to 4-6 ft (1.2-1.8 m) tall and have sprays of up to 12 nodding, reflexed flowers.

American and Bellingham hybrids — Division 4 — are adorned with 20 or more pendent, strongly reflexed flowers with prominent brown spots. They are borne on stems that grow 5-7 ft (1.5-2.1 m) tall. These plants prefer lime-free soil.

Longiflorum hybrids — Division 5 — are half-hardy, with horizontal trumpet blooms; they are best grown in pots.

Trumpet and Aurelian hybrids — Division 6 — include Asiatic hybrids not included in Division 1. They are strong-growing plants that bloom in late summer, with trumpet-shaped (6a), bowl-shaped (6b), pendent (6c), or flat, star-shaped flowers (6d).

Oriental hybrids — Division 7 — are derived from Japanese species, such as *L. auratum* and *L. speciosum.* They have enormous, spotted, generally bicolored flowers in huge sprays or clusters. These blooms may be trumpet-shaped (7a), bowl-shaped (7b), star-shaped (7c), or recurved (7d).

Miscellaneous hybrids — Division 8 — comprise those not included in any other division.

Species lilies — Division 9 — are the naturally occurring lilies and their varieties.

Choosing the site

Lilies vary in height from 1½ ft (45 cm) to 6 ft (1.8 m) — some even grow to 9 ft (2.7 m). Among the tallest are *L. superbum,* the panther lily *(L. pardalinum),* and *L. henryi.* The smallest include *L. × maculatum,* with its erect yellow to red flowers, which reaches only 2 ft (60 cm) high, and *L. pumilum,* which has scarlet Turk's-cap flowers.

Lilies grow naturally in such

Lilium pyrenaicum 'Aureum'
Division 9
species

'Shuksan'
Bellingham hybrid
Division 4
pendent, reflexed
flowers

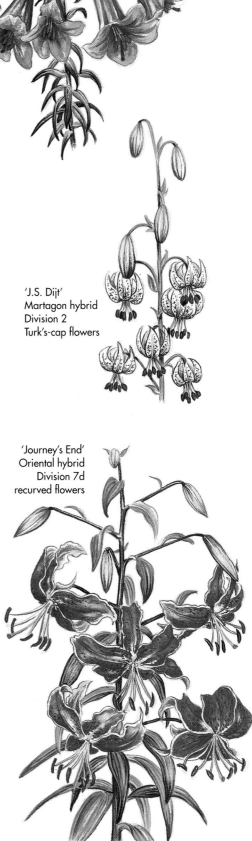

'Pink Perfection'
Aurelian/trumpet
hybrid
Division 6a
trumpet-shaped
flowers

'J.S. Dijt'
Martagon hybrid
Division 2
Turk's-cap flowers

'Journey's End'
Oriental hybrid
Division 7d
recurved flowers

varied situations that at least one species or hybrid can be found to suit almost any garden. Some — such as *L. pardalinum* and *L. auratum* — need neutral to acid soil. Others, including *L. longiflorum* and most of the hybrids, are tolerant of alkaline soils. And there are a few that actually prefer an alkaline soil — for instance *L. candidum* and *L. × testaceum.*

Many lilies are happiest in full sun, but certain ones like partial shade, such as *L. superbum.* All prefer a spot that will keep their roots cool, such as in the shade of small, shallow-rooted plants.

One species that thrives in most soils or positions is the tall regal lily *(L. regale),* which has white trumpet flowers tinged red-purple on the outside. Other robust and easy-to-grow species and hybrids are *L. martagon* and its cultivated offspring (for example, the white-flowered form, 'Album') and the bright Mid-Century hybrids.

Although a bed composed entirely of lilies can flower from late spring to midfall, you will find that most species need protection from wind, and some of the taller types also require support. In general, they do best when mixed with other plants. A background of shrubs, for example, will give some wind protection, as well as provide a beautiful backdrop for the blooms. And if taller lilies are grown among the shrubs, they can be supported naturally.

Lilies particularly suitable for woodland settings or wild gardens are the long-lived Bellingham hybrids, with their flowers in shades of red, orange, and yellow, spotted with maroon or black. Among the other woodland lilies are *L. auratum* and the fragrant Caucasus lily *(L. monadelphum).* For a large pocket in a rock garden, choose *L. pumilum,* with its scarlet Turk's-cap blooms.

Some species, notably *L. candidum, L. tigrinum,* and *L. × testaceum,* are likely to carry viral diseases, which are transmitted from plant to plant by aphids. Lest these susceptible species serve as a source of infection to other, healthy stock, they should be grown only in isolation.

Preparing the site

Most lilies will grow in any well-drained soil. If possible, choose a south-facing position on a slight slope to ensure good drainage.

Dig the soil well in advance of planting, to a depth of 1½ ft (45 cm), breaking it up well. If it is sandy, fork in leaf mold or well-rotted garden compost at the rate of one large bucketful per sq yd/sq m. For heavy clay or silt soils, add builder's sand at the same rate. Never use fresh manure around the roots of lilies — it can cause them to rot.

Ensure that the bed is well drained, as lilies die in stagnant conditions. If your garden is flat and tends to flood, make raised beds of prepared soil about 1 ft (30 cm) deep, ideally with timber or stone retaining walls.

Purchasing lily bulbs

Buy lily bulbs from a reputable nursery or garden center and choose ones that are plump and healthy looking. They should have firm, closely packed scales, as well as a good root system. Never plant a bulb with withered, loose scales. Also avoid any with roots trimmed too close to the bulb. The smaller, young bulbs are best, because they form roots that, after planting, pull the bulbs down to the ideal level.

If any of your bulbs are bruised or soft, remove the outer scales and bury the bulbs in moist peat for a day or two before planting.

Planting lily bulbs

You can plant most lilies outdoors any time between late summer and early spring, provided the ground is not frozen. Madonna lilies should be set out as soon as possible after their stems die down in the fall.

Some lilies root only from the base of the bulbs, but others, notably *L. auratum, L. bulbiferum, L. regale,* and *L. speciosum,* also produce roots from the stem just above the bulb. The base-rooting types should be planted in the very early fall.

If planting is delayed because of bad weather or soil conditions, grow bulbs temporarily in pots or store them briefly in shallow boxes of damp peat to prevent them from drying out.

For most lilies, dig out the planting hole until it measures 2½ times the depth of the bulb. Exceptions are *L. candidum, L. giganteum,* and *L. × testaceum,*

PLANTING LILY BULBS

1 For most lilies, dig the planting hole 2½ times the depth of the bulb. Line the base with builder's sand or fine gravel to improve drainage. Spread out the bulb roots.

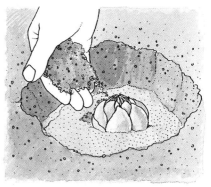

2 Cover the roots with more sand, then refill the hole with soil. Insert a label or short stick to mark each planting position. With a hand fork, scratch in a dressing of bone meal.

which should be planted just below the surface.

Line the base of the hole generously with builder's sand or fine gravel. Spread out the roots of the bulb. Cover the roots with more sand, then fill in with soil. Label the position of each bulb clearly.

After planting, scratch in a handful of sterilized bone meal per sq yd/sq m with a hand fork.

Growing lilies in pots

Shorter, earlier-flowering species of lily, such as the Mid-Century hybrids 'Connecticut King' (bright yellow) and 'Enchantment' (nasturtium-red), do best if they are grown in pots.

Although potting can be done from midfall to early spring, do it

as early as you can. Select a 6-in (15-cm) pot for a medium-sized bulb — about 2 in (5 cm) wide. Line the bottom of the pot with a scrap of clean newspaper.

With base-rooting lilies, fill the pot halfway with sterilized, peat-enriched but well-drained potting soil. Mound up the soil, place the bulb on top, and spread out its roots. Cover the roots with more soil and press them in. Then fill the pot with additional soil and label it. Bury the pot to the rim in sand outdoors and cover it with about 4 in (10 cm) of sand.

With stem-rooting lilies, quarter-fill the pot with potting soil before inserting the bulb. Then cover the bulb with 1 in (2.5 cm) of soil. Place it in an unheated greenhouse or frost-free shed or garage. Once the shoot reaches the top of the pot, fill the pot with more soil, almost to the rim.

In early spring — when the young growth of the stem-rooting lilies has pushed up — plant the bulbs outside or place them in a sunny spot indoors where the temperature ranges from 54-61°F (12-16°C). Don't move them to a warmer room until the flowers open.

Begin regular and moderate watering so that the soil stays constantly moist. Every 2 weeks, feed with weak liquid fertilizer until the buds show color.

Lilies can also be grown in tubs outdoors. Plant them in peat-enriched potting soil, but look after them as you would those growing in the garden.

Aftercare

Even though most lilies are cold

POTTING TWO TYPES OF LILY

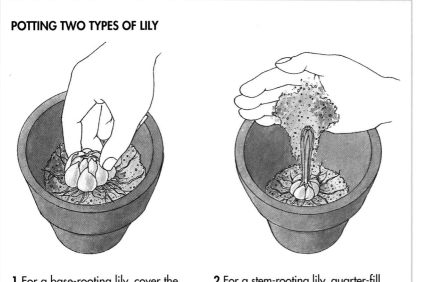

1 For a base-rooting lily, cover the bottom of a 6-in (15-cm) pot with a scrap of newspaper, then fill halfway with sterilized, well-drained potting soil. Make a mound and place the bulb on top. Fill the pot with more soil.

2 For a stem-rooting lily, quarter-fill the pot with sterilized, well-drained potting soil. Insert the bulb and just barely cover it with soil. When the shoot reaches the rim of the pot, cover with more soil, as shown.

hardy, the alternate freezing and thawing of the soil that is associated with early spring can harm the bulbs. A blanket of organic mulch around the planting site will help prevent any damage.

Garden lilies that flower in late summer need staking as protection from fall storms. Those with arching stems, such as *L. henryi*, and those over 3 ft (90 cm) high, also look better if supported. Insert the stakes in early spring. Whether wooden or metal, the stake should be two-thirds of the eventual length of the stem. As the lily grows, tie in the stem.

Do not allow the soil around the plants to dry out. During dry spells in the growing season, thoroughly water the site and mulch it with shredded leaves.

To prevent seeds forming and weakening the plant, deadhead faded blooms. In the fall, let the stems die down. When they are dead — but not rotted — gently pull them from the ground (don't cut them off, as the stems remaining in the soil will rot and damage the bulb). Bag and dispose of this material; be sure not to use it for composting, as it may be diseased.

If you want to increase lilies by seed, leave one or two seedpods on each plant. Harvest them when ripe (yellow) and dry them indoors. If they are left too long on the plants, the capsules will burst open, dispersing the seed.

Indoor lilies either can be planted out in the garden as soon as they have finished flowering or can be kept in their pots for another year. If they are to remain in their pots, remove the top 1½ in (4 cm) of potting soil and replace it with new soil. Then, bury them again under sand outdoors during the winter. Do not let them dry out completely.

Propagation
There are several successful ways of increasing stocks of lilies.
Detaching scales The easiest and most widely used method of propagating lilies is by separating scales from the bulbs and growing these on. Flowering plants will be produced 2 to 5 years later, depending on the species.

The best time for this operation is immediately after the bulb has flowered, although scales can be planted at any time between late summer and early spring. Use only healthy bulbs fresh from the

PROPAGATING FROM BULB SCALES

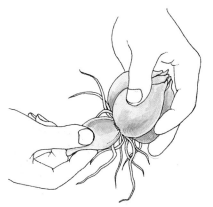

1 Soon after the lily bulb has bloomed, carefully lift it from the soil. Pull away any withered or damaged outer scales from the bulb. Then, gently detach as many of the plump scales as are needed.

2 Fill a seed flat or pot with well-moistened, sterilized potting soil. Plant each scale to half its depth and cover the container with a clear plastic top or plastic bag supported on a wire frame.

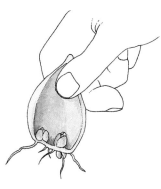

3 Within 6 weeks, bulblets should have formed at the base of each scale. Check by gently removing the soil around one or two scales. If bulblets have formed, remove the top covering.

4 Shoots will soon appear above the soil. Transfer each new plant into a pot, 2½-3 in (6-7.5 cm) deep, filled with sterilized potting soil. Sink the pots in sand outdoors; cover with more sand.

garden; otherwise, there is a risk of passing on infection.

Pull away any withered or damaged outer scales until plump, unbruised scales are revealed. Detach as many of these as are required — there may be 12 to 24 per bulb — gently but firmly, removing each one as close to its base as possible. If you wish to replant the parent, take off only five of its scales.

Plant each scale to half its depth, base down, in pots or flats of well-moistened but well-drained, sterilized potting soil. Space each scale ½-1 in (1.2-2.5 cm) apart and press in.

Cover the container with a clear plastic top or a plastic bag supported on a wire frame. If the scales have been taken early in the year, this container can be placed in a cold frame or unheated greenhouse, or set indoors on a cool windowsill. But

DIVIDING LILY BULBS

Some vigorous lilies, such as *L. pardalinum*, have elongated bulbs joined together like a rhizome. These need to be divided, even if you do not want to propagate from them; otherwise, flowering deteriorates. Sever the bulbs from one another with a sharp knife and then plant them in their new positions in the normal way. Don't divide all your stock at once.

if the scales have been taken in the fall or winter, they will need a bottom heat of 50-55°F (10-13°C), such as that provided by a heated propagation box.

When shoots appear above the soil, the young plants can be planted outside or transferred to small pots of well-drained potting soil, which you then sink into sand outdoors and cover with 1 in (2.5 cm) of sand. Alternatively, place the pots in an unheated greenhouse, cold frame, or frost-free garage or shed.

By the fall of the year after planting, bulbs of vigorous hybrids will be ready for moving out into the garden. Less vigorous varieties may not be ready for another 12 months; keep them in the same pot or, if needed, plant them in pots one size larger.

Division Some lilies, such as *L. pyrenaicum,* increase their bulbs so quickly that they need to be lifted and divided every 3 or 4 years. *L. regale* can also be propagated in this way.

When the stems have died down in late summer, carefully loosen and lift the clump with a fork. Gently separate the bulbs and replant them in fresh soil.

Stem bulbils are the tiny green or black-purple bulbs that grow on the stem in the leaf axils of some species, such as *L. bulbiferum* and *L. tigrinum.* Detach these only when they come away easily without pulling — usually around flowering time. Sow them ½ in (12 mm) deep and 1 in (2.5 cm) apart in a seed-starting mix and then put them in a cold frame or in pots outdoors that you cover with sand. Replant the bulbs into the

garden the following fall.

Bulblets are the offsets that grow on some lilies — for example *L. wardii* and *L. nepalense* — just below ground level, either among the stem roots or from the base of the bulb. Detach these and replant them straight into the ground or grow them on indoors in a seed-starting mix.

Seed can be used to produce larger quantities of new, disease-free bulbs. However, hybrid lilies won't breed true, and you must wait several years for flowers.

Lily seeds can be divided into two groups — epigeal (such as *L. regale* and *L. tigrinum)* and hypogeal (such as *L. canadense* and *L. superbum).*

When seeds are mature (in the fall), or in the early spring, sow them ½ in (12 mm) deep and 1 in (2.5 cm) apart in a seed-starting mix. Place them in a cool greenhouse or frost-free sun porch. Epigeal seeds germinate and produce top growth in a few weeks. Hypogeal seeds produce a bulb first, then develop their first shoots within a few months.

Lily troubles

Lilies may be damaged by slugs and snails, and mice may eat the bulbs. Aphids are particularly harmful to these plants because they spread viral diseases. Serious viral infections can result in yellow-streaked leaves and weak, stunted stem growth. They may even cripple or abort the flowers. While bulbs may live several years with such an infection, there is no cure. The best treatment is to remove and dispose of the infected stock.

BULBILS AND BULBLETS

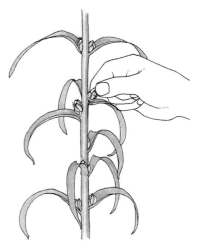

1 Tiny bulbs, known as bulbils, form in the leaf axils of some lily species, including the tiger lily; these can be used for propagation. Remove them in late summer and plant them in a pot or flat of seed-starting mix.

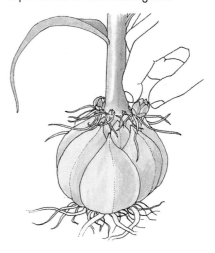

2 Small bulblets, which grow among the stem roots just below ground level or on the base of some lilies, can be detached and set out directly in a nursery bed in late summer. Or, you can plant them in pots indoors.

PROPAGATING LILIES FROM SEED

1 Harvest seed capsules in the fall when they turn yellow. Sow the seeds immediately, or in early spring, in a seed-starting mix. Space seeds 1 in (2.5 cm) apart and ½ in (12 mm) deep.

2 When the second leaf of epigeal types (those that produce top growth in a few weeks after sowing) appears, transplant into pots or deep flats. Set them 1 in (2.5 cm) apart on either side.

3 When the first leaf of hypogeal lilies (those that produce a bulb first and shoots later) emerges from the soil, replant each seedling individually in a 2½-in (6-cm) pot.

DELICATE IRISES

Exquisite irises flower from late winter until late summer — as tiny rock garden beauties, as stately residents of flower beds, and as true water plants.

Irises have been grown in gardens for centuries — some were cultivated in Asia thousands of years ago. Their uniquely shaped flowers come in a vast range of colors, and their generic name actually derives from the Greek word *iris,* meaning a rainbow. There are over 150 *Iris* species, most of which originated in the temperate regions of the Northern Hemisphere. They belong to the large Iridaceae family, which includes crocuses, gladioli, and freesias.

There are two main groups of irises — those that grow from rhizomatous roots (actually swollen underground stems) and those that grow from true bulbs.

The typical iris flower has three outer petals, known as "falls," which usually droop downward; three inner petals, called "standards," generally stand upright. Projecting between these are three narrow petallike "styles" — structures that serve as links between the pollen-receptive stigma and the seed-forming ovary.

The leaves of this hardy plant resemble large blades of grass that grow in a fan-shaped spray.

Classification
Botanically, irises are divided into several groups, according to parentage, origin, floral structure, and other features. Each group is further subdivided. The rhizomatous irises can be found in any of the following divisions:

Bearded irises have a tuft of fleshy hairs, commonly known as the "beard," on the outer fall petals. They also have thick, creeping rhizomes from which arise a fan of broad evergreen or semievergreen leaves. A single stem, bearing several blooms, emerges from each fan in a wide array of colors.

These irises are further

classified according to height — tall bearded (over 28 in/70 cm), intermediate bearded (15-28 in/37-70 cm), dwarf bearded (10-15 in/25-37 cm), and miniature dwarf bearded (under 10 in/25 cm). Species include the purple-flowered German iris *(Iris germanica), I. pallida,* and the tiny *I. pumila,* but the numerous hybrids of mixed parentage are much more popular.

Beardless irises have beautiful flowers, but the fall petals lack a beard. Their evergreen leaves,

which are long, dark, and narrow, rise from slender rhizomes. Beardless irises are divided into the following groups:
❏ Pacific Coast or Californicae beardless irises are indigenous to North America. They carry dainty flowers on wiry stems in late spring and early summer. *I. douglasiana, I. innominata,* and several hybrids are in this category.
❏ Siberian or Sibirica irises have grasslike herbaceous foliage and groups of profuse flowers borne on slender stems. Named hybrids,

▶ **Siberian irises** Hybrids of this beardless group give a superb show of slender-stemmed flowers in early summer. Easy to grow, they thrive in cool, moist borders or by the edge of a pool, in sun or shade.

A VARIETY OF IRISES

dwarf bearded hybrid

intermediate bearded hybrid

tall bearded hybrid

tall bearded hybrid

tall bearded hybrid

tall bearded hybrid

Iris pallida bearded iris variegated foliage

derived largely from *I. sibirica,* grow to about 3 ft (90 cm) high.

❏ Spuria irises are clump-forming, with tough, fibrous rhizomes and reedlike foliage. In the fall the old leaves die down, but the new foliage lasts through the winter. The flowers are robust and have a waxy texture. Named hybrids (butterfly irises) are more popular than the species.

❏ Louisiana irises descend from a group of species — *I. fulva, I. foliosa,* and *I. giganticaerulea* — that have hybridized naturally to produce a range of colors extending from yellow to red and blue. Their tolerance for heat and humidity have made these a favorite of Southern gardeners; many of the Louisiana hybrids and cultivars, however, are outstandingly hardy plants that flourish throughout most of the United States.

❏ Other beardless irises, forming a miscellaneous group, include the herbaceous Japanese iris *(I. kaempferi),* the rabbit ear iris *(I. laevigata),* the yellow flag *(I. pseudacorus),* and the evergreen stinking iris *(I. foetidissima).*

Crested irises, correctly called Evansias, have a cockscomblike linear crest on the falls. Both the falls and standards of their orchidlike pastel flowers lie in the same plane. The evergreen leaves rise from slender rhizomes. Crested irises include *I. cristata, I. japonica,* and *I. tectorum.*

Bulbous irises are divided into three main groups.

❏ Juno irises are distinctive but

uncommon in home gardens. The manner of growth is similar to that of sweet corn, with flowers appearing from leaf axils. Standard petals are reduced to little more than bristles. The spring-flowering, mauve and yellow *I. bucharica* is the easiest to grow.

❏ Netted or reticulata irises have bulbs netted ("reticulated") with fibers. Their leaves are tubular and pointed. The varieties and hybrids belonging to *I. reticulata*, together with *I. danfordiae* and *I. histrioides,* are excellent late-winter plants for a rock garden and for growing in pots.

❏ Xiphium types include English, Dutch, and Spanish irises. They have sparse, reedlike leaves and bear one to three elegant flowers per stem. Named hybrids or mixed-color selections make fine cut flowers, but the tender plants are usually short-lived.

Choosing irises

Tall bearded irises do best when planted in beds on their own because they have special cultivation requirements. However, they are also at home in a perennial or shrub border, blooming in late spring or early summer, when there are few other bold flowers. Their attractive foliage contrasts well with surrounding leaves.

Intermediate bearded irises flower in very late spring and are perfect either for the front of iris beds or borders of low-growing perennials or shrubs. They may also be planted in large pockets in a rock garden.

Dwarf bearded irises will not stand much competition, and are most successful when used as ground cover in a rock garden or grouped in front of small plants. Several varieties clumped together will create a striking effect. Their handsome flowers appear in midspring to late spring.

Among the beardless types, the Louisianas and Sibiricas make splendid plants for the center of a bed. They thrive in most soils, though the Sibiricas like more moisture. Plant Pacific Coast hybrids, which flower in late spring, at the front of borders. Ranging in height from 9 in (23 cm) to 1½ ft (45 cm), they prefer sun or semishade in acid, dry soil.

Spuria irises are an excellent choice for planting at the back of a border — they grow 3-5 ft (90-150 cm) tall and are long-lasting.

PLANTING BEARDED IRISES

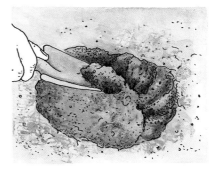

1 Before planting, trim the leaves to form a short fan shape — if left untrimmed, the leaves will be top-heavy and cause the shallowly planted iris to topple over.

2 Using a trowel, dig out a roughly fan-shaped hole. The point of the fan should face the sun and the hole must slope from ground level at the point to 4 in (10 cm) deep at the other side.

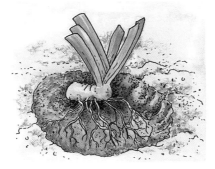

3 Place the trimmed rhizome at the point of the fan, with the leafy end lowest. Spread the roots downward into the hole, making sure they diverge as much as possible to give support.

4 Using your fingers, press in the soil around the roots, leaving the top of the rhizome exposed just above the ground level. Label each plant clearly and water it well.

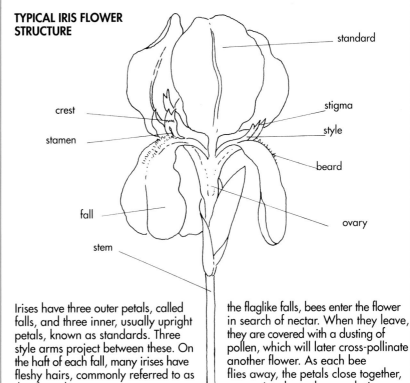

TYPICAL IRIS FLOWER STRUCTURE

standard

crest

stamen

stigma

style

beard

fall

ovary

stem

Irises have three outer petals, called falls, and three inner, usually upright petals, known as standards. Three style arms project between these. On the haft of each fall, many irises have fleshy hairs, commonly referred to as the "beard."

This petal formation is an adaptation for bee pollination. Attracted by the flaglike falls, bees enter the flower in search of nectar. When they leave, they are covered with a dusting of pollen, which will later cross-pollinate another flower. As each bee flies away, the petals close together, separating the anthers and stigma, and thus preventing undesirable self-pollination.

PLANTING BEARDLESS IRISES

1 Trim the leaves of beardless and crested irises to about 9 in (23 cm) before planting — as with bearded types, they are planted shallowly and would topple over if left too tall.

2 Using a hand trowel, dig a round hole that will be large enough to take the spread-out roots. Set the rhizome 1 in (2.5 cm) below the surface. The soil should not be too dry.

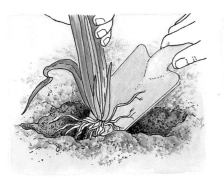

3 Spread the roots out well, with the trimmed leaf fan standing upright. Return the soil carefully and press it around the rhizome gently with your fingers. Label each variety clearly.

4 Space additional rhizomes 1½-2 ft (45-60 cm) apart in all directions. Spurias should be planted in clumps 2 in (5 cm) deep. Keep the soil moist until they are fully established.

Several flowers are carried on one stem toward the end of early summer. In winter, the Algerian iris (*I. unguicularis*) has lovely lilac flowers. It flourishes in warm regions, such as the Pacific and Gulf coasts, against a south-facing wall where the soil gets hot and remains fairly dry in summer.

Other beardless irises will grow only in boggy soil or with their roots submerged beneath water. The *I. kaempferi* hybrids can be planted in a bog garden, but will not tolerate alkalinity. They make a fine display of large flowers in early summer to midsummer.

The yellow flag and rabbit ear irises, *I. pseudacorus* and *I. laevigata* respectively, are very vigorous plants that flower in late spring and early summer. They should be planted in 2-4 in (5-10 cm) of water in pots or baskets, or directly into the bed of a pond.

Small bulbous irises are easy to grow indoors for winter flowering. The netted types bloom between late winter and early spring, and some are pleasantly scented. They are useful for growing both indoors and in a rock garden.

Of the bulbous Xiphium types, the Dutch irises flower first, starting in late spring. These are followed by the Spanish hybrids, then the English irises in late spring and summer. Growing 1½-2 ft (45-60 cm) tall, they are all suitable for pockets in a mixed bed.

Planting irises
Bearded irises have thick, fleshy rhizomatous roots that should be half-exposed on the soil surface. Beardless and crested irises have thinner rhizomes and should be planted below the surface.

Rhizomatous irises grow best in a rich soil containing plenty of humus. Select a sunny site that is not overshadowed by tall plants. Good drainage is essential, so amend heavy clay soils or build a raised bed. Dig and enrich the plot before planting, adding a dressing of bone meal. Neutralize acid soils with lime.

Pacific Coast hybrids and crested irises won't tolerate wet or alkaline soils. Create acid conditions by digging in amendments, making raised beds, or incorporating sand for better drainage.

Bearded irises should be planted in early July in the North, but in the South, wait until the heat of midsummer has passed. Set the rhizomes in groups of three or four, allowing 1½ ft (45 cm) between tall types; 9-12 in (23-30 cm) between intermediates; and 6-9 in (15-23 cm) between dwarfs.

Before planting, trim the leaves to form a short fan shape and remove any damaged roots. Using a trowel, dig a sloping, fan-shaped hole. The point of the fan should be close to the surface and face the sun; the semicircular end should be about 4 in (10 cm) deep. Place the rhizome at the point of the fan, with the leafy end lowest. Spread the roots downward into the hole. Cover the roots with soil, but leave the top of the rhizome exposed. Press in the soil, then label and water the plant.

Water as necessary for about 3 weeks, after which the rhizomes should be fully established.

Beardless irises and crested irises are also grown below ground. In early fall, plant Sibirica rhizomes, each with the foliage trimmed as for bearded types, in a sunny site. Set them 1 in (2.5 cm) deep in soil that is not too dry, ensuring that the roots are spread out well. Space the rhizomes 1½-2 ft (45-60 cm) apart. Water after planting and keep the soil moist.

In midfall, plant the fibrous rhizomes of Spuria irises in clumps 2 in (5 cm) deep. Any fertile soil is suitable as long as the site is sunny. Don't let the rhizomes dry out while you are working.

The Pacific Coast hybrids are difficult to transplant and often are most successful when started from seed. If purchased as seedlings, set them out in midfall, incorporating peat into the soil around the root ball. Press in with your fingers and water well.

Plant the slender rhizomes of crested irises in late spring or early fall, just below soil level, singly or in groups. They prefer a sheltered, semishaded spot that has moist acid or neutral soil enriched with peat or leaf mold.

Water-loving irises, such as *I. laevigata* and *I. pseudacorus* and its cultivars, need a water depth of

6 in (15 cm). In spring or late summer, they can be planted in an aquatic basket (available from aquatic-plant nurseries) or directly into a pool bed. Set out *I. kaempferi* just below the surface of boggy and humus-rich acid soil and fertilize frequently.

Bulbous irises require a sunny, well-drained site that contains plenty of composted manure or garden compost. Plant Dutch, Spanish, and English irises in early fall to midfall, setting them about 4-6 in (10-15 cm) deep.

English irises do well in rich, damp soil that will not dry out too quickly in hot weather. Easy to grow, they do not require lifting after flowering. Plant them 6-8 in (15-20 cm) apart. Set Dutch irises the same distance apart, but in a light soil. Spanish irises, on the other hand, produce more striking blooms if placed 4 in (10 cm) apart in light soil. They favor a warm site sheltered from winds.

In early fall to midfall, plant netted/reticulata irises 2-3 in (5-7.5 cm) deep and 2-4 in (5-10 cm) apart in clumps. Select a light, well-drained soil in a sunny spot.

Juno iris bulbs have thick storage roots attached to them, from which feeding roots develop during the growing season. Plant the bulbs singly or in clumps in a spot sheltered from summer rain or in very well drained soil. Set them 2 in (5 cm) deep and 6-9 in (15-23 cm) apart in early fall.

Routine cultivation

Encourage bearded iris rhizomes to harden for the winter by sprinkling potassium sulfate over the bed at the rate of 1 tablespoon (15 ml) per sq yd/sq m. If frost lifts

'Regeliocyclus'
bearded hybrid
cushion type

beardless
Pacific Coast
hybrid

Iris sibirica
hybrid; beardless
Siberian type

Iris foetidissima
beardless species
seedpods

Iris kaempferi
hybrid
beardless type

Iris pseudacorus
'Variegata'
beardless variety
water iris

Iris laevigata 'Alba'
beardless variety
water iris

Iris japonica
crested species

Iris bucharica
bulbous species
Juno type

Iris reticulata 'Clairette'
bulbous type
netted/reticulata

Iris danfordiae
bulbous species
netted/reticulata

Dutch irises
bulbous hybrids
Xiphium type

81

AFTERCARE OF IRISES

1 Winter frosts may lift the rhizomes of beardless irises. Do not press them down, or you may break their roots and weaken them. Instead, bank up sand or soil around the sides of the rhizomes.

2 In winter, dead leaves may harbor pests, such as slugs and snails. Peel off these leaves and trim back all remaining foliage to prevent wind damage, which could loosen the roots.

3 In spring, spread a mulch of garden compost or composted manure around clumps of shallow-rooted beardless irises. It will discourage annual weeds and conserve moisture.

4 In summer, break off seedpods from Sibirica irises to prevent seedlings from choking the bed. Seedpods of *I. foetidissima* are decorative when ripe, and should not be removed.

late-planted rhizomes out of the ground during the winter, do not press them down. Add light soil around the sides of the rhizomes or lift and replant them.

During winter, peel off dead foliage from bearded irises to discourage slugs. In early spring, carefully fork in a complete fertilizer, such as 5–10–5 with trace elements, at the rate of 3 tablespoons (45 ml) per sq yd/sq m.

Avoid hoeing around beardless irises, as the roots are near the surface and are easily damaged. Alternatively, weed by hand or mulch with a garden compost in the spring.

The leaves of the Sibirica beardless irises die down in winter. Clear them away to prevent slugs overwintering in this foliage, and to let light and air reach the roots.

After Sibirica blooms have faded, break off the developing seed-pods — they deprive the plants of energy and the resulting seedlings will choke the surrounding soil. To preserve their height and lush green color, apply a general fertilizer around mature plants in early spring.

Spuria beardless irises tend to bloom better in subsequent years if they are not watered after flowering. Both Pacific Coast and crested irises dislike alkaline conditions, so mulch them in spring with a layer, 1-2 in (2.5-5 cm) thick, of pine needles or shredded hardwood leaves.

Some bulbous irises must be lifted and stored dry over the winter; others can be left in the ground. English irises, for example, are quite hardy and will not need lifting in the fall until they become overcrowded. Lightly fork garden compost into the beds after the foliage has died down.

Lift and store Dutch iris bulbs only if the soil is wet and heavy. This work should be done after the foliage has died down in late summer. Replant the bulbs in the early fall when they have dried. Spanish irises should be lifted routinely. Keep the bulbs in a dry, airy, and frost-free spot. Before replanting, soak them in an approved fungicide.

Netted/reticulata irises require feeding after they have flowered to ensure good bulbs for the following year. Apply a general liquid fertilizer every 2 weeks until the leaves turn yellow.

Do not lift Juno bulbs unless they become congested. Fork compost into the bed, trying not to damage the roots. If the soil is acidic, amend it annually with 1 rounded tablespoon (15 ml) per sq yd/sq m of ground limestone.

Propagation

Most irises are increased by division — seed can be collected and sown, but seedlings will take several years to reach maturity and hybrids won't breed true.

Divide bearded iris rhizomes every 3 years to increase the stock and improve flower quality. The best time is immediately after flowering, but it can be done until the end of early fall.

Beardless, crested, and water irises also become crowded after a few years and must be divided. Take care with them — the rhizomes are easily damaged.

Large clumps of Sibiricas grow hollow in the center, where the soil has been exhausted. Divide them about every 3 years, either in fall or in midspring.

All bulbous irises are increased by division of the bulbs. Lift and divide English and Dutch irises when the clumps become overcrowded. Divide Spanish irises when they are lifted annually.

If netted/reticulata and Juno iris beds become overcrowded, carefully lift and divide the bulbs after the foliage has yellowed, then replant them in the fall.

Lift rhizomatous irises carefully and cut pieces, 2-3 in (5-7.5 cm) long, from the rhizome's outer sides, each with roots attached; discard the woody center.

Separate bulbous irises according to size. Replant the largest bulbs directly in the flowering site and grow smaller ones on in a nursery bed for 1 or 2 years.

ALLIUMS FOR SUMMER

Easy-to-grow alliums, which include culinary chives and wild garlic, make colorful contributions to summer beds and rock gardens.

The genus *Allium* contains about 400 species. Within this genus are some culinary plants, including onion, spring onion, shallot, leek, garlic, and chives, as well as a group of flowering plants, known as ornamental onions, which are grown for show. These have flower clusters in a choice of colors — purple, lilac, pink, yellow, and white.

The generic name allium comes from the ancient Latin word for garlic. Most species are bulbous, but some are rhizomatous. Nearly all are hardy; they grow wild in a wide range of habitats throughout the Northern Hemisphere, from the sun-baked, dry hills of Turkey to northern meadows and open woodlands.

Special features

Ornamental onions have a distinct odor, which is most noticeable when the foliage is bruised.

The small individual flowers are gathered in ball-shaped clusters on upright, leafless stems. Some of these clusters can be impressively large. The flowers themselves are either spread apart and star-shaped, or bell-shaped and pendent. The stems of drooping flowers often stand upright once the blooms are pollinated.

The blooming period for these flowers ranges from late spring to early fall. The grayish to midgreen leaves are of little interest. They are usually strap-shaped, but some species have rolled-round or broad foliage.

Border plants

A number of species will thrive in a sunny, well-drained border. Among these is *Allium giganteum,* one of the largest ornamentals. It grows up to 4 ft (1.2 m) tall and looks striking at the back of a border. In early summer, deep lilac star-shaped flowers form tight spherical clusters, 4-6 in (10-15 cm) in diameter. Its gray-green leaves appear early and can be damaged by spring frosts, but surrounding flowers should offer some protection.

Smaller border types with large spherical flower heads in the purple color range include *A. aflatunense,* which is 2½ ft (75 cm) tall. During late spring and early summer, it bears starry deep lilac-pink flowers in loose rounded clusters, 3-4 in (7.5-10 cm) in diameter. Use the foliage of other plants to mask its narrow leaves, which tend to die off early.

For semishaded spots, choose *A. christophii* (syn. *A. albopilosum),* which also grows to 2½ ft (75 cm) tall. It has narrowly pointed, star-shaped silver-lilac flowers. Each cluster, as much as 10 in (25 cm) wide, carries up to 80 flowers. The seedpods remain beautiful for a long time and are excellent for drying. However, its gray-green hairy leaves wither about the same time the flowers open.

A. rosenbachianum bears star-shaped rich purple flowers during late spring. Its stems, which grow up to 2-2 ½ ft (60-75 cm) tall, support the dense clusters that may be up to 6 in (15 cm) wide. *A. stellatum* (the prairie onion) is a decorative Midwestern native with umbels of pinkish-rose blossoms, in late summer and fall, atop stems that are 18 in (45 cm) tall.

A. cernuum (the nodding onion) carries loose clusters of bell-shaped deep lilac-pink flowers on

◀ **Allium giganteum** The perfect spheres of deep lilac flowers atop tall stems are most attractive when viewed against a background of silver-gray foliage plants. The leaves of these artemisias will later hide the alliums' bare stems.

stems 2 ft (60 cm) tall in early summer to midsummer. *A. siculum* (syn. *Nectaroscordum siculum*) displays loose, drooping clusters of greenish-purple bells on stems 2-4 ft (60-120 cm) high. After pollination, the flowers turn upright and are followed later by decorative, straw-colored seedpods.

In late spring and early summer, *A. roseum*, at least 2 ft (60 cm) tall, exhibits loose clusters of comparatively large bright pink flowers. And the slender 3-ft (90-cm) stems of *A. sphaerocephalon* support tight, egg-shaped heads of maroon-purple flowers from midsummer to late summer.

A. tuberosum (Chinese chives) has white blooms with flat-topped heads in late summer and early fall on stems 20 in (50 cm) long.

A. schoenoprasum (culinary chives) is an excellent choice for edging borders and paths and for setting out in the herb garden. If planted in moist soil, it forms clumps topped by tight spherical heads of rose-lilac flowers from late spring to early summer.

Rock garden types

Smaller species of ornamental onion are especially suitable for the free-draining soil, sunny setting, and shelter of rock gardens.

Blue-flowered species include *Allium caeruleum (A. azureum)*. Its stems, which may grow 2 ft (60 cm) tall, bear small but dense spherical heads of star-shaped deep sky-blue flowers in late spring to early summer. *A. cyaneum*, a good rock garden species, blooms in midsummer to late summer. It carries sparse, mauve-blue, roughly spherical flower heads on 10-in (25-cm) stems.

An excellent choice for yellow beds is *A. flavum*, which has pendent, bell-shaped, golden yellow flowers that open in midsummer, followed by bluish leaves.

Unlike several ornamental onions, *A. karataviense* has attractive foliage. The broad grayish-green leaves, tinted with metallic purple, appear in early spring. Later, the plant bears tight globular clusters of starry dull pink or grayish-white flowers on stems 8 in (20 cm) tall. This species is also ideal for a sunny border.

For pink rock garden schemes, try clump-forming *A. narcissiflorum*. Its sparse but graceful clusters of bell-shaped flowers open in midsummer to late summer. Another choice is *A. ostrowskianum*, which has larger, starry flowers in late spring or early summer.

In midsummer the grassy-leaved *A. pulchellum* (syn. *A. carinatum pulchellum)* shows

Allium christophii

Allium caeruleum

Allium triquetrum

Allium pulchellum

Allium sphaerocephalon

Allium ursinum
ramsons, or wild
garlic

drooping violet-red bells on stems that reach 1-2 ft (30-60 cm) in height. This species self-seeds.

A. cyathophorum Farreri, the Farrer onion from China, has keeled leaves. In late spring, it bears loose clusters of bell-shaped purplish-red flowers on angled stems that are 15 in (37 cm) tall.

Species with flowers in the violet-purple range include the ultra-hardy (to zone 4) *A. senescens.* Its blooms open in midsummer to late summer over a clump of flat, twisted leaves, making it an interesting ground cover. The variety *glaucum* has grayish leaves.

A. neapolitanum (daffodil garlic), is moderately hardy in zones 6-9, but you must plant it in a protected site if you live at the northern end of this range. In spring or early summer, loose heads of starry pure white flowers develop on stems 8-12 in (20-30 cm) tall. The form that is generally seen is the larger-flowered 'Grandiflorum.'

Woodland gardening

The self-seeding golden garlic *(A. moly),* with stems up to 1 ft (30 cm) high, is perfect for naturalizing in short grass or in an open woodland. In late spring or early summer, clusters of star-shaped bright yellow flowers stud the gray-green leaf clumps.

For carpeting dampish ground in dappled shade, try ramsons, or wild garlic *(A. ursinum),* which produce profuse, loosely packed clusters of white flowers. The broad leaves resemble those of lily of the valley.

Cultivation

Plant the bulbs in the fall or spring — they are available mostly by mail order — in well-drained soil of average quality. If the soil is heavy, improve drainage by mixing in sharp builder's sand before planting.

Most species prefer an open, sunny spot, and the bulbs should be set in soil three to four times their own depth. For example, a 1-in (2.5-cm) bulb should have 3-4 in (7.5-10 cm) of soil above it. Plant them in groups — the large species should be spaced about 9 in (23 cm) apart; the dwarf types, 4 in (10 cm) apart.

Don't disturb the bulbs until the clumps are so congested that their flowering is markedly reduced. When replanting, add just a little well-rotted compost to the soil to replenish nutrients.

In windy sites, the taller species may need staking. Unless you are keeping the seed heads for indoor decoration, deadhead them when the flowers fade (leave a few if you require seed for propagation). To

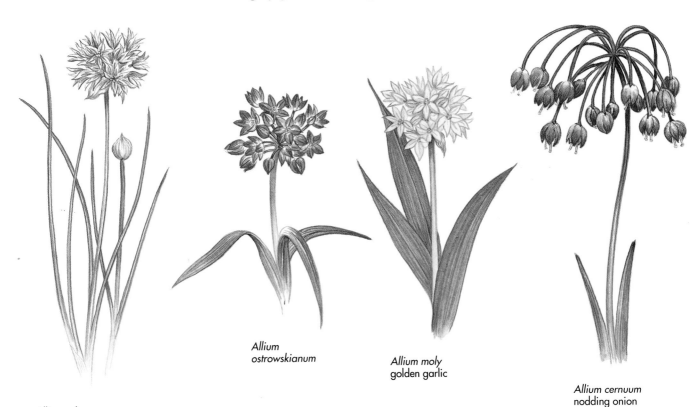

Allium schoenoprasum
culinary chives

Allium ostrowskianum

Allium moly
golden garlic

Allium cernuum
nodding onion

help feed the bulbs, allow the stems and leaves to die off naturally. You can hide the dying foliage by combining alliums with gray-leaved plants that thrive in the same soil conditions. Remove all dead material in the fall.

Dwarf species can be grown as potted plants. Keep them in a cold frame or greenhouse until they are nearly ready to flower, then bring them indoors.

Propagation

Most ornamental onions can be increased easily from seed, and many sow themselves. Sow them thinly in pots of a seed-starting mix. Keep the pots in a cold frame or unheated greenhouse for the first year, or plunge them in a protected spot outdoors and leave them for a year. Seeds of *A. aflatunense, A. karataviense, A. ostrowskianum,* and *A. roseum* are very slow to germinate, taking up to 2 years to sprout.

Once they have germinated, prick out seedlings into pots or flats. Alternatively, transplant them to nursery rows, where they should remain until they are large enough to move to their permanent positions. It will take 2 to 3 years to obtain flowering-sized bulbs from seed; *A. giganteum* is likely to take a year longer.

Many species multiply rapidly from offsets produced by the parent bulbs. Lift these in early fall, or in spring when growth commences, then detach and replant them immediately.

▲ **Border color** A clump of giant alliums looks striking in an early-summer perennial border. Growing up to 4 ft (1.2 m) high, the stems of this allium, topped with purple-red flower heads, tower above blue camassias and near-purple irises. A weeping ornamental pear provides a silver background.

► **Alpine alliums** In complete contrast, *Allium karataviense*, from central Asia, is no more than 6 in (15 cm) high. Its broad, curving, and purple-mottled leaves spread equally wide. In late spring, airy globes of pinkish-white stars rise above the foliage on short, stout stems.

GRACIOUS GLADIOLI

With tall spires of trumpet blooms, gladioli make an elegant sight grown in the garden or displayed in a large vase indoors.

The name *Gladiolus* comes from the Latin word for sword, which describes the shape of the plant's leaves. Indeed, these corm-rooted plants are sometimes known as "sword lilies," even though they belong to the iris family.

The popularity of gladioli can be attributed to their beautifully formed flowers. The individual florets, which all face in the same direction, are set on either side of a long, thick stem. Flower spikes measure up to 2 ft (60 cm) long

and consist of 16 to 26 closely set trumpet-shaped florets, each with six petals. The lower three fall petals are slightly reflexed. A few of the species are fragrant.

Flower color varies from very pale yellow to intense scarlet; there are no true blues. Blooms may be a solid color, or bicolored and tricolored with obvious markings in the throat of each floret.

Gardeners grow several true species in their gardens. Among these, *Gladiolus byzantinus* and

G. tristis perform the best. However, many gardeners prefer the large-flowered hybrids. They are of complex parentage and belong to two botanical groups: *Gladiolus × hortulanus* and *G. × colvillei*. Garden hybrids in the *G. × hortulanus* group are classified according to the size and shape of the flowers.

Large-flowered hybrids produce the tallest flower spikes, each up to 2 ft (60 cm) long. Their rather triangular, closely packed, and overlapping florets are 4-6 in (10-15 cm) wide and come in an enormous range of colors and shades. They flower from midsummer to early fall in the North, and all winter in zones 9-10.

In full bloom, the large-flowered hybrids stand 3½-4 ft (1-1.2 m) tall. They bear the characteristics of many *Gladiolus* species, notably *G. natalensis*.

Primulinus hybrids have more slender flower spikes, about 15 in (38 cm) long, with separate florets, 2-3 in (5-7.5 cm) wide, arranged in a zigzag pattern. Unlike the typical gladiolus flower, the upper petal of these hybrids is usually hooded and folded over the anthers and the stigma, a feature of this group's main parent, *G. primulinus*.

At 2-3½ ft (60-100 cm) tall, the primulinus hybrids make excellent cut flowers. They flower from midsummer to late summer.

Butterfly hybrids are similar to the large-flowered hybrids, but their spikes are shorter — up to 1½ ft (45 cm) long. The edges of their petals are often frilled and ruffled, and the individual florets are about 3 in (6.5 cm) wide. They have distinctive throat markings, giving them the appearance of exotic butterflies, and stand 2-3 ft

◀ **Large-flowered gladioli** For a vertical accent, set groups of these half-hardy but vigorous hybrids at the back of a bed. Suitable for cutting, the florets open in succession from the base upward, but you can hasten the production of fully open flowers by pinching out the top bud.

(60-90 cm) high when in flower from midsummer to late summer. **Miniature hybrids** are similar to the primulinus hybrids, but they have smaller florets — 1½-2 in (4-5 cm) wide — often with ruffled petals set closely together on spikes 15 in (38 cm) long.

These miniature hybrids, which grow to about 1½-2½ ft (45-75 cm) tall, bloom from midsummer to late summer. Garden centers usually sell them under the name *G. nanus*, but they are sometimes confused with miniature hybrids of the *G. × colvillei* group.

These *G. × colvillei* hybrids have been bred from a number of different species, including *G. tristis*. They have loose spikes, about 10 in (25 cm) long, of rather upward-pointing florets, each about 3 in (7.5 cm) wide, which open in midsummer to late summer. The flowers are distinguished by their blotched or marked throats. The plants generally grow to about 1½ ft (45 cm).

Planting corms

A plump, high-necked bulbous rootstock, or *corm,* with a small root scar produces better blooms than a large, flat corm with a broad root scar, so check carefully before buying.

Tall hybrids are ideal for the back of a border; shorter ones are more effective near the front.

Gladioli grown in a mixed bed benefit from the shelter provided by surrounding plants and will flower a few weeks earlier than those set out in an isolated bed or exposed site. If you intend to cut the flowers, plant the corms in a spare corner of the garden.

Prepare the planting site as soon as the soil is workable in late winter or very early spring. Gladioli grow best in well-drained soil and need a sunny position — spindly growth and poor flowers result from growing the plants in shade, however slight.

While turning over the soil, dig in a little composted manure. If the soil is heavy or sandy, work in plenty of organic matter. Rake a generous handful of bone meal into the surface of each sq yd/ sq m of the prepared site.

Once the danger of frost is past, plant the corms 4 in (10 cm) deep in heavy soil and 6 in (15 cm) deep in light soil. Corms that are planted too shallowly may topple over when they flower. Bed them

Gladiolus x hortulanus
large-flowered hybrid

Gladiolus x colvillei

Gladiolus tristis

PLANTING GLADIOLI CORMS

As soon as the danger of frost is past, plant corms 4 in (10 cm) deep in heavy soil, or 6 in (15 cm) deep in sandy soil, for extra stability. If the soil is prone to waterlogging, put a layer of sharp sand in the base of the planting hole. Then press the corms firmly in place before filling in with soil.

Gladiolus x hortulanus
primulinus hybrid

firmly in the base of each hole before filling it in with soil — air pockets around the corms will fill with water and cause rotting. On heavy soils, where drainage is a problem, put a layer of sharp builder's sand in the base of each hole before setting in the corm.

In a mixed border, arrange corms in clumps, setting them 4-6 in (10-15 cm) apart. If you want to cut the flowers, place the corms either in a single row or double rows, 12-15 in (30-38 cm) apart.

You can extend the floral display in summer by making successive plantings at 2-week intervals, right into July in the North.

Aftercare

Do not hoe or apply fertilizer until the young shoots appear — then hoe shallowly and often to prevent weed growth and to aerate the surface soil. Apply a light top-dressing of complete fertilizer, such as 5–10–5.

To encourage good rooting, do not water until 8 or 10 weeks after planting. Then, after the flower spike has appeared, water generously, particularly during dry periods. Regularly apply a liquid fertilizer once the embryo flower spike is evident in the center of the leaf fan. Reduce water loss from the soil by applying a surface mulch of bark chips or grass clippings. To control thrips and aphids, spray regularly with an appropriate insecticide.

To avoid wind damage, stake tall hybrids, as their flower spikes are top-heavy. Shorter types need no support, except in exposed sites. To support tall gladioli grown in rows, insert a strong stake at each end of a row. Tie long pieces of string at parallel points on the stakes. Stretch these strings between the stakes and on either side of the plants. Then secure each plant to the strings with soft twine or wire rings.

For decorative plantings, support each spike individually with a bamboo stake. Make sure it is long enough to support the full length of the stem at maturity. To avoid damaging the corms, place

Gladiolus x hortulanus
butterfly hybrid

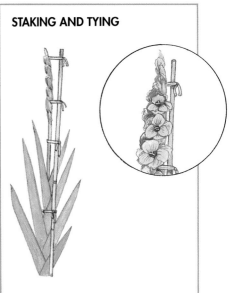

STAKING AND TYING

For flawless blooms, support each spike individually with a bamboo stake and soft twine. Insert the stake as soon as you can tell which way the flower spike will face — positioning it behind the spike and a couple of inches away from the base.

Gladiolus x hortulanus
miniature/nanus hybrid

89

the stake a couple of inches (centimeters) from the base of the stem, and at the back of the spike, as all flowers face one way.

Tie in both the stem and the flower spike. As the spike gains height and weight, add more ties between the florets to prevent it from bending and breaking.

Lifting corms for winter

None of the garden hybrid gladioli will survive the winter outdoors north of zone 9. However, a few of the species are much hardier, notably *G. byzantinus*, which will overwinter successfully as far north as zone 5.

North of these temperature zones, lift hybrid gladioli with a fork when the foliage turns yellowish brown, generally in midfall, and before the first hard frost. Remove any soil sticking to the corms, then cut off the main stem ½ in (1 cm) from each base.

Put the corms in a dry, airy place. They will dry in 7 to 10 days under normal conditions, but the process can be speeded up by directing a fan over the corms.

When they are quite dry, clean the corms thoroughly. Break away and discard the old, shriveled corms that are at the base of the new corms — if they are sufficiently dry, they should be easy to remove. Pull off the tough outer skin on large corms, and also remove any small cormels. These can be stored separately and used as propagation material.

Store the cleaned corms in a cool but frost-free place, such as a shed, cellar, or attic. Good circulation of air around the stored corms should prevent fungal rots from damaging them; a large paper bag hung from a ceiling or a wall hook makes an ideal container. Check the corms occasionally during the winter months and throw away any that show signs of mold or other disease.

To obtain earlier flowers the following year, place the corms in a well-lit position in a greenhouse in late winter or early spring. Stand them in empty flats at a temperature of 54°F (12°C). When the corms sprout in early spring they can be planted out.

▶ **Gladiolus byzantinus** Exceptionally hardy, this species can be left to overwinter outdoors to zone 5. Every summer, it bears spikes, 15 in (38 cm) long, of loosely set wine-red flowers.

OVERWINTERING DORMANT CORMS

1 Lift corms as soon as leaves begin to turn yellow-brown, before the first hard frost. Ease away any soil sticking to them and trim off the main stem ½ in (1 cm) above each corm.

2 Lay the corms on newspaper in a shallow box or flat and put them in a dry, airy place until they are thoroughly dry. This process can be speeded up by directing a fan over them.

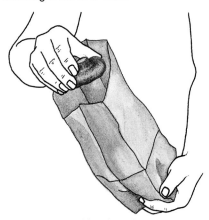

3 When the corms are fully dried, clean off all loose outer skin and break away the old, shriveled corms at the base of the new corms. Also remove any small cormels.

4 Store in a cool but frost-free place over the winter. To prevent fungal rots, pack corms in paper bags and hang up in a dry, well-aerated location.

CROCUSES AND COLCHICUMS

Though similar in appearance, these small bulbs are unrelated. Their showy goblet flowers are indispensable in the spring and fall garden.

Members of the genus *Crocus* belong to the Iridaceae family, which makes them relatives of irises, freesias, montbretias, and gladioli. *Colchicum* species and varieties, on the other hand, are in the Liliaceae family, which includes lilies, tulips, fritillaries, scillas, and hyacinths.

The botanical name *Crocus* comes from the Greek word *krokos*, meaning saffron. The threadlike filaments of the styles of one species, *Crocus sativus,* are the source of an intense orange saffron dye that is used for coloring and flavoring foods. *Colchicum* is named after Colchis, an ancient country on the Black Sea. Although the seeds and corms of all colchicums are poisonous, the dried corms of *Colchicum autumnale* contain the medicinal colchicum *(tinctura colchici)* — a painkiller used in the treatment of gout.

Both crocuses and colchicums produce goblet-shaped, bowl-shaped, or starry flowers on slender stalklike tubes that emerge directly from the corms. Their resemblance to each other is so close that colchicums are frequently called autumn crocuses. This name tends to cause confusion: Although most colchicums bloom in the fall, there are also certain crocus species that flower in the fall. Of course, crocuses are best loved for the colorful carpets that they create in the spring.

Crocus flowers always have six petals surrounding a prominent flared stigma — the pollen-receptive tip of the female reproductive organ. Colchicum flowers also have six petals, though doubles are known, but the stigma is less prominent.

If you have trouble distinguishing a crocus from a colchicum, wait until the leaves appear. Crocuses have grasslike slender leaves, usually colored midgreen to dark green, with a silvery midrib; colchicums have much larger and broader, usually strap-shaped, glossy green leaves. Colchicum leaves are bigger and taller than their flowers, and are often regarded as too messy for a flower bed. They are better suited to shrubbery underplantings or to naturalizing in a yard.

A further distinction between the two lies in the shape of the bulbous rootstock, or corm, of each genus. Crocus corms are flat and round; those of colchicums are oval and upright.

Crocuses are much neater in habit and suitable for planting in the front of a bed and for small pockets in a rock garden. They, too, can be naturalized in a yard. The more delicate ones can be grown in a pot or forced indoors, if placed on a cool windowsill.

◀ **Fall-flowering colchicums** Bright clumps of *Colchicum speciosum* provide welcome splashes of deep pink, lilac, mauve, or white when planted in a garden or naturalized in rough grass.

Choosing crocuses

There are about 80 species of crocus, with many more varieties. Dozens of these can be grown in home gardens. They are mostly very hardy, originating from high ground in countries north and east of the Mediterranean.

Crocuses are exclusively dwarf plants, generally reaching just 3-6 in (7.5-15 cm) in height when in flower. The leaves, which develop after the blooms, may be slightly taller. Flowers and tufted leaves emerge directly from the small corm — there is no stem. Flower color and flowering season are the main features that will affect your choice of species or variety.

The blooms open upward and outward to face the sun, but remain closed during dull weather. Semiclosed flowers, often with beautiful markings on the outside of their petals, may be just as attractive as fully open ones. Colors cover a wide range, including many shades of purple, mauve, red, lilac, pink, yellow, and cream, as well as white. There may also be feathery markings or suffused blotches on the outside of the petals in deeper shades of purple, mauve, chocolate-brown, or bronze.

Most crocuses bloom in late winter to spring, but several types flower from fall to early winter. Of the spring types, the Dutch hybrids bred from *Crocus vernus* are the most popular. They have the largest and most robust flowers — standing up to 6 in (15 cm) tall — in an extensive range of bold colors. Varieties and hybrids of the late-winter-flowering *C. chrysanthus* are also favorites; their softer flower colors are always marked with contrasting blotches or feathering.

Among the other late-winter and early-spring crocuses are *C. ancyrensis*, with long-lasting tangerine to rich yellow flowers; *C.*

biflorus (the Scotch crocus), with white flowers flushed with purple-blue; *C. sieberi,* with pale mauve flowers marked with yellow at the base; and *C. tomasinianus,* with slender lavender to red-purple flowers.

Fall and early-winter crocuses are planted less often, but are well worth seeking out. As with the spring types, these crocuses generally bloom before the leaves develop. In this group are *C. longiflorus,* which has fragrant, deep lilac long petals; *C. cancellatus,* which bears slender pale blue flowers striped on the outside; *C. sativus* (the saffron crocus), which produces rose-purple flowers; and *C. speciosus,* which produces blooms in shades of lavender, blue, and white, some of which have darker veins.

Choosing colchicums

The choice of *Colchicum* species or varieties will depend largely on your preference for color and petal markings. Almost all of them flower in the fall; their leaves appear in spring and die down again in early summer. However, *C. luteum* — the sole yellow-flowered species, and a plant that is rare — displays both its leaves and flowers in the spring.

Colchicum flowers generally stand 6-8 in (15-20 cm) high, but their leaves may reach a length of up to 16 in (40 cm), with a width of 2-4 in (5-10 cm). The broad foliage can easily smother low-growing and delicate neighbors, and therefore colchicums should be grown only where such a risk is not possible.

Most colchicum blooms are pinkish-lilac or white, but shades of rose-purple, rose-pink, and mauve are not unusual. Many have distinctly checkered markings on the petals. The flowers have an unfortunate habit of flopping over in wet or windy weath-

er, so these plants are best grown through other low-growing ground covers for support. Tall grass, as in a meadow, provides similar support.

The two main hybrid groups, belonging to *Colchicum autumnale* and *C. speciosum,* have white, pink, rose-lilac, or rose-purple flowers. Double-flowered varieties — usually with "Plenum" in their name — have fuller blooms. A further group of hybrids of mixed parentage, but mainly from *C. speciosum* subspecies, have large and robust flowers; these include 'Violet Queen,' which has thin white stripes on its deep mauve petals, and the ever-popular hybrid 'Waterlily,' which, as its name suggests, has lilac-mauve flowers with many petals that open wide.

Other attractive colchicums are *C. cilicicum,* which displays deep rose-lilac flowers, and *C. byzantinum,* which exhibits profuse pale pinkish-lilac blooms.

Planting crocuses

Most crocuses like a well-drained soil and a sunny position where their corms can ripen fully in summer. *Crocus vernus* and *C. cancellatus,* however, prefer moist soils and dislike prolonged dryness in summer. The corms are best left undisturbed for several years, so a rock garden pocket or the front of a border that you do not cultivate deeply is the most suitable.

If you want to plant crocuses in grass, choose winter and early-spring types, such as *Crocus speciosus* and *C. vernus* hybrids. These will maintain sufficient leaf growth to restore the corm's food supply for the following season before the grass needs to be mowed for the first time.

Soil type is not important, but increase the pH of very acid soils by incorporating lime (unless you

SPRING-FLOWERING TYPES

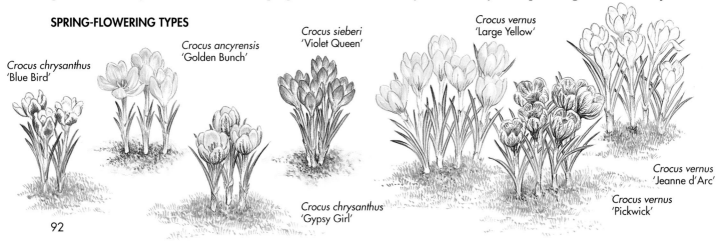

Crocus chrysanthus 'Blue Bird'

Crocus ancyrensis 'Golden Bunch'

Crocus sieberi 'Violet Queen'

Crocus chrysanthus 'Gypsy Girl'

Crocus vernus 'Large Yellow'

Crocus vernus 'Jeanne d'Arc'

Crocus vernus 'Pickwick'

are placing them between acid-loving plants, such as rhododendrons). Improve the drainage of heavy soils by adding plenty of sharp sand and organic matter.

Crocuses are always sold as dormant corms, either unpackaged, in aerated plastic packages, or in boxes. Make sure they are firm and free from obvious signs of fungal rots or pest damage. Plant them as soon as they are available: spring-flowering types in early fall; fall-blooming ones in summer.

Set crocus corms 2-3 in (5-7.5 cm) deep and 3-4 in (7.5-10 cm) apart. On light soils, where summer cultivation might disturb the corms, plant them up to 5 in (13 cm) deep. All crocuses look best in small informal drifts or clumps. When planting under turf, use a special bulb planter, which will allow you to replace the plug of soil and grass over the corm.

Planting colchicums

Colchicums are also commonly sold as dormant corms, and these should be planted once they become available in late summer. Alternatively, plants can be lifted and moved to a new site as soon as their leaves die down in early summer or midsummer.

Any well-drained soil in a sunny or partially shaded, sheltered site will do, but fertile soils encourage better multiplication of the corms. Each corm may produce several flowers, but for the best effect, place six or more corms in small drifts. Set them 3-4 in (7.5-10 cm) deep and the same distance apart, pressing them in lightly.

Aftercare

Both crocuses and colchicums require minimal aftercare. Deadheading is unnecessary because faded flowers disintegrate very rapidly (sometimes almost overnight) without harming the corm.

FORCING CROCUSES INDOORS

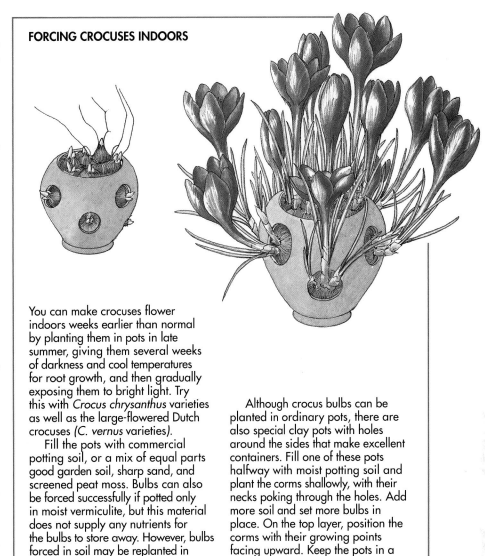

You can make crocuses flower indoors weeks earlier than normal by planting them in pots in late summer, giving them several weeks of darkness and cool temperatures for root growth, and then gradually exposing them to bright light. Try this with *Crocus chrysanthus* varieties as well as the large-flowered Dutch crocuses (*C. vernus* varieties).

Fill the pots with commercial potting soil, or a mix of equal parts good garden soil, sharp sand, and screened peat moss. Bulbs can also be forced successfully if potted only in moist vermiculite, but this material does not supply any nutrients for the bulbs to store away. However, bulbs forced in soil may be replanted in the garden after they flower. It may take several years before these bulbs bloom again.

Although crocus bulbs can be planted in ordinary pots, there are also special clay pots with holes around the sides that make excellent containers. Fill one of these pots halfway with moist potting soil and plant the corms shallowly, with their necks poking through the holes. Add more soil and set more bulbs in place. On the top layer, position the corms with their growing points facing upward. Keep the pots in a cool (but frost-free), dark place until the shoots have reached 1-2 in (2.5-5 cm).

Never remove a plant's green leaves; wait until they have turned yellow-brown and are easier to pull off.

Crocuses are frequently mutilated by birds. The yellow varieties seem most prone to this kind of damage, and the culprits are often sparrows that seem intent on mere vandalism rather than gaining any food from the flowers. If bird damage is severe, protect blooms in the following years by crisscrossing black thread across the site, tying it to small sticks set around the perimeter. Of course, this system does little to enhance the beauty of crocus blooms.

A less obtrusive way of overcoming bird damage is to sprinkle napthalene moth crystals among the emerging plants. The smell will discourage the wildlife without harming it and the odor

FALL-FLOWERING TYPES

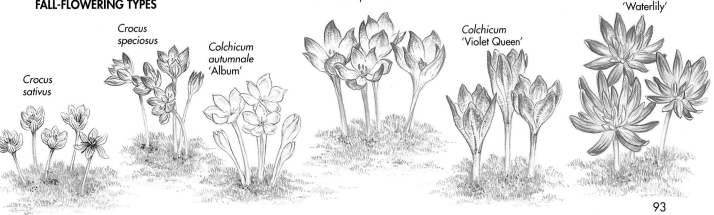

Crocus sativus

Crocus speciosus

Colchicum autumnale 'Album'

Colchicum speciosum

Colchicum 'Violet Queen'

Colchicum 'Waterlily'

should remain imperceptible. Repeat the treatment as necessary, especially after heavy rain.

In some gardens, mice and squirrels may be a problem — they eat crocus corms in the soil. A sprinkling of moth crystals at planting time provides some initial protection, discouraging the rodents from digging in the newly turned soil. Planting slightly deeper may also help, but if the pests persist, you may be forced to plant corms inside cages fashioned from wire mesh.

Propagation

Both crocuses and colchicums can be propagated from seed or by separating and growing on the small cormels that develop around each main corm. The number of these cormels varies, depending on species and variety. They will soon grow on to flowering size.

Seedlings take much longer to reach flowering size — generally 2 to 6 years, occasionally longer. Neither crocus seeds nor colchicum seeds are generally available commercially — you will have to collect your own. Cultivars do not breed true.

Crocus cormels should be removed as soon as the parent's leaves turn brown. Lift the corms and ease away the cormels. Dry them off in flats in a warm greenhouse or shed for a few days.

Once dry, remove any dead leaves, roots, loose scaly skins, and any remains of the old corm. Separate the cormels into two or three sizes. Replant the largest for flowering the next year and put the rest in a nursery bed in rows far enough apart for a narrow hoe to be used to control weeds; within the rows, set the cormels 2-3 in (5-7 cm) deep and 1-2 in (2.5-5 cm) apart. The young plants will grow fastest in well-drained soil in a sunny position. The bed should be kept free of weeds during the growing season. These smaller corms should flower in 2 years.

Colchicum cormels can be treated similarly, lifting the parent corms in early summer or midsummer when the foliage has died down. Grow the cormels on in a nursery bed for 2 years.

Crocus seeds are freely produced by some species, resulting in plants that are fairly true to type unless cross-pollination has accidentally occurred. The seeds from garden hybrids are not likely to breed true.

Crocus seed capsules rise up quickly on short stalks in early summer and midsummer. Collect the capsules as they begin to split open. Sow the seeds in flats or pots of sterilized seed-starting mix. Cover them with ½ in (12 mm) of seed mix and place in a cold frame or protected spot outdoors. If left outdoors in the winter, the containers should be dug in so that their upper surface lies flush with the ground. Cover the flats or pots with a mulch of evergreen boughs.

Leave the seedlings in their flats or pots for 2 years, then plant them in their flowering positions if they are large enough; otherwise, transplant them to an outdoor nursery bed and grow on for another year.

Colchicum seeds form a viable means of propagating all species, except *Colchicum byzantinum*. Sow the seeds when they are mature, in early summer to midsummer, in pots, 6-8 in (15-20 cm) deep, filled with sterilized seed-starting mix. In a cold frame, germination may take 18 months.

A year after germination, plant out the seedlings into a nursery bed. Each seedling will have a small corm at its base. Seedlings take from 3 to at least 6 years to reach flowering size.

▶ **Spring crocuses** The Dutch hybrids bred from *C. vernus* form ever-widening clumps of bright-colored goblet flowers that open fully to show off their orange stigmas.

NARCISSI AND DAFFODILS

No spring garden is complete without these cheerful trumpets. There are thousands of hardy varieties in a wide range of colors from which to choose.

Narcissi are among the best bulbs for naturalizing in the garden. These ornamental flowers, which appear in spring, are particularly suitable for planting under deciduous trees, in corners of lawns, and on grassy banks; most can also be grown successfully in beds, rock gardens, and planters.

All narcissi have a central trumpet or cup, called the *corona,* which is surrounded by six petals, collectively known as the *perianth.* Although the name narcissus is applied to any member of the genus *Narcissus,* it is popularly used for varieties with a short central trumpet that is no deeper than a shallow cup.

However, trumpet narcissi, more commonly referred to as daffodils, bear a single blossom on each flowering stalk, with a trumpet as long as, or longer than, the petals. In addition, the trumpet, which may be narrow or widespread, is frilled or flared at its outer edge. Usually, the overlapping petals are pointed at the tips. Colors vary among the many cultivars: some, including the old favorite 'King Alfred,' have clear, bright yellow trumpets and petals. There are also bicolored daffodils, which have yellow trumpets and white petals, as well as another group that has both white trumpets and white petals. As for the so-called reverse-bicolored daffodils, their trumpets are paler than their surrounding petals.

Between the true daffodils and the short-cupped narcissi are those with assorted-sized cups. They have a wide range of colors, from white to cream, yellow to pink, red, and orange. Sometimes the petals and cups are the same shade; other times, they contrast.

Double-flowered varieties are characterized by trumpets that split into many ragged parts, indistinguishable from the petals. This trait gives them a different appearance from other narcissi. The blooms may be white, cream, pale yellow, or orange. Many double narcissi are strongly fragrant.

Classification

As a result of a great deal of hybridizing over the years, the genus *Narcissus* has been split into 12 divisions, based on flower shape and parentage. The true daffodil hybrids are grouped in Division 1. Those with trumpets more than one-third but less than half the petal length — known as large-cupped narcissi — form Division 2. Small-cupped narcissi, with trumpets less than one-third of the length of their petals, make up Division 3.

▼ **Spring shows** Early-flowering white daffodils and yellow cyclamineus narcissi, with their long, narrow trumpets and backswept petals, are a welcome sight in spring. They thrive in light shade beneath deciduous trees, where they can be left to multiply. A mulch of leaf mold helps them to strengthen their bulbs for next year's flowers.

CLASSIFICATION

Within each of the first three divisions there are several subdivisions in which varieties are classified according to the color of their trumpets/cups and petals — all-yellow, all-white, bicolored, or reverse-bicolored. For example, all-yellow trumpet daffodils form Division 1a, and all-white small-cupped narcissi comprise Division 3c. Double-flowered narcissi and daffodils, whose trumpet or cup is replaced by a tuft of irregular petals, are represented in Division 4. These are all scented.

Divisions 5 to 9 encompass those plants that display floral features characteristic of a particular wild narcissus species. Tri-andrus narcissi varieties (Division 5) and cyclamineus (Division 6), for example, resemble their parents *Narcissus triandrus* and *N. cyclamineus* respectively, with their pendent, bell-shaped trumpets and backswept petals.

Jonquils (Division 7) also are similar to their parent plant, *N. jonquilla*. They have rushlike leaves and are notable for their sweet fragrance. Each stem bears a small cluster of flowers with shallow cream, yellow, or orange cups and rounded or pointed petals that are sometimes in contrasting colors.

The tazetta narcissi of Division 8 also carry several blooms on each stem; they are not hardy north of zone 7 and are mainly grown for forcing and blooming indoors. Within Division 9 are the

'King Alfred'
Division 1a
trumpet daffodil
all-yellow

'Mount Hood'
Division 1c
trumpet daffodil
cream-white

'Spellbinder'
Division 1d
trumpet daffodil
reverse-bicolored

'Fortune'
Division 2b
large-cupped narcissus
bicolored

'Carlton'
Division 2a
large-cupped
narcissus
all-yellow

'Birma'
Division 3a
small-cupped narcissus
yellow-petaled

'Barrett Browning'
Division 3b
small-cupped narcissus
white, with colored cup

'Snowshill'
Division 2c
large-cupped narcissus
all-white

'Actaea'
Division 9
poeticus narcissus

'Trevithian'
Division 7
jonquil narcissus

'Yellow Cheerfulness'
Division 8
tazetta narcissus

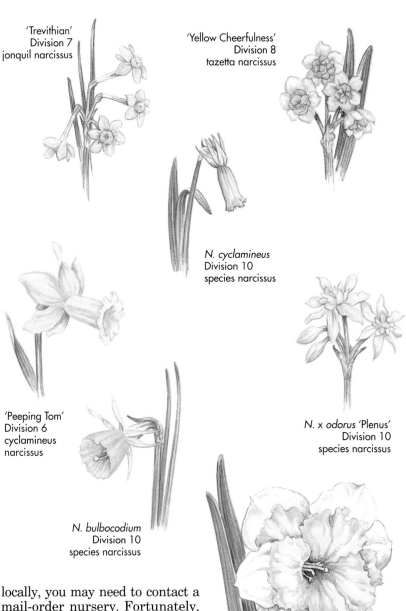

N. cyclamineus
Division 10
species narcissus

'Peeping Tom'
Division 6
cyclamineus
narcissus

N. x odorus 'Plenus'
Division 10
species narcissus

N. bulbocodium
Division 10
species narcissus

'Cassata'
Division 11
split-corona narcissus

poeticus narcissi, which are derived from the species *N. poeticus*. They have flat, brightly colored, and usually frilled cups and conspicuous white petals that do not overlap each other.

The distinguishing features in Divisions 5 to 9 are the number of flowers per stem; the manner in which the flowers are held — horizontally or pointing downward; the shape of the petals, which may be reflexed or swept forward from the cup; and the slenderness of the trumpets or petals.

The true species and wild forms make up Division 10. All varieties in Division 11 have a split corona, which gives them an orchidlike appearance. Division 12 includes a few miscellaneous varieties.

Buying bulbs

An increasing number of narcissus and daffodil varieties, together with a handful of old favorite species narcissi, are available as dormant bulbs in late summer and fall from garden centers. For varieties that are hard to find

'Angel'
Division 3c
small-cupped narcissus
all-white

'Petit Fours'
Division 4
double narcissus

locally, you may need to contact a mail-order nursery. Fortunately, bulbs travel well, so transporting them should not be a problem.

Do not buy bulbs that show signs of shooting — small yellowish-green growths at their tips — because they will be damaged by cold winter weather when you plant them. Also, do not buy bulbs that you know have been stored in a warm room. If possible, check that the bulbs are very firm to the touch, uniform in size, and free from fungal diseases. Bulbs with lots of small offsets (small bulbs that develop around the base of the bulb) attached to them, though larger in overall size, may give a relatively poor show of flowers. Of course, it may be difficult to inspect bulbs that are sold in sealed boxes.

Bargains can often be found in garden centers that sell bulbs loose. This type of display allows you to make your own selection and fill a bag for a set price. Be careful, though, as such bulk dis-

plays usually include lower-quality bulbs, and other customers can mix up the various cultivars.

If you don't intend to plant the bulbs immediately, store them in a cool, airy place. Remove boxed or bagged bulbs from their wrapping and lay them on open flats.

Preparing the site

Narcissi are tolerant of most fertile soils, whether alkaline, neutral, or slightly acid. Dig in ground limestone only if the soil is very acid. Open up the texture of heavily compacted soils by digging thoroughly before planting.

Most narcissi do not like very

water-retentive soils; the bulbs are apt to rot. If the soil is poorly drained, dig in plenty of sharp builder's sand and organic matter. However, soil that dries out in late spring, between flowering and the time the foliage dies, can be a disadvantage — drought retards regrowth of the bulbs and leads to smaller and possibly fewer flowers.

Apply a handful of complete fertilizer per sq yd/sq m, or one with potassium (which improves flower color) and phosphorus only, at planting time. Don't dig in fresh manure immediately before planting, but if you are preparing the planting bed well ahead of time (several months at least), you may add it then.

Planting the bulbs
Plant newly purchased bulbs as soon as possible in late summer or

▼ **Hoop-petticoat daffodils** These tiny species narcissi, no more than 6 in (15 cm) tall, are surrounded by grasslike leaves. They are ideal for rock gardens or raised beds. The deep yellow trumpets dominate the spiky petals and appear in late winter and early spring.

early fall. Use a dibble for small bulbs and a trowel or special bulb planter for bigger ones. Flatten the bottom of the planting holes so that the bulbs can rest on the soil — gaps remaining under planted bulbs may fill with water and cause rotting. On heavy soils, sprinkle a ½-in (12-mm) layer of builder's sand in the bottom of the hole to assist drainage.

In ground that otherwise will not be cultivated, the hole should be three times the depth of the bulb. For example, place a bulb that is 2 in (5 cm) deep in a 6-in (15-cm) hole. Cover with 4 in (10 cm) of soil. Bulbs planted in cultivated beds that will be hoed in summer and forked over in winter should be set a little deeper.

See that the bulbs are positioned correctly in the holes. The pointed tip must face upward, with the rounded base that bears the remnants of the previous season's roots facing downward.

You can also plant several bulbs in one large hole. Dig such a hole to the appropriate depth and place several bulbs in the bottom, then refill and press down the soil.

The spacing of narcissus and

daffodil bulbs depends on the purpose for which they are being grown, the number of times you will lift them, and the size of the bulb. For naturalizing grassy or woody areas, scatter the bulbs onto the ground wherever you want them to go. Just make sure that the distribution is fairly irregular before planting. In permanent beds or borders, space them 4-8 in (10-20 cm) apart.

For producing cut flowers, which entails lifting every 2 or 3 years, set the bulbs 4-6 in (10-15 cm) apart, depending on their size, in rows that are spaced 1½-2½ ft (45-75 cm) apart.

The more frequently the bulbs are lifted, the closer together you may plant them. Set small species, such as *Narcissus bulbocodium, N. cyclamineus,* and *N. triandrus,* 2-3 in (5-7.5 cm) apart in groups of a dozen or more.

If your planting plan features many varieties of narcissi or daffodils, with little or no separation of groups, it is often difficult to lift them without getting the varieties mixed up. A good solution to this problem is to plant bulbs of the same variety in a single large hole

GROWING NARCISSI IN BOWLS INDOORS

1 Bulbs should be planted in pots for forcing in late summer or early fall. If they have old roots attached, cut these off with sharp scissors, as close to the base as possible.

2 If the bowl has drainage holes, cover them with pieces of broken pot. Otherwise, put a few pieces of charcoal at the bottom to absorb surplus water and keep the potting soil sweet.

3 Partly fill the bowl with moist potting soil and position three to five bulbs so that their necks are just visible above the surface. Press soil down well, adding more if necessary.

and wrap them completely in a sheet of plastic netting or a large plastic mesh bag. Provided the mesh is large enough for the shoots to grow through, but small enough to retain the bulbs, the netting or bag can be used to lift all the bulbs at once after loosening the surface soil.

Naturalizing in grass

If you wish to grow narcissi or daffodils in grass, remember that their leaves must be allowed to die down before being sheared off. In effect, this practice means that the grass cannot be mowed for the first time each year until at least early summer — much too late for a formal lawn. Instead, consider naturalizing bulbs in a less formal area or a grassy bank, where they will provide a wash of color.

Ideally, use a bulb planter to plant the bulbs. This tool lets you extract a plug of soil completely with its grass top, and then replace it entirely intact after you have placed a bulb in the hole. Models with a hinged cutting head easily release the soil plug — a handy feature when you are working with damp, heavy soils.

Aftercare

Narcissi and daffodils require little or no aftercare once planted, and so can be left for several years. Bulbs should not be watered in; normal rainfall generally supplies all the moisture essential for healthy growth. Stakes or other forms of support are also unnecessary.

Cut off dead flower heads to conserve the bulb's energy, but leave most of the flower stem. Let the leaves die down completely, or at least become yellow, before

removing them. It is important to keep as much green material as possible intact, since the food held in the bulb must be replenished for the following flowering season.

Many gardeners like to knot the leaves or bend them over and tie them with twine or elastic bands. However, this practice is not recommended — it strangles the leaf tissues and prevents vital nutrients from traveling down to the storage bulb.

Lifting and storing

In general, the time to lift narcissi is when they become congested and tend to flower less freely. Wait until the leaves have turned yellow but have not died down — it is easier to find each bulb, and bulb flies will not have had time to attack. Choose a day when the soil is dry, then you will be able to lift the bulbs without damaging them.

Ideally, replant the bulbs immediately, at the recommended spacing, where they are to flower. If that is not possible, heel them in temporarily so that they can complete their growth. To do so, dig a trench 6 in (15 cm) deep and 1 ft (30 cm) wide. Lay the bulbs very close together on the trench bottom, then fill the trench with soil. Be sure that at least half the length of the stems and leaves protrude above the surface.

When the leaves have withered, remove the bulbs from the trench; pull off dead leaves, shriveled skins, and old roots. Discard damaged and diseased bulbs and sort the rest according to size, for later replanting or propagation. Store them in a cool, airy place until setting them out in early fall.

A MASSED POT DISPLAY

1 Prepare the bottom of a pot, 5-6 in (12-15 cm) deep, as you did the bowl above. Place three narcissus bulbs on a 2-in (5-cm) layer of moist potting soil.

2 Cover the three bulbs with more moist soil until it reaches just below their necks. Press the soil firmly around the bulbs with your fingers.

3 Set three more bulbs in the spaces between the first group and continue filling the pot with soil. A larger pot can hold two layers, each with five bulbs.

Bulbs for forcing

Many of the hardy narcissi that bloom outdoors during spring can be forced to flower indoors several weeks earlier. Just pot them up in late summer, then water and place them in a cool area. After several weeks, roots will develop. Bring the bulbs into a warm, bright room and the flowers will soon grow.

Bulb catalogs usually indicate those varieties that respond to indoor forcing — tazetta varieties, such as 'Paper White' and 'Soleil d'Or,' and miniatures, such as 'Tête-a-Tête,' are particularly suitable. Daffodils, such as 'Golden Harvest' and 'King Alfred,' will also flower well indoors.

The best potting soil to use is a sterilized blend of equal parts good garden soil (loam), builder's sand, and screened peat moss, or a commercial soil-based mix. Bulbs can also be forced in moist vermiculite. However, this material does not supply any nutrients, and so starves the bulb. Some narcissi, notably the tazetta types, can also be grown in shallow containers of pebbles just topped with water.

To create a more interesting indoor display, it is better to set several bulbs close together in one large pot than to plant a few in several small pots. After flower-ing, place them out in the garden. They will bloom again in a year or two.

Propagation

In general, gardeners find it easier to buy narcissi and daffodils as dormant bulbs that will flower within a few months of planting. However, it is possible to propagate these plants yourself — the only disadvantage is that it will take several years for the new plants to reach flowering size.

Most bulbs self-propagate by producing offsets. These immature bulbs can be detached during routine lifting and grown on separately in a nursery bed.

Certain narcissi produce seeds (often at the expense of offsets), and you can sow these outdoors. The quality of resulting plants, however, is often erratic in terms of the number of blooms produced, and the color and shape of the flowers. Named varieties will not breed true from seed.

Collect ripened seeds in midsummer and sow them within a few weeks. Use a relatively large pot filled with sterilized potting soil, as the seedlings need a deep root-run. Cover the seeds with ¼-½ in (6-12 mm) of potting soil and water in gently. Add a thin layer of builder's sand to deter slugs. Place the pot in a sheltered, semishaded spot in the garden, keeping the soil just moist.

Seeds usually take several months to germinate. Expect only a single, rather thin leaf per plant the first year. When it dies down, gently scrape off and replace the top ½ in (12 mm) of soil — you won't injure the seedling bulb, as it will have already pulled itself deeper into the soil. Cover with a fresh layer of builder's sand.

In the second year, repeat this procedure and also apply a dilute liquid fertilizer in midspring and again in late spring. Once the leaves have died, carefully knock out the bulbs from the pot. Thoroughly clean the soil from the bulbs, check them for signs of disease, and store the healthy ones until late summer.

Replant the bulbs in a place where they will not be disturbed. After 3 more years, move the bulbs to their permanent sites. Flowers may bloom in the fourth to seventh year after sowing. Keep species narcissi grown from seed in their pots until the first crop of flowers is produced.

▼ **Naturalized narcissi** Most daffodils and narcissi can be grown in grassy meadows and on sunny banks. Here, large- and small-cupped bicolored narcissi are mixed with golden and white trumpet daffodils.

A MANIA FOR TULIPS

Matched only by daffodils for popularity in spring flower beds, tulips are highly decorative and come in a myriad of colors, shapes, and sizes.

The genus *Tulipa* belongs to the lily family — Liliaceae — and consists of about one hundred species, most of which originated in the Middle East. Some, however, grow naturally in Europe and as far east as Asia. The name "tulip" derives from the corruption of a Middle Eastern word for turban, which the flower is thought to resemble.

Tulips have been popular garden plants in Europe for more than 300 years. In the seventeenth century, seeds and bulbs were brought there from Turkey, and it was not long before the attractive flowers were very much in demand. Within 100 years of their introduction, tulip mania had swept Holland, and fortunes were made on the sale of the bulbs.

Today, specialist growers in Holland cultivate hundreds of named varieties. In addition, plant collectors continue to seek original species in their native countries, further widening the range of colors, shapes, and sizes.

All tulips grow from rounded or somewhat egg-shaped bulbs. These have thin outer skins and a pointed nose that should face upward when set in soil. Most plants carry a solitary flower on an upright stem, but a few species have two or more per stem. The flowers are goblet-shaped, with six petals that can vary from slender and pointed to broadly rounded. Mature blooms generally open wide in sunlight. Double tulips are easily distinguished by their numerous petals per bloom.

Each bulb has one or two leaves growing at or near ground level, and two or three smaller ones farther up the stem. A few species, including *T. tarda,* have a tuft of narrow leaves at ground level.

Many of the attractive color irregularities, known as *breaks,* found in tulip flowers are due to a virus. When sharply defined splashes of a second color appear on the petals, the virus can be isolated and bred into a new color strain. Natural mutation also causes fluctuations in color, resulting in plants called "sports."

As natives of temperate regions, tulips require a period of chilling during dormancy. In frost-free regions, gardeners must refrigerate bulbs for 6 to 8 weeks before planting them in early winter.

Nearly every form of tulip flowers well in the first year after the bulbs have been planted, if they were bought from a reputable supplier. Only a flooded garden or an attack by a serious pest or disease can prevent a glorious display. More cultural attention is

◀ **Single late tulips** These May-flowering hybrids include many of the best-loved old garden tulips. Superb for flower beds, their sturdy stems carry squared-off flower bowls. A harmless virus sometimes causes a break in the flower color.

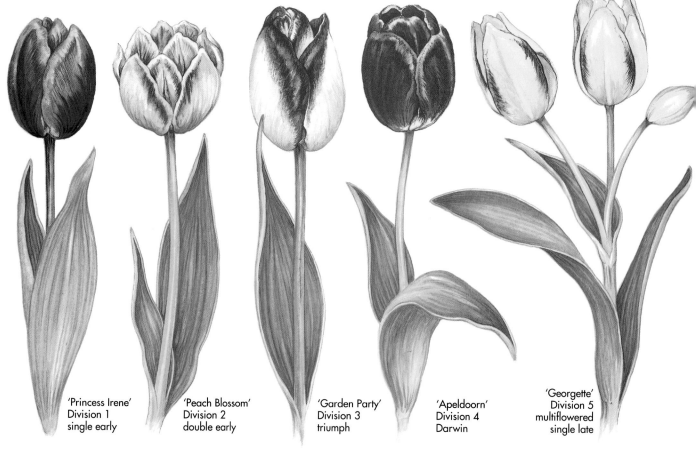

'Princess Irene'
Division 1
single early

'Peach Blossom'
Division 2
double early

'Garden Party'
Division 3
triumph

'Apeldoorn'
Division 4
Darwin

'Georgette'
Division 5
multiflowered
single late

needed to ensure blooming in subsequent years.

Classification

The official classification of the genus *Tulipa* encompasses 14 divisions of cultivated varieties, based mainly on flower shape, flowering season, and parentage. A fifteenth division contains all the naturally occurring species.

There have been several reorganizations of the divisions over the years, so some tulip enthusiasts may know particular varieties under different categories. The current classification follows.

Single early varieties — Division 1 — include some that were once grouped in the Darwin section. Their bold flowers are 3 in (7.5 cm) wide, cup-shaped, and round-petaled. They open from early spring to midspring; these tulips stand 10-24 in (25-60 cm) tall.

Double early varieties — Division 2 — are generally carried on shorter stems than the single early — they may grow up to 2 ft (30 cm) tall. Their double, peony-like flowers are 3-4 in (7.5-10 cm) wide and bloom in midspring.

Triumph varieties — Division 3 — incorporate some of those formerly called Mendel tulips. Their conical flowers open to a more rounded shape and can be up to 4 in (10 cm) wide. Borne on sturdy stems, triumphs stand 16-24 in (40-60 cm) tall and bloom from midspring to late spring.

Darwin hybrid tulips — Division 4 (formerly Division 5) — have huge, cuplike flowers that usually measure up to 6 in (15 cm) wide; some, however, are as wide as 8 in (20 cm). Available in many colors, often with contrasting markings, they open in late spring. These tulips stand 22-28 in (55-70 cm) tall on strong stems.

Single late tulips — Division 5 (sometimes called May-flowering, and including many former Darwins) — are among the tallest types, reaching 32 in (80 cm) tall. The flowers appear squarish to oval in profile, frequently with pointed petals. They open in midspring to late spring and often last until very early summer. As with previous divisions, these have one flower per stem, but the so-called 'Bouquet' varieties are multiflowered.

Lily-flowered varieties — Division 6 (previously 7) — have narrow-waisted flowers, with long, pointed petals that flare outward at their tips to a width of up to 6 in (15 cm), occasionally more. They open in late spring or sometimes a little earlier; these tulips are 20-26 in (50-65 cm) tall.

Fringed varieties — Division 7 (formerly part of the Cottage division and sometimes known as orchid-flowered tulips) — are distinguishable from all other types because of their sharply fringed petals. In other respects, they are similar to the single late varieties. They are commonly sold as mixed-color selections.

Viridiflora varieties — Division 8 (previously part of the Cottage group) — are also known as green tulips. They, too, are like the single lates, but are characterized by green streaks or suffusions on their petals.

Rembrandt tulips — Division 9 — have flowers with striped or feathery patterns caused by a harmless virus. In other respects, they resemble the single lates.

Parrot tulips — Division 10 — are also like the single lates in habit and flowering season, but have frilled, incut, and twisted petals. Many parrot tulips are bicolored and have weak stems.

Double late varieties — Division 11 (sometimes called peony tulips) — have large, fully double, rather squat flowers that may open up to 5 in (12 cm) wide. These tulips are 16-24 in (40-60 cm) high and bloom in late spring.

Kaufmanniana hybrids — Division 12 (also known as water-lily tulips) — are derived primarily from *Tulipa kaufmanniana*, a starry-flowered species from

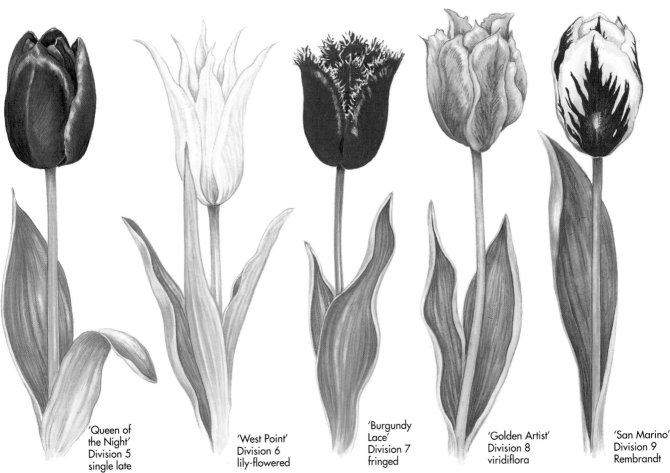

'Queen of
the Night'
Division 5
single late

'West Point'
Division 6
lily-flowered

'Burgundy
Lace'
Division 7
fringed

'Golden Artist'
Division 8
viridiflora

'San Marino'
Division 9
Rembrandt

Turkestan, named for the famous Russian botanist Kaufmann. These hybrids have water-lilylike flowers that open out flat, to 2½ in (6 cm) wide, in early spring. The plants are 4-10 in (10-25 cm) tall, with usually bicolored flowers. Some have brownish-purple spots or stripes on the leaves.

Fosteriana (or Fosterana) hybrids — Division 13 — have been bred mainly from *T. fosteriana*. This shiny-leaved species, with its bright red flowers, comes from the limestone mountains of central Asia. The hybrids share this brilliance of flower color — ranging from scarlet to yellow or white. The midspring flowers are slender when closed; in full sun, they open to a width of 7-8 in (18-20 cm). These plants stand 8-16 in (20-40 cm) high.

Greigii hybrids — Division 14 — are derived largely from *T. greigii,* and are also native to central Asia. Their leaves have distinctive wavy edges and bold purple-brown or maroon markings. The plants are usually 8-12 in (20-30 cm) tall, but occasionally reach 20 in (50 cm) in height. The large, brightly colored flowers bloom in early spring to late spring.

Species tulips — Division 15 — cover a wide range of flower colors, shapes, and sizes. Most are smaller and more delicate in appearance than the modern hybrids, but are equally hardy.

Choosing tulips

Tulips are virtually synonymous with spring flower beds and make good partners for biennials such

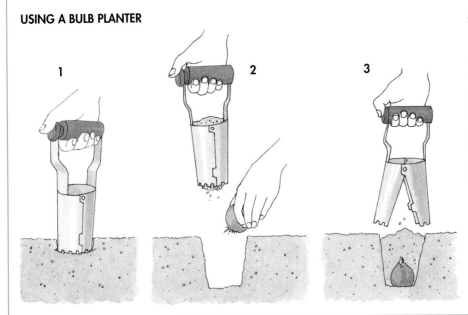

USING A BULB PLANTER

1

2

3

A bulb planter makes the job of planting bulbs less laborious. Push the planter firmly into the ground to the desired planting depth (some tools provide calibrations on the outside) **(1).** Use a twisting action if the soil is heavy. Then gently pull the cylindrical blade out of the ground, along with a plug of soil. To improve drainage, especially in clay soil, place a small amount of sharp sand in the bottom of the hole, then set a bulb in the hole **(2).** Finally, release the soil plug from the planter, dropping it back into the hole **(3).** Press the soil down with the tips of your fingers.

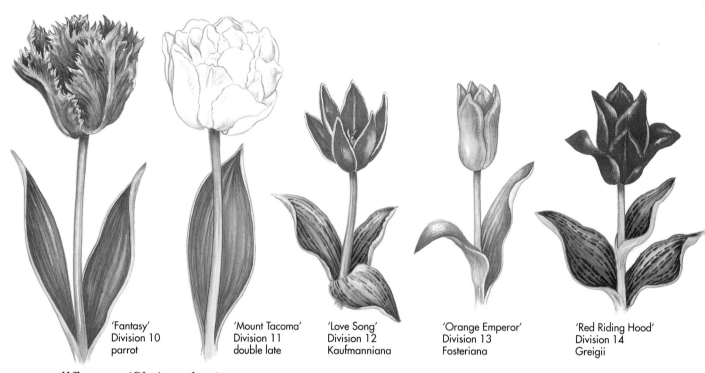

'Fantasy'
Division 10
parrot

'Mount Tacoma'
Division 11
double late

'Love Song'
Division 12
Kaufmanniana

'Orange Emperor'
Division 13
Fosteriana

'Red Riding Hood'
Division 14
Greigii

as wallflowers *(Cheiranthus),* forget-me-nots *(Myosotis),* and daisies *(Bellis perennis).* The taller and more robust modern hybrids in Divisions 1 through 9 are best suited to bedding schemes. Less robust types need the shelter of other border plants, while the smaller species and their hybrids are perfect for raised beds and containers.

Among the named hybrids, you'll find colors and heights to complement any scheme. In addition to these hybrids, many nurseries offer mixed selections, often from just one division. But they cannot be guaranteed to flower simultaneously and may be disappointing.

Similar in size to those found in the first nine divisions are the parrot tulips. Their heavy heads are easily damaged by winds and rain, so plant them in a sheltered spot. The two double-flowered groups need the same protection.

For pockets in a sunny, well-drained rock garden, the edges of a bedding scheme, or outdoor containers, choose among the Kaufmanniana or Greigii hybrids. Many of the true species, such as *Tulipa biflora, T. clusiana, T. pulchella,* and *T. tarda,* will also thrive in these situations.

Tulipa sylvestris is one of the few species that likes shady conditions, particularly dappled woodlands. All the other species and hybrids prefer full sun.

Planting bulbs outdoors
Tulip bulbs flourish in sandy, well-drained but humus-rich soil, which not only enhances their growth, but makes the task of lift-

ing them after flowering much easier. Though tolerant of a fairly wide range of soil pH, these bulbs favor mildly alkaline conditions. If your soil is especially acid, amend it with lime when you prepare it for planting — a couple of handfuls of ground limestone per sq yd/sq m is generally sufficient.

Dig the soil to at least one spade's depth, adding well-rotted compost to poor soils, together with a slow-release fertilizer. Also, incorporate builder's sand into clay soils to improve drainage.

In late fall, plant the bulbs in a sunny site. Earlier planting often results in premature shoot growth, which is then susceptible to frost damage.

The ideal planting depth and spacing depends on the soil type and the display you want. In light soils, bulbs can be planted up to 1 ft (30 cm) deep, which provides the best stability for taller-flowering types and allows for subsequent surface cultivation and interplanting without disturbance to the bulbs. However, a 6-in (15-cm) planting depth is more common, and you will find it easier to lift the bulbs in summer from that level. Never plant deeper than 6 in (15 cm) on heavy soils.

Place bedding tulips 4-12 in (10-30 cm) apart, depending on the effect you want to create. For formal beds, space bulbs 4-6 in (10-15 cm) apart, depending on the bulb size, in rows or groups. Leave room between the bulbs so

T. tarda
Division 15
species

T. pulchella
'Violacea'
Division 15
species

T. acuminata
Division 15
species

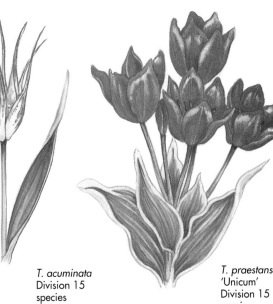

T. praestans
'Unicum'
Division 15
species

◀ **Lily-flowered tulips**
The gold-edged, crimson 'Aladdin' blooms in late spring; it is a graceful companion for such late-flowering narcissi as the tazetta cultivar 'Geranium,' with its rich orange cups and broad white petals.

▶ **Greigii tulip hybrids** Bred from the species *T. greigii,* these hybrids have inherited handsomely wavy-edged, striped leaves and slightly waisted goblet flowers. They are perfect for rock gardens, pot cultivation, and small flower beds that feature low-growing plants, such as pansies and English daisies.

you can interplant other plants.

When using tulips as garden perennials in a permanent site, smaller ones, such as *T. turkestanica* and *T. tarda,* can be set out in groups of 7 to 12 bulbs. Well-drained soil and a south-facing position sheltered from strong winds offer the best conditions.

There are two basic ways to plant tulip bulbs — either placed in individual closely spaced holes, or in a bed that has been excavated to the appropriate depth. For the first method, use a bulb planter rather than a trowel. It will enable you to lift out a plug of soil at the right depth, then drop it back into the hole once you have positioned each bulb.

In some gardens, rodents like to

dig up tulip bulbs. Protect against these pests by scattering new plantings with moth crystals, or else plant bulbs within cages fashioned from fine chicken wire.

To reduce the risk of rotting, position tulip bulbs on builder's sand. See that each bulb has its flat side facing downward. Press the soil firmly around the bulbs so that no air pockets remain.

Aftercare
Deadhead all tulips as the first petals fall, but don't cut off stalks or foliage. Leave as much green tissue as possible so that each bulb can build up its strength for the next season. Remove any fallen petals from the soil; these can harbor viruses.

Some species, such as *T. kaufmanniana,* and their cultivars will ripen in the soil, then bloom and increase naturally for many years. But most tulips, especially the modern hybrids, produce progressively smaller flowers and eventually die if they are left in the ground permanently. They should be dug up and stored dry every year after flowering.

Ideally, lift tulips from the ground when the foliage and stalks are yellowish brown in early summer. Use a garden fork to lever the soil below the bulbs. Do not pull them up by the leaves, or the bulbs may break away and be lost in the soil.

However, tulips can be lifted while the foliage is still green if the site is needed for other plantings. In this case, replant them in a temporary bed until the leaves die down naturally. Then dig them up and dry them as you would narcissi (p.99).

Place the lifted plants in shallow boxes and store them in a garage or dry shed. Remove the leaves and stems when they are dry and brittle. Also, rub away the roots, old bulb scales, and soil. Store the cleaned bulbs in a dry, airy place under cover and out of reach of mice. Check regularly for any sign of mold or pest attack.

Growing tulips in pots

The smaller species and hybrids can be grown successfully in an unheated greenhouse or cool, frost-free sun-room or windowsill. *T. pulchella* and *T. batalinii* are particularly suited to this type of cultivation. In midfall to late fall, place 5 to 7 bulbs, 2 in (5 cm) deep, in a shallow pot, 5-6 in (12-15 cm) deep, filled with sterilized, well-drained potting soil.

Water the bulbs at planting time, then keep them moist until the leaves turn yellow after blooming. Once the flowers fade, give the bulbs 3 or 4 weekly feeds of liquid fertilizer until watering is stopped. Allow the soil to dry out for the resting period during summer and early fall.

Single and double early hybrids can be planted in bowls to flower indoors during midwinter, just as some hyacinths and narcissi are. Plant forced bulbs from late summer to midfall. Triumph tulips, with their sturdy stems, respond especially well to this treatment.

Pack the bulbs into potting soil so that their "noses" barely emerge above the surface. For the best display, set them close together. Put the bowl in a cool, dark place, such as a basement or frost-free garage, to encourage root and leaf formation. Alternatively, set the bowl outdoors against a north-facing wall, covering it with black plastic and a layer of soil or sand to exclude light. Water it occasionally.

When the tips of the leaves are showing 1-2 in (2.5-5 cm), move the bowl to a windowsill in a cool room or to a greenhouse — 50°F (10°C) is ideal. As leaves grow, raise the temperature gradually to 64°F (18°C). Tall tulips may need support as the flowers develop. Keep them well-watered.

PLANTING BASKETS

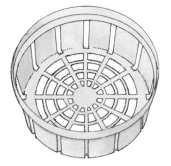

1 Because tulip bulbs should be lifted every year, the use of special plastic planting baskets — available at some garden centers — makes it easy to locate and raise bulbs from the ground.

2 Put a shallow layer of soil in the bottom of the basket, then place the bulbs in it. Dig a large hole that is wide and deep enough to accommodate the entire planting basket.

3 Set the basket in the bottom of the hole, checking that the bulbs will lie at the correct depth in the ground. Finally, refill the hole, covering both the basket and the bulbs inside.

4 Once the flowers have faded and the tulip leaves and stalks have turned brownish yellow, lever the entire basket, together with the bulbs and soil, from the ground with a spade or fork.

5 Clean each of the bulbs by hand, rubbing away loose soil, flaky scales, old roots, and small offsets. The offsets can be stored and replanted separately to increase your stock.

6 Lastly, wash the plastic baskets, then use them to store the bulbs until fall. The perforated sides and bottom allow air to circulate between the bulbs, which helps to prevent rotting.

Propagation

Although tulips can be propagated by seed, this method is very slow. In addition, seedlings from garden varieties are extremely variable.

Propagation is usually from the offset bulbs produced by all tulips. These are mostly true to type — any color sports do not vary in shape from the parent.

When lifting bulbs for storage, remove the offsets clustered at the base of the stems. Store them at 61-64°F (16-18°C) in a dry place. Plant offsets at the normal time, sorting them by size. Place the smallest ones 2 in (5 cm) deep and the largest ones 6 in (15 cm) deep. Space them so that they are twice their own width apart.

Climbers and wall plants

Honeysuckle, trained around an ornamental arch or other garden structure, is a delight to behold. On a warm summer's evening, its fragrance fills the air. A garden without any climbers or plants that have been trained to grow up against a wall lacks one of the fundamental dimensions of a truly balanced arrangement: vertical growth. This type of planting can adorn walls and fences, frame doorways or windows, provide shaded sitting areas, or create wonderful screens to conceal unattractive views.

It is essential to prepare the ground carefully before planting climbers, however, or they will not reach their full potential. Many people make the mistake of digging too small a planting hole; it must be wide and deep enough to allow the roots to expand.

When healthy climbers fail to thrive, it is frequently caused by one of the following: lack of soil, water, nutrients, or circulating air. For example, plants growing against an absorbent surface, such as a wall, are prone to dehydration — the wall draws water from the soil and holds the heat of the sun — and thus, during dry spells, many species, especially clematis, need a full bucket of water once a day if they are to survive.

Climbers show great variability in their patterns of growth. Some are slow-growing — wisteria takes at least 7 years before it begins to flower — while others quickly dominate the space given to them. In the latter group are the Virginia creeper, which rapidly covers a wall with foliage, and honeysuckle, which soon gets out of hand unless controlled by judicious pruning.

Wall climbers *Solanum crispum* 'Glasnevin' is smothered with clusters of star-shaped purple petals.

CHOOSING CLIMBERS

Versatile and colorful, climbing plants mask eyesores and furnish walls and fences with flowers and foliage.

With their wide range of handsome flowers and foliage, climbing plants add color and interest to the vertical surfaces in a garden. Moreover, they can camouflage eyesores or act as focal points in their own right.

Many climbers grow quickly and can easily cover an expanse of wall, yet they occupy only a tiny bit of ground — a bonus for those with small gardens. Some plants, such as honeysuckle, will even thrive in a large pot or tub, and thus can be grown on decks and balconies, in addition to open beds. Others, notably ivies and certain clematises, are so versatile that they will clothe both horizontal and vertical exteriors.

If you choose carefully among the numerous types of climbers, it is possible to have a year-round display of them in your garden. Evergreen ones exhibit brilliant fall colors, others flower in winter and spring, and still others bloom profusely in summer.

Although climbers are usually trained against walls or other garden structures, they can be allowed to scramble through shrubs or grow up trees, as they would naturally. Careful management is needed, however, so that the climber doesn't completely smother its host plant.

The most common mistake made by those buying climbers is that of selecting ones that grow too vigorously. Wisteria, for example, is among the most popular of climbers, yet unpruned, it can reach a height of 100 ft (30 m).

▲ **Variegated ivy** The variegated Persian ivy *(Hedera colchica* 'Dentata Variegata') retains its yellow leaf edges best in a sunny situation.

▼ **Canopy of clematis** The popular 'Jackmanii Superba' drapes its huge blooms over a garden wall in midsummer, firmly secured by its twining leaf stalks.

Although you can control climbers by regular hard pruning, it is wiser to select a smaller species if your space is limited.

Keep in mind that a climber growing against a painted wooden surface, such as a wall, may need careful untying and retying, or pruning back hard when the structure requires repainting or other maintenance work. To avoid this situation, train the plant on a trellis that is mounted a few inches (centimeters) away from the wall. Then the whole panel, complete with climber, can be swung away from the wall as necessary.

Defining climbers

Many climbing plants grow well in the United States. They may be annuals, such as the morning glory and sweet pea; perennials,

▶ **Woodbine honeysuckle** The native *Lonicera periclymenum* is a fast-growing woody twiner. It is happiest with its base in cool shade and its yellow and red flowers facing the sun.

such as the flame creeper *(Tropaeolum speciosum)* and ornamental hops; or shrubby, with a permanent woody frame of trunk and boughs, such as ivy and wisteria.

A climber needs a host or other support in order to grow well. Although ornamental shrubs, such as camellia, pyracantha, and Japanese quince, are often set against walls and rigorously pruned, these plants are not, strictly speaking, true climbers.

There are several ways in which climbing plants cling to their support. The so-called self-clinging species are the easiest for the gardener to grow. Some of them, such as English ivy and climbing hydrangea, adhere by means of aerial roots. Others, such as Virginia creeper, grasp onto a surface by means of threadlike adhesive tendrils. As a general rule, self-clinging climbers should be grown against solid walls or tree trunks. (These climbers, especially ivy, can harm old brick walls that have crumbling lime mortar, but sound walls are unlikely to suffer damage.)

◀ **Chinese wisteria** At maturity, *Wisteria sinensis* may reach a height of 100 ft (30 m). In early summer, it is covered with magnificent, fragrant pale mauve flowers that are carried in racemes up to 1ft (30 cm) long.

Climbers, such as honeysuckle and Chinese gooseberry (*Actinidia deliciosa),* have stems that twine around woody branches, a trellis, or wires for support. Similarly, the ornamental grapevine and the Chilean glory-flower (*Eccremocarpus scaber)* have tendrils that twine or curl, and the clematis has twining leaf stalks, or *petioles.* All these plants are excellent for training on freestanding pergolas or arches, or along fences.

Other climbing plants, such as the winter-flowering jasmines *(Jasminum nudiflorum),* do not have any special mechanism for attaching themselves. Their long, lax stems simply scramble through other plants. Climbing and rambling roses have thorns that hook onto available supports. Lax climbing shrubs, such as forsythia, must be tied to a support system, such as wires or a strong trellis, to grow vertically. These shrubs also grow through hedges.

Choosing climbers

It is a matter of personal preference whether you select a self-clinging plant, a twining type that needs wires or a trellis, or a rambler that must be tied in to a support system. But before buying one, decide how much time and effort you are able to give the plant, as well as its eventual height and spread.

Also consider the amount of sunlight and shelter the climber will need. It is better to have a particular spot in the garden in mind and choose a plant that will thrive there, rather than buy a climber simply on the basis of its appearance and not on its growing requirements. Keep in mind that south- and west-facing exposures receive the most sunlight; east-facing sites have only morning light; and north-facing situations get no direct sunlight and are therefore cool.

Tolerant climbers for north- and east-facing positions include climbing hydrangeas, Boston ivy, and the true ivies, especially the all-green types and those with white variegations, such as *Hedera colchica* 'Dentata Variegata' and *Hedera helix* 'Little Diamond.' Several climbing roses, such as the coral-pink 'Aloha,' the fragrant pink 'Mme Grégoire Staechelin,' and the scarlet 'Sympathie' grow well against sunless walls. *Clematis* 'Nelly

CLIMBING METHODS

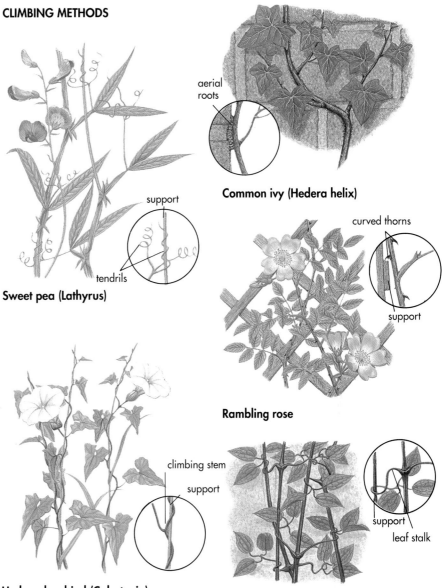

Sweet pea (Lathyrus)
support
tendrils

Common ivy (Hedera helix)
aerial roots

Rambling rose
curved thorns
support

Hedge glorybind (Calystegia)
climbing stem
support

Clematis
support
leaf stalk

▲ **Climbing mechanisms**
True climbers attach themselves to their supports by means of curling, twining, or adhesive tendrils or stems, aerial roots, hooked thorns, or winding leaf stalks. Others simply scramble their lax stems through surrounding plants, trellises, or netting.

◄ **Passionflower** The evergreen *Passiflora caerulea* is not hardy north of zone 8, except in sheltered sites. It produces its distinctive blue-and-white flowers in late summer and early fall.

Moser' also prefers a north-facing spot, as its mauve-pink flowers will fade in direct sun.

Many honeysuckles and clematises are grown in the shade, where their roots can be kept cool. Most flower best, however, when the stems are exposed to full sun. Try planting either of these climbers on the north side of a low structure, such as a fence, and then allowing it to clamber over the top. You could also train a large species clematis, such as *Clematis montana,* against a north-facing wall; it should produce masses of white flowers in spring. Alternatively, set it in full sun, but shade the roots with paving stones, a thick mulch, or another dense planting.

Among the climbers that will flourish in south- and west-facing

◄ **Boston ivy** Self-supporting and hardy, *Parthenocissus tricuspidata* 'Veitchii' will quickly cover an expanse of wall. In the fall, the leaves turn a glossy bright crimson before dropping.

▼ **Himalayan clematis** One of the easiest clematises to grow, *C. montana* is smothered with white spring flowers.

exposures are the ornamental grapevines, wisteria, the slightly tender Canary Island ivy, and ivies with yellow variegations, such as *Hedera helix* 'Goldheart.' Many plants that enjoy a sunny situation, such as passionflower and summer-flowering jasmine, also require shelter from winds.

Climbers are frequently used to conceal eyesores in the landscape. Those with evergreen foliage can be relied on to do the job year round. If you choose a different type, make sure that it has enough woody growth — the silver lace vine *(Polygonum aubertii),* for example — to partially obscure the unsightly feature, even when it is leafless. The more restrained *Akebia quinata,* with its semievergreen palmate leaves, can nicely mask a smaller object. Also consider erecting a freestanding trellis screen in front of an eyesore, then covering it with your choice of climber.

If you want to adorn a house wall, select a planting that will complement the wall's color. Deep purple clematis, for example, provides a stunning contrast against a white-stuccoed wall, as does summer-flowering white jasmine against a dark brick wall. And the foliage of certain climbers can also produce dramatic effects: crimson glory vine *(Vitis coignetiae),* for instance, will enliven a pale wall in the fall, while *Hedera helix* 'Goldheart' will spruce up a dark wall throughout the year.

For a climber to train on a pergola or trellis, look at some that are relatively small — perhaps one of the clematis hybrids, the annual black-eyed Susan vine *(Thunbergia alata),* or the perennial climbing sweet pea *(Lathyrus latifolius),* which has rosy purple flowers.

Climbers that serve as focal points depend largely on color for their effect, whether it comes from the plant's flowers, its interesting foliage, or even its decorative fruits. When choosing an eye-catching climber, try to assess what it will look like when not blooming. Think, too, about the amount of time the climber is "putting on a show," compared to the months when it may be subdued. A climbing plant that is reasonably attractive year round may be a better choice than one that produces spectacular blooms for a very short period.

Mixing climbers

If you grow certain types of climbers together, you can get double or even triple displays of blooms in one space. For a magnificent floral show, plant some roses and clematises together. Another possibility is to find a combination of climbers that will follow one another into bloom: a winter-flowering jasmine inter-twines nicely with a spring-flowering clematis, for example, or try planting that same clematis with a summer-flowering jasmine.

A striking contrast can be created by using the evergreen foliage of a climber, such as ivy, as a backdrop for the exquisite flowers of a more delicate climber, such as the frost-sensitive Chilean glory-flower *(Eccremocarpus scaber).*

▲ **Flame creeper** In cool, shady gardens, the perennial *Tropaeolum speciosum* bears scarlet flower clusters throughout summer. The blooms glow against a background of the variegated ivy *Hedera helix* 'Goldheart.'

◄ **Morning glory** This heat-loving annual *(Ipomoea tricolor)* shoots wiry stems up a trellis or wire supports. Its huge blue or purple trumpets open in the morning, then close again by the late afternoon.

Place only plants with similar cultivation needs together — they should also be compatible in growth rate. In addition, their individual pruning requirements must be taken into consideration. A climber that demands hard annual pruning, for example, would be an unsuitable partner for a permanent twining species.

Whichever climbers you choose, your garden will benefit from them, both decoratively and functionally. Just pay attention to their growth and flowering characteristics and plant them in the right place.

▶ **Wall coverage** A stunning mixture of climbers creates a colorful display for many months. The heart-shaped leaves of *Actinidia kolomikta*, prominently tipped with white and pink, blend with the yellow-green foliage of the evergreen Japanese honeysuckle *(Lonicera japonica)*, whose scented pale yellow flowers compete with the flame-orange tubes of the tender Chilean glory-flower *(Eccremocarpus scaber)*.

CLIMBERS

NAME	DESCRIPTION/HARDINESS	HEIGHT	SPREAD	EXPOSURE
Akebia *(Akebia quinata)*	Quick-growing woody twiner, with palmate evergreen leaves; red-purple flowers in midspring; to zone 5	30 ft (9 m)	16 ft (5 m)	N/E
Boston ivy *(Parthenocissus tricuspidata)*	Quick-growing woody and deciduous self-clinger; tiny flowers; crimson leaves in the fall; to zone 4	60 ft (18 m)	33 ft (10 m)	Any
Canary island ivy *(Hedera canariensis)*	Quick-growing evergreen self-clinger; large, heart-shaped green leaves; to zone 8	20 ft (6 m)	10 ft (3 m)	S/W
Chilean glory-flower *(Eccremocarpus scaber)*	Quick-growing annual twiner; red/yellow flowers in summer and fall; to zone 9	10 ft (3 m)	10 ft (3 m)	S/W
Chinese wisteria *(Wisteria sinensis)*	Strong-growing deciduous twiner; mauve-blue or white flowers in late spring; to zone 5	30 ft (9 m)	20 ft (6 m)	S/W
Clematis *(Clematis armandii)*	Vigorous woody twiner; evergreen leaves; white flowers from midspring to late spring; to zone 7	30 ft (9 m)	10 ft (3 m)	S/W
Clematis *(Clematis 'Jackmanii Superba')*	Quick-growing, large-bloomed purple hybrid; flowering in profusion from midsummer to early fall; to zone 5	15 ft (4.5 m)	10 ft (3 m)	S/W
Clematis *(Clematis 'Nelly Moser')*	Quick-growing woody twiner; pink-mauve flowers in late spring/fall; to zone 5	9-15 ft (3-4.5 m)	10 ft (3 m)	N/E
Climbing bittersweet *(Celastrus orbiculatus)*	Quick-growing deciduous twiner; bright yellow leaves in the fall; fruits not edible; to zone 5	30-40 ft (9-12 m)	16 ft (5 m)	S/W
Climbing hydrangea *(Hydrangea petiolaris)*	Vigorous deciduous self-clinger; massed creamy white lacecap flowers in early summer; to zone 4	50 ft (15 m)	33 ft (10 m)	N/E
Crimson glory vine *(Vitis coignetiae)*	Quick-growing deciduous twiner; crimson leaves in the fall; inedible black fruits; to zone 5	50 ft (15 m)	50 ft (15 m)	S/W
Everlasting sweet pea *(Lathyrus latifolius)*	Quick-growing perennial climber; summer flowering; pink-lilac; to zone 5	10 ft (3 m)	3 ft (1 m)	S/W
Honeysuckle *(Lonicera periclymenum)*	Quick-growing deciduous twiner; midgreen leaves, cream-tinged red-purple flowers; to zone 5	20 ft (6 m)	10 ft (3 m)	N/E
Ivy *(Hedera colchica 'Dentata Variegata')*	Moderate- to quick-growing woody self-clinger; creamy yellow-edged evergreen leaves; to zone 7	20-30 ft (6-9 m)	30 ft (9 m)	N/E
Ivy *(Hedera helix 'Goldheart')*	Moderate- to quick-growing woody self-clinger; gold-centered leaves; to zone 6	20 ft (6 m)	15 ft (4.5 m)	S/E
Kolomikta vine *(Actinidia kolomikta)*	Slow-growing deciduous climber; white and pink-tipped leaves; edible fruits; to zone 5	20 ft (6 m)	10 ft (3 m)	S/W
Morning glory *(Ipomoea tricolor)*	Quick-growing half-hardy annual twiner; blue summer flowers	8 ft (2.4 m)	3 ft (1 m)	S/W
Nasturtium *(Tropaeolum majus)*	Quick-growing annual twiner with round leaves; yellow, orange, or red flowers in summer	12 ft (3.5 m)	6-10 ft (2-3 m)	S/W
Passionflower *(Passiflora caerulea)*	Moderate- to quick-growing semihardy climber; white/blue flowers in summer and fall; to zone 8	30 ft (9 m)	3 ft (1 m)	S/W
Porcelain vine *(Ampelopsis brevipedunculata)*	Strong-growing woody twiner; turquoise fruits; yellow fall foliage; to zone 4	25 ft (7.5 m)	25 ft (7.5 m)	S/W
Potato vine *(Solanum jasminoides)*	Quick-growing twiner; deciduous; pale blue flowers midsummer to fall; to zone 9	15 ft (4.5 m)	10 ft (3 m)	S/W
Silver lace vine *(Polygonum aubertii)*	Quick-growing deciduous twiner; greenish-white fragrant flowers in summer/fall; to zone 4	25 ft (7.5 m)	25 ft (7.5 m)	N/E
Virginia creeper *(Parthenocissus quinquefolia)*	Quick-growing deciduous self-clinger; leaves turn bright red in the fall; to zone 3	70 ft (21 m)	33 ft (10 m)	N/E

SHRUBBY WALL PLANTS

**A vast range of nonclimbing shrubs
can be used to adorn house walls, decks, and fences
with year-round color, regardless of exposure.**

Even if your garden is small, you can make the best use of a limited space by carefully choosing plants to range along its borders. Many of these will reward you with a large-scale display of flowers and foliage. In larger gardens, they can bring color and interest to long stretches of boundary fence or to an exposed wall.

Wall plants are usually divided into climbers and nonclimbers. Those in the former group — self-clinging types such as ivy, thorny types such as climbing roses, or twining types such as wisteria — have their own means of clambering up walls or fences.

Nonclimbing wall plants, on the other hand, do not cling, twine, or hook onto supports. Most become free-standing shrubs or trees if grown in the open, but they can be trained to grow against a vertical surface. When planted in this way, however, they need both training and regular pruning.

Choosing wall plants
The most important factor to consider when buying a wall plant is its intended position in the garden. Most species need full sun to grow well. North- and east-facing walls are shady and often receive the worst winds in winter and spring. In a Philadelphia garden, for instance, this type of exposure would certainly kill a camellia that would flourish if grown against a south-facing wall.

Walls, and to some extent fences and trellises (depending on how solid they are), create a warm, sheltered microclimate. The heat retained in south- or west-facing walls also ripens woody growth, encouraging the production of flower buds. Some nonclimbing wall plants, such as *Abutilon,* are frost sensitive and survive north of zone 10 only with this kind of protection. Others, for

▶ **Flowering quince** Hardy to zone 5, this elegant shrub spreads its red, pink, or white flowers over a wall of any exposure. After its spring blooms fade, it should be pruned to shape.

▲ **Tender evergreen** Grown against a warm, sunny wall, *Abutilon megapotamicum* will thrive only in the most sheltered regions. Its conspicuous yellow-and-red pendent flowers appear from late spring until fall. Its relative, *A. vitifolium*, which has white or lavender bell flowers, is hardy to zone 7 if it is well protected by a south-facing wall.

◄ **Hardy forsythia** Even in the darkest city garden, *F. suspensa* will cover its bare, arching branches with a mass of bright yellow flowers in spring. Because the shrub can grow up to 10 ft (3 m) against a wall, it should be pruned severely after flowering.

example flowering quince *(Chaenomeles speciosa —* hardy to zone 5), are tough and do not require this type of setting.

In addition, look for shrubs that offer more than a short flowering season — such as evergreens and shrubs with berries, as they will add color to the garden in winter.

Also consider your soil type and conditions. Generally, the area at the foot of a wall tends to be drier than the surrounding ground, for a number of reasons. A wall can create a rain shadow and a foundation absorbs soil moisture. And sometimes overhanging eaves and gutters can prevent rain from reaching the soil underneath.

The soil at the base of a wall can vary in its texture and pH. A few shrubs, such as fig, thrive in poor soil, but most need a planting bed that is fertile, moist, and well-drained. If necessary, add amendments to rectify a poor soil.

Lastly, try to match the plant's vigor and size to the available space in your garden. Some wall plants, such as *Abelia,* remain relatively compact. Others, such as winter jasmine *(Jasminum nudiflorum),* can reach the top of a two-story house, but will respond well to pruning. There are a few wall plants, such as evergreen magnolia, that grow so large that they are suitable only for a very large property.

Color and scent
Most flowers are seen within the setting of their leaves, which act as a visual buffer between the wall and the shrubs. However, if the foliage or growth habit of the climber is sparse, choose species that will harmonize with the color

▲ **Sunny outlook** The evergreen *Carpenteria californica,* a West Coast native, is hardy to zone 8 if planted near a wall that protects it from cold, high winds. Tolerant of alkaline soil, the shrub bears glossy green foliage. In midsummer, it is enhanced by glistening white fragrant flowers.

◀ **Foliage shrubs** Another evergreen from California, *Garrya elliptica,* tolerates poor soil but appreciates protection even in zone 8. It is most likely to thrive against a south- or west-facing wall. Male specimens are outstanding for their magnificent late-winter displays of long yellow-green catkins; they are more ornamental than the female types, which bear shorter, silver-gray catkins.

of the wall. Pale flowers provide a more interesting contrast than vivid ones, especially at night.

Fortunately, all the winter-flowering wall shrubs, such as the evergreen camellias, the mahonias, the pink-tinged white *Viburnum tinus,* and the yellow winter jasmine, come in clear shades. They can be relied on to add color to a bare garden.

To enhance a garden wall, consider scented shrubs such as the delicate wintersweet *(Chimonanthus praecox)* or the fragrant summer-blooming *Buddleia davidii* in the North. In the South, try the aromatic true myrtle.

Training and support

Train individual plants for the effect you want — rigidly formal fans or espaliers, for example, or an evenly dense covering of flowers and foliage. It is essential, however, to start training wall plants when they are young.

Generally, training establishes a main framework. Any crowded or diseased wood should be removed. Maintenance pruning usually promotes the growth of young flowering wood and keeps the plant within its allotted space.

Choose a support system to complement the vigor and ultimate size of the climber and, to avoid damaging it, put the system in place before you plant.

To train the main stems and branches, use plastic-coated or galvanized wire, combined with screw eyes inserted into shields set into the wall. (Garden twine will eventually rot.) This system can be arranged vertically, horizontally, or diagonally, as well as singly or in parallel rows.

A plastic, metal, or wooden trellis is another popular means of support and has a charm of its own. A rigid, traditional square-mesh trellis and extending, diamond-mesh trellis panels are available at garden centers and from catalogs. Sturdier trellises that have been stiffened and braced make excellent free-standing features. In addition, there are types that combine arches with *trompe l'oeil* effects. When attaching a trellis to a wall, use wooden blocks as spacers to allow for ventilation between the wall and the plant. Attach young plant growth to a trellis with soft twine, but as the wood ages, use plastic-covered wire instead.

▲ **Winter blooms** Camellias can flourish as far north as Delaware, or even Philadelphia, if set against a wall with a sunny exposure. Avoid east-facing sites.

▼ **Abundance of blue** Few wall shrubs can compare with the evergreen *Ceanothus impressus.* In full sun, it is covered with deep blue flowers.

FRAGRANT HONEYSUCKLES

**This large, wide-ranging group of plants
includes numerous deliciously scented climbers
and bushy wall shrubs.**

Honeysuckles belong to the genus *Lonicera*. This large group of deciduous and evergreen shrubs includes many twining climbers, totaling more than 150 species distributed worldwide. The plants are named after sixteenth-century German naturalist Adam Lonicer. About a dozen members of this genus, along with another dozen cultivars and hybrids, are commonly grown in home gardens.

Lonicera is part of the botanical family Caprifoliaceae, which contains abelias, beauty bushes *(Kolkwitzia)*, elders *(Sambucus)*, Himalayan honeysuckles *(Leycesteria)*, snowberries *(Symphoricarpos)*, viburnums, and weigelas. The flowers in each of these plant groups are tubular, with five flaring petal lobes, and are borne in close pairs, either singly, doubly, or in clusters.

Small clusters of red or orange berries, usually with each one fused to another, appear on many of these plants. But it is the berries of certain shrubby honeysuckles that are most striking — red, violet, bluish or purple-black, and sometimes translucent types are displayed. Though eaten by birds, all these berries are poisonous to humans; warn children to stay away from them.

Honeysuckle leaves are mostly oval or rounded, and often taper to a point. Those at the branch tips may be stalkless and joined in pairs around the stem like small collars. The leaves are midgreen in most deciduous species, but there are also golden yellow and net-veined types. Evergreen and semievergreen honeysuckles have glossy, rich green foliage. Two examples are *Lonicera nitida,* a hedging plant, and *L. pileata,* a good ground cover plant.

Choosing climbers

The climbing or twining species, varieties, and hybrids are certainly the most familiar honeysuckles. Almost every East Coast gardener knows the Japanese honeysuckle *(L. japonica),* an evergreen vine that, despite its foreign name, runs wild through woodlands east of the Mississippi, often becoming a weed. But many of the less rampant, cultivated strains of this vine make excellent garden plants. Cultivar 'Halliana,' also known as Hall's honeysuckle, bears perfumed white flowers that yellow as they age, while its relative 'Purpurea' offers purple foliage. The tamest and yet most picturesque of the Japanese honeysuckles is 'Aureoreticulata,' which is grown for its golden-veined foliage. It is also less hardy than its parent (which

◀ **Woodbine** A fixture of the Old World cottage garden, the common honeysuckle *(Lonicera periclymenum)* is beloved for its clouds of sweetly scented flowers in summer.

119

Lonicera japonica 'Halliana'
vigorous climber

Lonicera fragrantissima
bushy shrub

Lonicera sempervirens
vigorous climber

Lonicera tatarica
bushy shrub

is hardy to zone 5). 'Aureo-reticulata' is frequently cut down by frosts in northern states, but basal growth invariably survives the winter.

A plant often found in the hedgerows of England also flourishes here — the common honeysuckle, or woodbine *(Lonicera periclymenum)*. This beautifully fragrant climber, with its cream-and-purple summer flowers, is considered an essential element of the traditional cottage garden. Woodbine's flowering season can be extended by intertwining it with the species-type cultivars *L. periclymenum* 'Belgica,' the Dutch honeysuckle, which blooms in late spring, and the cultivar *L. p.* 'Serotina,' which flowers into midfall. All three are hardy to zone 5 and vigorous enough to smother a 20-foot wall. They need support, but little other routine care and attention.

For color variation, select *L.* × *brownii*, which has orange-scarlet trumpets in late spring (often repeating in late summer), or its scarlet-red and longer-flowering cultivar 'Dropmore Scarlet.' Or choose *L.* × *tellmanniana*, with its slender orange-red to yellow flowers. If planted in the shelter of a south- or west-facing wall, this climber will grow in areas as far north as southern Canada.

Hardy to zone 4, *L. sempervirens* earns its common name of coral honeysuckle by bearing slender terminal clusters of orange-scarlet flowers throughout the summer. The giant honeysuckle *(L. hildebrandiana)* produces the largest flowers of all the cultivated varieties — its cream or orange blooms are 4-6 in (10-15 cm) long.

Choosing shrubby types
Among the shrubby honeysuckles are two that are particularly useful in the garden. Box honeysuckle *(L. nitida)* forms a dense, compact evergreen bush that grows up to 6 ft (1.8 m) tall and has small, glossy dark green leaves that resemble those of boxwood. Its flowers are unexceptional, but they are followed by translucent violet berries. Tolerant of coastal salt spray, winds, and shade, this shrub is perfect for adding to a bank of shrubbery or for making a hedge. *L. n.* 'Baggesen's Gold' provides a wonderful backdrop of golden foliage, but it needs full sun to produce its richest color.

Privet honeysuckle *(L. pileata)* is a semievergreen shrub that makes good ground cover. Like box honeysuckle, it can tolerate shade and salt spray. Its dense, glossy foliage forms a carpet of arching branches, 2-3 ft (60-90 cm) high. A single plant can spread to 6 ft (1.8 m) wide.

Other shrubby types that are useful for background planting or screening are *L. tatarica*, with lovely red, pink, or white flowers, and *L. syringantha*, with gray-green leaves and clusters of small mauve-pink lilac-shaped flowers.

In addition, there are a few shrubby honeysuckles that flower in winter or very early spring, mainly on leafless branches. Although not very showy, the white flowers of *L. fragrantissima*, for example, will bring fragrance to the winter garden.

Suitable sites
Honeysuckles do well in ordinary, well-drained soils, but they don't like a boggy site. Climbers prefer to have some added humus, such as well-rotted compost.

All honeysuckles will grow in sun or partial shade, but most of the climbers should be positioned so that their roots are in shade and their top growth is in the

Lonicera ×
tellmanniana
climber

Lonicera japonica
'Aureo-reticulata'
climber

Lonicera periclymenum 'Belgica'
vigorous climber

sun. If this is not possible, place some shallow-rooted ground cover plants around the base of each honeysuckle.

Unfortunately, climbing honeysuckles are prone to aphids. If these pests prove to be very troublesome, consider planting the honeysuckles in full shade (aphids thrive in warmth). However, a shady spot will mean that the plants produce fewer flowers.

Since support is needed for the twining climbers, choose a position against a wall or fence, if possible, where it will be easy to erect a trellis. Almost any site is suitable for the shrubby types; in order to enjoy the fragrance of the winter-flowering varieties, grow them close to your house, deck, or porch.

Planting honeysuckles
Weather and climate permitting, deciduous climbers and shrubs can be planted at any time between early fall and midspring, and container-grown nursery stock can be set out successfully at any time of year. Evergreen honeysuckles should be placed in the ground only during midspring to late spring.

Remember to install the support system for climbers before planting them, though extra wires or wooden trellising can be added in subsequent years.

Dig a hole large enough to accommodate the entire root ball of plants in containers, or to hold the spread-out roots of plants lifted from open ground. Ensure that the honeysuckle will stand at the same height in the soil as it was in the nursery. When planting against a wall or fence, set the hole about 1-1½ ft (30-45 cm) from the base, as the soil near the base of a wall or fence is almost always very dry and infertile.

Put the plant in its hole, leaning the main stem toward the support surface, and fill it in with soil. If the young stem is damaged, insert several stakes around the perimeter of the root ball and wrap chicken wire or netting

▲ Scarlet trumpet honeysuckle
Otherwise known as *Lonicera* × *brownii,* this spectacular semievergreen climber is a marvelous selection for a sunny wall. The flowers appear in late spring and again in late summer.

around them to form a protective frame. Remove the frame once the plant is established and has a woody, trunklike stem.

For honeysuckle hedges, space plants 1 ft (30 cm) apart in a row. Other types should be spaced at distances equivalent to half their expected ultimate spread.

As soon as a plant is in the ground, press the soil in firmly around its base. Train climbers back to their support. Water the plant and apply a mulch of leaf mold or other organic material. Encourage hedging plants to grow bushy by pruning back all young growths by one-half to two-thirds at planting time.

Aftercare
Climbing honeysuckles need little routine care, other than to tie

121

their branches to suitable supports. To maintain vigor, thin out old wood of both climbers and shrubby types every few years after flowering. Annual pruning is undesirable, as the honeysuckles would lose flowers. Apply a new organic mulch each spring.

In the first summer after setting out hedging plants, trim off the young tips two or three times to promote strong, bushy growth. In subsequent summers, cut back by half all new growth until the desired height is reached. Afterward, shear hedges in late spring and again in early fall to maintain their shape.

Keep an eye out for aphids. Should you notice them on your honeysuckles, spray the plants with insecticidal soap or another recommended insecticide. If honeysuckles are left untreated, aphids can seriously damage the foliage, and the insect's honeydew secretions will soil the leaves below the point of infestation. Black sooty mold grows on this sticky honeydew, further disfiguring the plants.

Propagating honeysuckles

In the wild, honeysuckles regenerate themselves by layering. Their drooping branches come in contact with the ground and root

quite freely. Use this technique to propagate your own stock of shrubby and low-growing honeysuckles. On sites where climbers are supported on a wall or fence, however, it may be difficult to find a branch that can be bent to the ground. The best time for layering is between late summer and late fall. Roots should develop by the following fall.

For climbing honeysuckles that cannot be layered, take stem sections, 4 in (10 cm) long, in midsummer to late summer. Insert these in a well-drained rooting medium in a cold frame or other shaded, cool but frost-free spot. By the following midspring to late spring, cuttings should have rooted. Transfer them into pots, 3½-4 in (9-10 cm) deep, filled with an organic-enriched potting soil and grow them on outdoors. Plant them in their permanent positions the following fall.

Alternatively, take hardwood cuttings, 9-12 in (23-30 cm) long, in early fall to midfall and insert them in a sheltered nursery bed.

▼ **Shrubby honeysuckle** In a mixed planting of wall shrubs, *Lonicera nitida* 'Baggesen's Gold' glows above rose-purple *Berberis thunbergii* 'Rosy Glow' and purple-leaved sage *(Salvia officinalis* 'Purpurascens').

SUPPORTING CLIMBERS

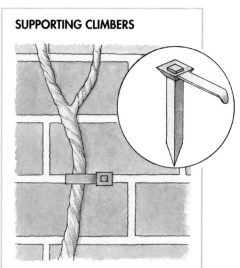

1 Lead-headed nails are useful for securing woody stems to brickwork. The nail itself can be driven directly into a mortar joint, then a metal strap attached to the head is wrapped around the stem.

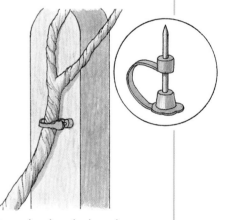

2 Special nails with plastic-loop cleats make an ideal alternative for fixing to brickwork, and can be used on posts or fences. Wrap the cleat around the stem before hammering in the nail.

3 Alternatively, stretch galvanized wire between two or more vine eyes, or two screw eyes. Space wires at about 2-ft (60-cm) intervals up the wall. Tie in each stem loosely but firmly with plastic-coated wire.

LUXURIOUS IVIES

**Thriving in most soils and almost any site,
tolerant of atmospheric pollution and hard pruning
into topiary shapes, ivies offer year-round color.**

Ivies are an important group of evergreen creeping and climbing shrubs belonging to the genus *Hedera,* which contains only 15 species. Their natural habitat, however, stretches from Europe through the Himalayas to the Far East. In addition, they are widely naturalized throughout North America.

Hedera is a member of the family Araliaceae, which also includes *Aralia* and *Fatsia.* There are hundreds of ivy varieties, most of which are easy to find. The majority are forms of *Hedera helix* (common or English ivy), and have a large range of leaf shapes and coloring. Ivies are often sold as indoor plants, but most are completely hardy.

Easy to grow, ivies have many uses in the garden. As climbers, they will cover walls, fences, and tree trunks, as well as disguise sheds and garages. They look decorative throughout the year, growing up trelliswork, posts, pillars in borders, and tree stumps. Many make ideal ground cover in shady places, and will quickly fill in any bare spots. The less vigorous types are attractive in containers, window boxes, and alongside steps.

Ivy characteristics

The typical ivy leaf is palmate (handlike), with three or five lobes, but there are many variations, including heart-, arrowhead- or oval-shaped leaves, as well as crinkle-edged ones. They range in size from 1-8 in (2.5-20 cm) long and are poisonous. Many ivies grow fast and will rapidly climb a wall 50-100 ft (15-30 m) high, but there are also a number of less vigorous types.

The foliage is available in shades of green or it may be variegated with splashes of cream, gold, yellow, gray, silver, or pink. Some leaves have bronze or purple tints in the fall.

Ivies have two types of growth: juvenile and adult. The former bears the characteristic compound lobed leaves and uses aerial roots to climb surfaces. When it reaches the top of a support, it produces adult growth, which is bushier, and does not climb. (The difference between these types of growth is most obvious in *Hedera helix.*) The stems carry entire leaves and bear clusters of small, star-shaped greenish-yellow flowers in midfall to late fall. These are followed by poisonous, fleshy fruits, which usually ripen to black the following spring.

Bush or tree ivies, which are propagated from adult flowering shoots, are shrubby plants that produce only adult growth and develop into dense, leafy mounds.

Climbing ivies

Perfect for covering a wide expanse of wall, the impressive Persian ivy *(Hedera colchica* 'Sulphur Heart') has large, variable leaves, up to 5 in (12.5 cm) long, decorated with central

▼ **Canary Island ivy** The rapidly growing *Hedera canariensis* 'Gloire de Marengo' is perfect for covering eyesores. The erect climbing stems are clothed with large, leathery dark green leaves that turn silvery gray to creamy white at the edges.

Hedera canariensis
'Gloire de Marengo'

Hedera colchica
'Dentata Variegata'

Hedera helix
'Buttercup'

Hedera colchica
'Sulphur Heart'

'Dentata Variegata,' with bright green leaves that are broadly edged in creamy yellow, helps to enliven a shady spot.

Hedera helix has several varieties that can carpet any area with highly decorative ground cover. For example, *H. helix* 'Ivalace' has dark green, crinkled, five-lobed leaves that give a lacy effect; and *H. helix* 'Parsley Crested' has bright green unlobed leaves, with crimped edges.

For a dainty cover between snowdrops and crocuses — and a pretty choice to disguise their untidy dying leaves — plant the slow-growing *H. helix* 'Königer's Variegata,' which has small, arrow-shaped gray-green leaves with silvery edges. And *H. helix* 'Chicago Variegated,' with three-lobed leaves thickly edged in creamy white, blends well with other types of ground cover, such as dead nettles *(Ajuga).*

Winter color
Any of the variegated ivies will bring color to a winter garden. The slow-growing *H. helix* 'Tricolor' (also sold as 'Marginata Rubra,' or 'Elegantissima'), with its small, roughly triangular gray-green leaves and a cream-yellow edge, often has a narrow margin of pink during the winter months.

For bronze winter-foliage tints, try *H. helix* 'Brokamp,' which is also drought-resistant. For crimson hues, choose the cultivar 'Parsley Crested' (its leaves turn a purplish-green with bright green veins in winter) or *H. helix* 'Glymii' (oval, twisted leaves). Both work well as ground cover or for background planting.

Ivy screens
You can also use ivies to make good hedges or screens by training them to cover a fence of wire, pickets, or plastic netting. For the best coverage, select a large-leaved type, such as Irish ivy *(H. helix* 'Hibernica'), with its five-lobed, dark green leaves, or *H. colchica* 'Dentata,' which has leathery leaves. For added color, intersperse either with a vigorous variegated variety, such as *H. helix* 'Goldheart.'

To provide year-round interest in a shady rock garden, try *H. helix* 'Congesta.' This slow-growing variety has stiff, upright shoots and arrow-shaped leaves.

splashes of yellow or light green. The species itself has leaves up to 10 in (25 cm) long that hang down somewhat like an elephant's ears.

For an even brighter effect, consider the colorful *H. helix* 'Buttercup.' Its small, five-lobed leaves change color with the seasons: They are lime-green in spring, butter-yellow in summer, and midgreen in winter. Unlike other ivies, this variety needs plenty of light for good leaf color.

Another excellent ivy for clothing a wall is *H. helix* 'Goldheart,' a neat climber that has small dark green leaves with a conspicuous splash of gold in their centers. A good choice for growing on a low wall is the small-leaved,

less vigorous *H. helix* 'Glacier.' Its lobed grayish-green leaves are marked with silver-gray, and may be edged with cream.

The popular variegated Canary ivy *(H. canariensis* 'Gloire de Marengo,' also known as *H. canariensis* 'Variegata') is suitable for training up a post in a mixed bed. Its large leaves are deep green in the center, shading to gray-green, with thin cream margins. This ivy may die back during a severe winter, even in zone 7, but usually recovers in time to make a good summer display.

Ground cover ivies
Ivies will carpet shady ground where almost no other plant will grow. One of the best types for this purpose is the vigorous, large-leaved Persian ivy *(Helix colchica).* The handsome variety

Cultivation

Although green ivies do well in sun and deep shade, they grow more slowly in sunny sites. Variegated types are susceptible to leaf scorch in south-facing sites and will revert to green in total shade. Thus, a lightly shaded, sheltered site is best.

Ivies tolerate all soils, except highly acid ones, which need amending with ground limestone.

Plant container-grown ivies at any time during frost-free weather, but set out ivies propagated from cuttings during cool, moist weather in fall or early spring.

When positioning ivy against a wall, dig the planting hole at least 6 in (15 cm) away from the base. If you are growing a climber against a tree trunk, make the hole wherever possible between the tree roots. Set a

Hedera helix 'Glacier'

Hedera helix 'Goldheart'

Hedera helix 'Tricolor'

Hedera helix 'Ivalace'

JUVENILE AND ADULT IVY GROWTH

▲ The juvenile growth of ivy is easily distinguished by its leathery, lobed leaves and woody climbing stems. The tendrils growing on the stem are aerial roots that cling to almost any rough surface, enabling the plant to clamber up walls, fences, and tree trunks.

◀ The adult growth is bushier and does not climb. The stems are more succulent, bearing softer, oval leaves that are unlobed and undivided. In midfall to late fall, it produces clusters of nectar-rich, star-shaped greenish-white flowers. These are followed by round, fleshy, poisonous fruits that ripen to blue-black, with a grapelike bloom, the following spring. *H. nepalensis* has yellow or sometimes orange fruits.

IVY CUTTINGS

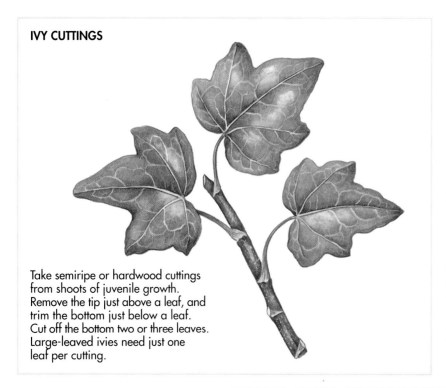

Take semiripe or hardwood cuttings from shoots of juvenile growth. Remove the tip just above a leaf, and trim the bottom just below a leaf. Cut off the bottom two or three leaves. Large-leaved ivies need just one leaf per cutting.

well-drained rooting medium and place them in a closed cold frame or other cool but frost-free spot that is also moist and shaded.

Four to six weeks later, transplant the rooted cuttings into individual 3-in (7.5-cm) pots of well-drained, sterilized potting soil; grow them on and harden them off before planting out.

You can also propagate from trailing shoots, which usually produce roots all along the stems, mainly at the leaf nodes. Cut off a section of stem, pot it up, and treat it as a cutting. A climbing stem pegged to the ground roots rapidly. Once rooted, remove it from the parent and plant it out. Or, root a section of stem in a pot.

To propagate a bushy ivy, take semiripe cuttings from adult flowering shoots in midsummer to late summer; they take longer to root than juvenile growth.

stake in the ground at an angle to encourage the plant to grow toward its support.

Clip ivies extensively in midspring to late spring to prevent them from becoming top-heavy and to control their size. On named cultivars, remove any shoots bearing ordinary leaves that do not conform to the type; on variegated ivies, take off any shoots with all-green leaves.

Ivy will not damage masonry walls in a good state of repair, but it can damage those that already have crumbling mortar. Also, ivy must not be allowed to reach the eaves of a house because it may block the gutters and grow between shingles or slates.

Propagation

Most ivies are easy to propagate from cuttings. Take 6-in (15-cm) cuttings from ripe shoots in late fall, remove the tips, and insert them in sandy soil outdoors. Some will root in a glass of water.

Alternatively, take tip cuttings, 3-5 in (7.5-12.5 cm) long, in midsummer to late summer. Trim them just below a leaf node, removing the lower leaves. Insert the cuttings in a peat-enriched,

▶ **Trailing ivies** Young ivies are as likely to trail as to climb. They fill containers with welcome foliage colors throughout the year. Later they can be transplanted to the garden, where they eagerly climb walls and fences or scramble along the soil as permanent ground cover.

THE GRAPE FAMILY

**Providing fruits and brilliant fall colors,
ornamental grapes, Virginia creepers, and other vines
cover high expanses of wall.**

Americans are so accustomed to thinking of grapevines in connection with vineyards that they often forget that the grape family, the Vitaceae, also includes many outstanding ornamental plants. Although this group may not help you fill a fruit bowl, jelly jar, or wine bottle, it can furnish you with rich harvests of colorful berries and leaves.

Of course, grapevines grown for their edible fruits also have considerable decorative value. Anyone who has ever picnicked beneath a backyard arbor hung with succulent, blue-black bunches of Concord grapes can attest to their beauty.

True grapevines belong to the genus *Vitis,* which encompasses all the types cultivated for their edible fruits as well as several purely ornamental species.

Some other decorative types in the Vitaceae family are *Tetrastigma voinierianum* (the chestnut vine) and *Ampelopsis brevipedunculata.* Other members of the grape family offer some of the finest fall-foliage tints, as well as fresh colors in spring and summer, along with fruits that sparkle among the green leaves.

Many grapevines are remarkably vigorous growers that will clamber up a wall within a short period of time, tying themselves to trellises with tendrils or gluing themselves to masonry or wood with adhesive-tipped discs.

Some, such as the grape ivies (*Cissus* spp.), flourish only in the South, but others, such as Virginia creeper *(Parthenocissus quinquefolia)* and Boston ivy *(Parthenocissus tricuspidata)* — actually a native of central China and Japan — are fully hardy in zone 4 or 5 and can survive the worst urban air pollution.

True grapes
Most *Vitis* species climb to 12 ft (3.5 m) or more, and some, such as crimson glory vine *(Vitis coignetiae),* can grow to 80 ft (25 m) if proper support is available. Left free, these plants will also cover an expanse as wide as they are tall. As a result, they must be cut back hard each year to limit their growth.

Their hand- or heart-shaped leaves are deciduous, typically shallowly lobed, and often prominently veined and toothed. They generally measure 2½-8 in (6-20 cm) wide.

After the insignificant flowers appear, they are followed by clusters or bunches of small, usually edible grapes that may be green, wine-purple, or purple-black, often with a blue-gray bloom.

Vine stems climb by means of branched tendrils that clasp neighboring plant stems, stakes, or wire.

Since the edible grapes are primarily regional plants, most gardeners let their location dictate

◄ **Boston ivy** Indifferent to atmospheric pollution, *Parthenocissus tricuspidata* 'Veitchii' rapidly clothes the highest wall without any assistance. In the fall, its glossy leaves turn brilliant orange and yellow.

*Ampelopsis
brevipedunculata*

their choice of species. For instance, the classic grape used in winemaking, the European species *Vitis vinifera,* flourishes mainly on the Pacific Coast, but is also being grown successfully in microclimates on the East Coast. Varieties and hybrids of the muscadine *(V. rotundifolia)* are reliable standbys in the South, and those of the fox grape *(V. labrusca)* are the traditional favorites of the Northeast and upper Midwest. In each case, there are dozens of cultivars available.

If you are growing grapes mainly for the vines' ornamental value, then you should check carefully to make sure the cultivars you select will be disease-resistant in your area. The common table and wine grapes often require continual spraying, since farmers will tolerate a less-than-robust vine if it bears superior fruits.

In addition, consider the color of a vine's fruits or foliage. A purple-fruited or reddish-leaved type, for example, makes a good foil for tall white or pink flowers at the back of a bed, and contrasts well with the mauve-blue or pink blooms of clematis hybrids. By contrast, the cool, greenish fruits of a white grape such as 'Niagara' (a seedling of 'Concord') can help temper the hot yellows and oranges of chrysanthemum flowers.

❏ *Vitis coignetiae,* the crimson glory vine, is a true grape, but has only ornamental value. It is an imposing grapevine, with huge midgreen leaves up to 1 ft (30 cm) wide. The leaves, which are rounder and less toothed than most vine foliage, turn superb shades of orange-red, yellow, and crimson-purple in the fall. The vine's purple-black berries are inedible.

❏ *Vitis californica,* the California grape, produces edible fruits, which are somewhat dry though flavorful. Its foliage turns red in the fall.

Other ornamentals

There are three important species of *Parthenocissus,* all noted for their fall colors. They are distinguished from grapevines by their leaves, which are more deeply divided or separated into leaflets, and by their tendrils, which are tipped with adhesive pads or hooks that will grip any vertical surface firmly.

❏ *Parthenocissus henryana,* the silver-vein creeper, is the least vigorous species, reaching a maximum height of 25-30 ft (7.5-9 m), but it has distinctive foliage. An individual leaf is composed of three to five separate leaflets, each about 2½ in (6 cm) long. Their silver veins stand out against the velvety green blades. To encourage the best foliage color, this vine should be protected from the full sun and set in a lightly shaded spot. After producing a crop of insignificant flowers in the summer, it bears small blue fruits that are attractive to

Parthenocissus quinquefolia
Virginia creeper

Parthenocissus henryana
Silver-vein creeper

birds. In the fall, the leaves turn a brilliant red, making their silvered veins even more prominent.

❏ *Parthenocissus quinquefolia,* the true Virginia creeper, is a woodland plant that grows naturally throughout much of eastern North America. Though similar in habit to *P. henryana,* it grows much more vigorously, and its five leaflets are two or three times larger in size, but lack the whitish veins. Although the fall coloration and fruits are similar to the silver-vein type, this creeper can climb to 70 ft (21 m). The cultivar 'Engelmannii' has smaller, more delicate foliage than the species type; the variety 'hirsuta' produces leaves that have downy undersides.

❏ *Parthenocissus tricuspidata,* the Boston ivy, with its tolerance for air pollution, is a good choice for an urban garden. Boston ivy is easily distinguished from Virginia creeper by its leaf shape, which resembles that of the grapevine, except that the margins are less toothed. Each leaf is entire rather than split into separate leaflets, but it has three deep lobes. The foliage turns a spectacular deep crimson in the fall. Even though the blue fruits of this climber are hidden by the foliage, they are attractive to birds. The cultivar 'Veitchii' has purple-hued, smaller leaves when young, and is somewhat less vigorous than the species. 'Robusta'

is a superior strain of the species because it is vigorous and disease-resistant, with glossy green leaves.

❏ *Ampelopsis brevipedunculata* is not common but is well worth searching out. After a long, hot summer and mild fall, this vigorous climber produces unique porcelain-blue berries. Its three-to five-lobed hoplike leaves are decorative in their own right. The cultivar 'Elegans,' which is sometimes also listed as 'Tricolor,' or 'Variegata,' is less rampant and is suitable for more restricted spaces. Its deciduous foliage is attractively mottled with white and pink spots.

❏ *Cissus* spp., the grape ivies, are familiar to most gardeners as houseplants, but can be planted in the garden in warmer regions. *C. striata,* the miniature grape ivy from Chile, will survive an occasional frost and is often trained over screens and lattices in southern California. *C. incisa,* the ivy treebine, is a North American native with handsome, deeply cut leaves. Thriving in shade or sun, this deciduous vine rapidly climbs to 30 ft (10 cm). With protection, it will survive into the southern part of zone 6.

❏ *Tetrastigma voinierianum,* the chestnut vine from Southeast Asia, throws up a thick, if coarse, screen of toothed leaves, 4-8 in (10-20 cm) long. Grown in zones 9 and 10, it provides a quick cover for fences and lattices.

Site and soil

All *Vitis* vines do best on well-drained, loamy soil that is alkaline or neutral; however, they can tolerate a wide range of soil types and pH. The site can be sunny or shaded, but in the North, a south- or west-facing position is needed to produce a good show of fruits.

Silver-vein creeper is the least hardy of the *Parthenocissuses* (to zone 8 only), and requires a sheltered situation against a south-or west-facing wall to survive farther north). *P. quinquefolia* is hardy to zone 4, and *P. tricuspidata,* to zone 5; both will tolerate any exposure.

Because ornamental vines cannot support themselves, they should be planted against a vertical surface, which may be a wall, fence, railing, trellis, latticework screen, pergola, or even a tree stump. The tendrils of self-clinging species like *Parthenocissus* adhere to windows, doors, gutters, and drainpipes, so keep them trimmed back from such architectural features. Likewise, allowing Boston ivy or Virginia creeper to climb a wooden house or a living tree trunk may encourage its decay.

Planting

Plant vines during mild weather between late fall and midspring. Most nurseries and garden centers sell these plants in pots or containers, as bare-rooted vines

Parthenocissus tricuspidata 'Veitchii'
Boston ivy

Vitis coignetiae
crimson glory vine

GRAPE SUBSTITUTES

Although they are not members of the Vitaceae family, the vines below share the same overall growth habit and work well in partnership with grapes, or can substitute for them satisfactorily. Unlike grapes, these plants bear flowers that are as striking as their foliage, and usually their fall color is not a major feature. In the case of the golden hop, however, its lush, grapelike foliage is the main attraction — its gilded fruits are more colorful than its insignificant flowers.

Campsis radicans
trumpet vine

Solanum crispum
'Glasnevin'
potato vine

Polygonum aubertii
Silver-lace vine

port, tying them with soft string to more stakes if necessary.

Aftercare
Ornamental vines require little routine maintenance once they are established. If they spread too quickly and space is limited, thin out old growths and cut back young ones in late summer. *Parthenocissus quinquefolia* in particular will quickly cover all but high walls, so cut shoots back hard before they become woody.

Over time, grapevines can grow into drains and gutters, causing blockages and subsequent moisture problems. It is best to cut away any such stems at an early stage of development. However, unlike ivies and other aerial-rooting climbers, ornamental vines will rarely do any damage, even to older masonry. In fact, the vines may help preserve the masonry by insulating it somewhat from rapid changes in temperature.

Propagation
The simplest way to propagate vines is to take hardwood cuttings, 10-12 in (25-30 cm) long, in the late fall. Insert them up to half their length in a sheltered spot in the garden.

Alternatively, take stem cuttings of half-ripened growth, 4-5 in (10-12.5 cm) long, in late summer or early fall. Insert them individually into pots of sandy, sterilized potting soil. Place the pots in a propagation box with a bottom temperature at 55-61°F (13-16°C), or cover with a clear plastic bag supported on a wire frame and set in a shaded, cool but frost-free place.

Long shoots can be layered in midfall to late fall; these should root by the following fall, when they can be detached.

Pests and diseases
Grapes, Boston ivy, and Virginia creeper are especially attractive to Japanese beetles, which will almost completely destroy the foliage. In regions where the beetles are endemic, the leaves should be regularly sprayed with a recommended insecticide during the summertime. In many regions, a fungal disease, black rot, will cause the fruits borne on grapevines to wither before they ripen unless the plants are treated with fungicidal sprays.

do not transplant very well. Handle them carefully to prevent root disturbance.

Prepare the planting site well. Remember that the ground close to a high wall or building is likely to be dry and poor, containing very little humus. Dig a planting hole, 2 ft (60 cm) square and 1½ ft (45 cm) deep, close to the base of the support. Fill the hole with well-prepared, moist, loamy soil and press it down firmly. Add a generous topdressing of organic material and fork it in lightly.

Position the young vine so that the top of the soil ball is level with the surface of the ground and press it in well. Water the vine and insert twiggy sticks or stakes angled toward the wall. The tendrils will cling to these until they can get a more permanent hold.

Pinch out the growing tips of all upright stems to encourage branching. If the stems are very tall and slender, with few branches, prune them back to about 9-12 in (23-30 cm) after planting. For the next few months, train all stems toward the main sup-

THE MAJESTIC CLEMATIS

Foremost among climbers, the well-loved clematis plants range from dainty and elegant species to flamboyant and exuberant large-flowered hybrids.

Clematises may be the most popular of all climbers, and with good reason. They are cultivated for their mass of blooms, which are found in a vast range of colors. The large-flowered hybrids come in many glorious shades of purple, mauve, red, pink, and white, as well as bicolors; and the species clematises also include yellows. Many of these vines are vigorous enough to be used for screening an unsightly feature, such as a storage shed or garage, or for enhancing a tree or high wall. Others are excellent for training on pergolas, fences, posts, or even around a window or doorway. And there are certain species that bring color and interest to a garden by simply scrambling through other woody-stemmed shrubs and climbers.

Most clematises are deciduous. Though often vigorous, they are weak-stemmed and attach themselves to a support by means of twining leaf stalks. The flowers, which may be cup-, bell-, or urn-shaped, are made up of four to eight petallike sepals. Some of the clematis species have attractive fluffy seed heads that follow the blooms and remain until the following spring.

Choosing and buying

Before purchasing large-flowered hybrid clematises, check their flowering times. Those that bloom early in the year are likely to produce a second show in late summer or fall. Because the early flowers grow on the previous year's growth, the plant should be lightly pruned after the first flowering. Late-flowering hybrids, however, bloom on new growth and must be pruned nearly to the ground every spring.

This difference may affect the suitability of a particular hybrid for growing among other plants. If paired with roses, for example, which require regular pruning, choose a clematis that needs hard cutting back. You can strip the clematis down first, thus leaving other plants accessible for selective pruning.

Most nurseries grow clematis plants either in rigid plastic pots or in various types of flexible containers. They are sold this way because climbers hate root disturbance during transplanting. Bare-root plants are available but are less reliable.

Don't be tempted by large plants offered by nurseries. Young, modestly sized ones that have not outgrown their containers do better when set out in the garden. However, they shouldn't be so immature that soil falls away from the root ball when it is removed from the container.

You can buy clematises in either spring or fall, but the largest selection is available in spring. Healthy plants will have several fat buds spaced along their shoots.

Soil and site

All clematises prefer rich, alkaline soil, but they will tolerate any good neutral or slightly acid

▶ **'Ville de Lyon'** This large-flowered hybrid has been around for almost a hundred years and has never lost its popularity. The bright carmine flowers, with their golden stamens, are borne from midsummer until fall on the current year's shoots.

type. They do, however, require deep soil to allow a long root-run, and cool, moist, well-drained conditions for the roots beneath.

There is a good choice of species and hybrids for all exposures; many will grow in a variety of settings, from full sun to continuous light shade. Most good nurseries state the plant's preference on the container label.

When planting one of these climbers against a wall, keep the root ball at least 9 in (23 cm) away from it. Soil directly under a wall is too dry for moisture-loving clematis roots.

Planting clematis

Container-grown plants can be set out at any time of year, but the best season for this task is spring or fall. Unless you have the perfect soil for clematises — rich, crumbly loam — it's worth preparing the planting site well.

Dig a large hole, at least 18 in (45 cm) wide and deep. With a garden fork, turn over the soil in the bottom of the hole, then mix in a couple of handfuls of bone meal. Top with organic material.

▶ **Traveler's joy** This almost-forgotten common name aptly describes the small-flowered clematis species that can weave its way through rows of shrubs and other host plants.

PLANTING CLEMATIS

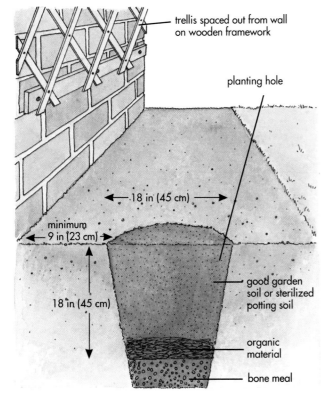

trellis spaced out from wall on wooden framework

planting hole

18 in (45 cm)

minimum
9 in (23 cm)

18 in (45 cm)

good garden soil or sterilized potting soil

organic material

bone meal

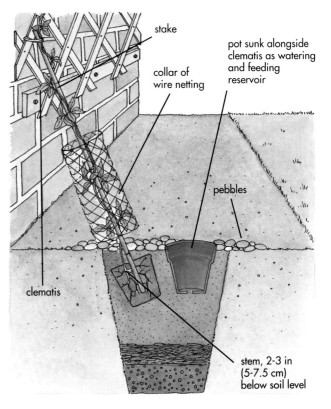

stake

collar of wire netting

pot sunk alongside clematis as watering and feeding reservoir

pebbles

clematis

stem, 2-3 in (5-7.5 cm) below soil level

PRUNING CLEMATIS

1 Clematis hybrids that bloom late in the year, from midsummer onward, flower on new wood produced earlier the same year. Cut them down almost to the ground every year in late winter or early spring to encourage new, strong growth. Make cuts above fresh new buds or shoots.

2 When pruning late-flowering hybrids, cut back each stem to just above the lowest strong growth bud. Make a downward-sloping cut away from the bud. As shoots develop, see that they attach themselves evenly along their support structure. Tie them in gently with garden twine if necessary.

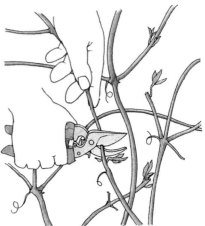

3 Early-flowering clematises do not require any routine pruning, as they bloom on old wood. Stems that have outgrown their allocated space or those that are too straggly can be removed after flowering. Space out and tie in stems that have been loosened during this pruning.

If the soil you excavated from the hole is of good quality, use it to fill the hole, but mix in some peat and a few handfuls of bone meal. If the soil is poor, fill the hole with well-drained, sterilized potting soil or good garden loam.

Before planting, install a support system, such as a trellis or plastic-coated wire mesh nailed to a wooden framework. Ensure that a container-grown clematis is well watered. (Immerse a dry plant in a bucket of water for about an hour). Remove the clematis, still tied to its stake, from the pot. If some roots have grown tightly around the inside of the pot, gently ease them away from the root ball but keep the roots as intact as possible.

Refill the planting hole halfway with soil and position the root ball so that about 2-3 in (5-7.5 cm) of the main stem sits below the surrounding soil level. Check the planting depth with a stake laid across the hole. Refill with more soil and press it firmly around the plant.

Shade the roots by covering the planting area with a layer of gravel or pebbles. You can pave over the roots, but this covering may prevent rainwater from penetrating the soil around the roots. Alternatively, plant shallow-rooted ground cover around the base of the clematis. Avoid vigorous types that will compete for soil nutrients and water.

If the surface covering is likely to inhibit future watering and feeding, sink a pot near the clematis root ball and place a slate or tile over it. The pot can be filled with water or dilute liquid fertilizer, which will be released through the drainage holes to the clematis roots.

The stems of a young clematis plant are fragile, but it is easy to protect them from accidental injury. Just put a collar of wire netting around the base of the plant. Bury the bottom few inches (centimeters) in the soil to anchor it.

Aftercare
For the first year, plants require minimal attention, other than an occasional watering in warm weather. Tie in any stems that flop from their support stake.

Deter slugs and snails, especially during humid weather. The stems of young plants can be completely stripped of leaves by severe infestations.

In the spring following planting, cut back the stems of all large-flowered hybrids to the lowest pair of strong buds. This type of light pruning will encourage the growth of several wide-spreading stems. Naturally vigorous and branching species clematises, such as *C. montana*, do not require pruning now.

If the plant still produces only one main shoot, despite pruning, pinch out the tip in summer. This action will also slow down soft growth, thought to be the cause

of clematis wilt, a fatal disorder.

In subsequent years, clematises require annual pruning and feeding to maintain their vigor and flowering potential.

Feeding In the fall, expose the soil and sprinkle a few handfuls of bone meal around the base of the plant, or work organic material lightly into the soil.

In spring, apply a handful of potassium sulfate and water it in well. In summer, water often during dry weather, at least once a week throughout the hot months.

▲ **Tree climbers** A vigorous clematis, such as *C. montana,* looks spectacular as it twines around a tree, and the flowers lend the tree a second season of bloom. Plant the clematis on the north side so that the roots are in shade; lead the stem to the tree branches along a stake.

Use a liquid fertilizer weekly during the growing season, except for the time the plant is in flower. **Support** Clematises are self-supporting, provided they have an open framework to cling to, such as a trellis, sturdy netting, or close-spaced wires. If you grow a clematis against a tree or through a shrub, the partners will provide enough support. After the first year, no further tying in is necessary.

Pruning This job depends on the plant's flowering period and growth habit. Early-flowering species and large-flowered hybrids do not need regular pruning. They produce blooms on the previous year's growth, so pruning would remove blooming shoots. After flowering, trim off dead shoots or those that are too rampant for their allocated space.

The late-flowering species generally die back in winter and regrow from ground level the following year. Cut back this type almost to the ground in late winter or early spring, leaving short stumps, each with just one strong shoot bearing healthy buds.

Some of the double-flowered hybrids produce their blooms only on old wood. Single flowers appear on new wood during the second blooming, which occurs later in the season. Do not prune this type of clematis; otherwise, you won't get any double flowers. Remove old wood soon after the first show is over.

▼ **Climbing company** Two intermingling clematises create a brilliant midsummer display. The harmony of wine-red 'Mme Julia Correvon' and purple 'Victoria' is enhanced by pinkish-white tree mallows.

Garden shrubs

Shrubs are the backbone of the garden; they are the permanent features that vary the landscape. If chosen carefully, they provide year-round interest. Once established, shrubs are less trouble to look after than perennials, annuals, and bedding plants. Most require minimal maintenance pruning, whether they are grown in mixed beds or on their own.

The shrubs described in the following pages are as attractive in leaf as in flower, with the exception of roses, which have their own special charm. Many of these plants have more than one feature to make them interesting throughout the year. Barberry and viburnum, for example, have pretty, scented flowers and handsome foliage (whether summer green or autumnal bronze), as well as magnificent massed berry color. In addition, evergreen shrubs can keep the garden alive throughout the winter. Consider, for example, the constant splendor of sheets of flowering heathers, whose dead flower heads can often be left in place to glow in the winter sun. Dwarf conifers are magnificent when planted as specimen trees or as part of a rock garden.

Roses are, of course, the glory of summer. Bearing the best-loved of all flowers, these shrubs will live for decades with care — and their enormous variety means that the perfect example can be found for every garden. Not only does the shape of their blooms inspire lifelong enthusiasm, they are also enjoyed for their characteristic scent, exquisite colors, and fiery fall hips.

Winter shrubs Camellias bear their splendid flowers from early fall until spring.

EXQUISITE CAMELLIAS

**Set against handsome and glossy evergreen foliage,
the magnificent blooms of the camellia highlight lightly shaded
gardens in winter and spring.**

A member of the tea family, Theaceae, the genus *Camellia* consists of 82 species of evergreen shrubs and small trees, native to tropical and subtropical regions of India, China, Korea, Taiwan, and Japan. Of these, only a handful are cultivated, but, as the result of extensive breeding programs, there are now some 2,000 cultivars.

Camellias were named in honor of George Joseph Kamel, or Camellus, a seventeenth-century priest and botanist who traveled widely in the Far East.

The young foliage shoots of *Camellia sinensis* are the commercial source of tea — the world's most popular caffeine drink. Other camellias, including *C. oleifera,* are sources of seed

oils. But it is for their glorious blooms that camellias are valued. Cup- or bowl-shaped, these may be single, semidouble, or double. The petals range in color from pure white through soft shades of pink to rich rose-pink and red.

The leathery leaves are also attractive. They are glossy, very finely toothed, and frequently prominently veined, making a splendid year-round display, equaled only by the evergreen laurels and rhododendrons.

In their natural habitat, camellias live below shady evergreen trees on mountain slopes, often enjoying high levels of humidity. In the home garden, they also thrive in light shade below taller trees. Generally, they dislike full sun in exposed sites.

Most of the camellias commonly grown in the United States belong to just two species, *Camellia japonica* and *C. sasanqua.* These are similar in overall habit, leaf shape, and flower formation, but there are some minor differences between them. The leaves of *C. sasanqua* are somewhat smaller — 2 in (5 cm) long — than those of *C. japonica* — 4 in (10 cm) long. *C. sasanqua* blooms from September to December, but *C. japonica* flowers from October to April. In addition, *C. sasanqua* usually reaches the height of a large shrub, while *C. japonica* may grow as tall as a small tree.

Both species are reliably hardy only to zone 8, though they may also survive for many years farther north if set out in a protected spot. When used as landscape plants, they are reliably hardy from North Carolina southward to Florida in the East, and on the Pacific Coast from California to British Columbia. North of southernmost areas of zone 7, camellias are best kept in a cool greenhouse at 50-60° F (10-16° C), where they will provide an unforgettable wintertime display.

Classification

Camellias are grouped according to flower form and size. This classification does not affect their cultivation needs, but it is useful for distinguishing the many cultivars and hybrids.

Since flower color may vary slightly depending on soil type and light intensity, it does not provide an effective means of differentiating varieties. With only subtle tonal differences from one cultivar to another, even the best color photos may be misleading.

Flowering seasons also vary from year to year, and depend on

◀ **Hardy camellias** Grown in sheltered woodland conditions, *C. japonica* cultivars are generally hardy from zone 8 southward. Set them in a spot where early morning sun can't strike still-frosted flower buds. A thaw that occurs too quickly causes the bloom to abort.

Camellia japonica
'Elegans'
anemone-form

the locality. For example, a hard winter delays flowering, and a long, hot summer encourages flower buds to develop early. However, camellias can be loosely grouped into early-flowering, midseason, and late types. The early ones flower from late fall to midwinter; midseason types bloom from midwinter to early spring; and late types blossom from early spring to late spring.

Camellias are divided into the following groups by flower shape:
Single flowers have one ring of no more than eight petals, with conspicuous stamens.
Semidouble flowers have two or more rings of petals surrounding a prominent cluster of stamens.
Anemone-form flowers have one or more outer rings of petals that lie flat or are slightly wavy, surrounding a mass of petallike stamens, or *petaloids*.
Peony-form flowers are deep and rounded, consisting of a convex mass of petals and petaloids; stamens may also be present.
Double/rose-form flowers have

overlapping petals in a rounded mass that opens to reveal a concave center with some stamens.
Formal double flowers are similar to the rose-form types, but their symmetrically overlapping petals never open out completely. Since they have no stamens, they are sterile.

Size forms an important part of the classification of blooms, particularly for flower-show judging. The categories are:
❏ Very large: over 5 in (12.5 cm) in diameter.
❏ Large: 4-5 in (10-12.5 cm) in diameter.
❏ Medium: 3-4 in (7.5-10 cm) in diameter; sometimes divided into medium-large (3½-4 in/9-10 cm in diameter) and medium (3-3½ in/7.5-9 cm in diameter).
❏ Small: 2-3 in (5-7.5 cm) in diameter; sometimes overlapping with a miniature category (less than 2½ in/6.5 cm in diameter).

Choosing camellias

Camellia japonica cultivars are mainly hardy and survive outdoors through zone 8. They are among the easiest camellias to grow. However, as they come into flower very early, their blooms are prone to frost damage. (Those with pink or white blooms are most susceptible.) In cooler regions of zone 8, they are best grown in tubs in unheated greenhouses or outdoors in a warm microclimate.

Hundreds of named cultivars,

Camellia japonica
'Adolphe Audusson'
semidouble

*Camellia
japonica
'Mathotiana
Rosea'*
formal double

Camellia japonica
'Swan Lake'
double/rose-form

Camellia reticulata
formal double

Camellia
'Donation'
semidouble

TAKING LEAF-BUD CUTTINGS

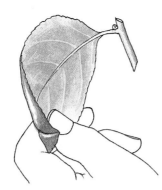

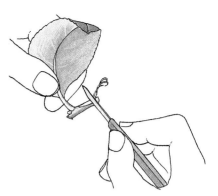

1 In summer, cut off a semihard lateral shoot (one that began growing in the spring) that has several mature, healthy leaves on it.

2 Divide the stem into several pieces, each with just one leaf and a single bud. Trim each piece just above and about ¾ in (2 cm) below the leaf axil.

3 Using a sharp knife, scrape off some bark from the base of the stem, then dip the wounded part into hormone rooting powder.

4 Insert each prepared cutting in a 50:50 mix by volume of peat and sand so that the leaf axil just shows. Press them in firmly and water with a hand sprayer.

5 When well rooted, generally after about 6 months, transplant the cuttings individually into 3½-in (9-cm) pots filled with an acid potting soil.

6 Unlike many shrubs, camellias mature very quickly. The cuttings often produce some flowers even in the first year after rooting.

with single or mottled colors, are available; these have a graceful bushy habit and shiny foliage. They reach a height of 20-25 ft (6.0-7.5 m). 'Flame' (late, red, semidouble) is an exceptionally cold-hardy cultivar, as are 'Kumasaka' (late, dark pink, double), 'Lady Vansittart'(mid to late, semidouble flowers vary from white to red), and 'White Empress' (early, white, incomplete double).

Camellia sasanqua 'Yuletide' single

Camellia sasanqua is somewhat less frost tolerant than *C. japonica*. The *C. sasanqua* cultivars are beautiful, but do well only when grown against a sheltered wall north of zone 9. Their flowers, which appear in winter and early spring, are small, exquisitely formed, and mainly single. These often-fragrant blooms are borne on shrubs 6-10 ft (1.8-3 m) tall. 'Bonanza' has semi-peony-form deep red flowers and 'Daydream' produces large, single white blossoms edged with deep rose.

Site and soil
Plant camellias outdoors in early fall to late fall or early spring to midspring during fine weather. The plants thrive in the same type of soil as do rhododendrons. The soil should be rich, well-drained, lime-free (acid to neutral), and preferably mixed with leaf mold. Most types prefer a westerly or sheltered northerly exposure. Or, you can plant them against a wall or below trees where they will be protected from

frost and early morning sun. They flourish in dappled shade with some full sun late in the day.

Set plants shallowly but firmly in the soil, never burying the main stem any lower than it was in the nursery. Mulch the area with shredded bark or leaf mold.

At the northern end of their range, do not put camellias in an east-facing exposure — after a heavy frost, bright morning sun will scorch frozen flower buds as they thaw. Southerly exposures are also unsuitable, since camellias like a cool root-run.

A garden that is sheltered by vegetation or buildings is warmer than an exposed space, and also offers wind protection to delicate camellia blooms. At planting sites where winds are unavoidably high, stake young plants until they are established and protect them with a windscreen.

Tub-grown camellias
Even in areas where camellias thrive, the early-flowering types grow best in pots, 8-12 in (20-30 cm) deep, or in small tubs so that

the budded plants can be moved under cover during cold nights. Use a potting soil made of 4 parts by volume lime-free loam, 2 parts leaf mold or peat, and 1 part sharp sand. Add a handful of bone meal per bucketful. Or, use commercial potting soil formulated for acid-loving plants.

From late spring to midfall, stand the containers outdoors in a sheltered, semishaded position, then take them into a cool greenhouse or unheated porch where a temperature of 40-45°F (4-7°C) can be maintained until late spring. For very early flowers, raise the temperature to 48-53°F (9-12°C). Camellias can be grown all year round if planted in the soil within a cool greenhouse.

Aftercare

Once established, camellias require little routine care. You do not need to prune camellias regularly; to maintain a good shape, snip off straggly shoots in midspring after the plants have flowered. If you want to encourage especially large blooms for show purposes, thin out the flower buds before they swell or open.

Deadhead spent camellias to retain their form and to prevent fruits from appearing. These are not decorative and sap the plants' strength.

Apply a generous mulch of leaf mold, shredded bark, or other organic material every year in midspring; a 2-in (5-cm) covering over the entire root-run is ideal.

Propagating camellias

In summer, take cuttings, 3-4 in (7.5-10 cm) long, from half-ripe lateral shoots. Root these in a well-drained but moist rooting medium. For the best results, keep the medium at a temperature of 55-61°F (13-16°C).

To obtain large numbers of plants, take leaf-bud cuttings during the summer, as shown on the previous page.

Some camellias do not root easily from cuttings. These are best propagated by layering in early fall. Choose pliable stems from mature plants, wound a section of each stem, and peg them at the point of this wound into pots of moist rooting medium. The bruised stem portion should develop roots after 18 months; then the young plants can be severed from the parent and grown on in individual pots.

Pests and diseases

Several types of scale insects, including camellia scale and mealybugs, may infest camellias. If left unchecked, they may rob the plants of their vitality. Check with your garden center or local Cooperative Extension or Agricultural Service for recommended insecticides in your area.

Camellias that suffer from physiological disorders exhibit unusual symptoms. Cold night temperatures may cause a bronzing of the leaves. Frost damage is the main cause of bud drop, but this condition can also be associated with dry soil. Plants grown in alkaline soil may show brown or black spots on their leaves. In addition, the leaves may turn a poor shade of green and begin to slightly pucker around the spots.

If the foliage starts to yellow, the change may be due to chlorosis on alkaline soils. To remedy the problem, apply iron chelate in the spring.

◀ **Elegant camellias** In dappled shade and a protected site, *C. japonica* 'Elegans' shows its natural vigor, assuming treelike proportions and an abundance of rich, glossy leaves. In midspring, it is festooned with huge anemone-shaped blooms that vary in color from deep pink to bright salmon-rose.

VERSATILE VIBURNUMS

**Beloved for their scented flowers, shapely foliage,
bright berries, and rich autumnal tints, viburnums
make rewarding garden shrubs year round.**

If you choose wisely, you will probably be able to find a viburnum with desirable characteristics for every month of the year. Some types have winter flowers; others have spring or summer blooms. There are deciduous and evergreen species, often with attractively shaped or textured leaves. Many viburnums have long-lasting clusters of berries from late summer to winter, and several species acquire beautiful fall colors. Frequently, a single species provides a year-round, everchanging attraction.

The genus name *Viburnum* comes from the Latin name for the European wayfaring tree, *Viburnum lantana*. These woody plants belong to the Caprifoliaceae family, which includes many shrubs, such as abelia, elder, honeysuckle, and weigela.

In the wild, viburnums grow throughout the Northern Hemisphere. They are usually very hardy and suitable for gardens in most parts of North America, except for the extreme South.

Special features
Viburnums produce their flowers in rounded or flattened clusters. Though each five-lobed, funnel-shaped bloom is very small, the whole cluster may be up to 6 in (15 cm) wide.

Flower color varies from pure white or cream through very pale pink to midpink. The flower buds are usually more richly colored than the open blooms.

Many viburnums have exceptionally fragrant flowers that will certainly add to any hedge or mixed border. Thus, it is not surprising to learn that gardeners

commonly plant them near a house door or window.

In some species, such as *V. alnifolium, V. opulus, V. plicatum tomentosum,* and *V. sargentii,* the flowers are of two types — sterile and fertile — forming a "lacecap" head. The sterile flowers, which have striking white petals that attract pollinating insects, are arranged in a ring around a flattened cluster of smaller, much less showy, fertile flowers.

The casual observer might confuse lacecap-flowered viburnums

▼ **Snowy 'Mariesii'** A favorite variety of the Japanese snowball bush, *Viburnum plicatum tomentosum* 'Mariesii' is distinguished by tier upon tier of horizontal branches. These are laden in late spring and early summer with pure white lacecap flowers that are similar to those of the hydrangea.

Viburnum lantana
wayfaring tree
(late-summer berries)

Viburnum davidii
(fall berries)

Viburnum plicatum
tomentosum 'Mariesii'
(early-summer flowers)

Viburnum ×
bodnantense 'Dawn'
(winter/early-spring flowers)

Viburnum
opulus
guelder rose
(berries and
fall foliage)

Viburnum rhytidophyllum
(late-spring flowers)

with lacecap hydrangeas, even though they are unrelated, and have distinctly different leaves.

The flowering season of viburnums stretches from winter to summer. Some deciduous viburnums will produce a flush of flowers whenever there is a mild spell in winter (in mild climates), or in early spring on leafless twigs. The best among these is *V. × bodnantense,* though its blooms may turn brown after a hard frost. In cold areas, the variety 'Dawn' (hardy from zones 5-8) is less prone to frost damage. The deciduous shrub *V. farreri* also blooms in early spring, at the first hint of warm weather, carrying pendent, richly fragrant pinkwhite clusters.

V. tinus, an evergreen type, and its cultivars flower in succession from midwinter (January, in the South) to early spring, often staging a simultaneous show of white or pale pink flowers and blue-black berries. Evergreen viburnums are especially useful for mixed beds containing bright plants, as well as for hedges.

Among the spring- and summer-flowering types, the deciduous *V. carlesii, V. × carlcephalum,* and *V. plicatum tomentosum* (Japanese snowball) are particularly attractive and showy. Like the evergreen *V. × burkwoodii,* low-growing *V. davidii,* and *V. japonicum,* they almost all have sweetly scented flowers.

Viburnum leaves vary enormously between species. Some have distinct textural qualities — *V. rhytidophyollum,* for example, has large, dark, lance-shaped leaves, with a wrinkly surface and gray, nappy underside.

Viburnum tinus, in contrast, has shiny, leathery leaves with a smooth surface. A number of other species, such as *V. opulus* and its cultivars, have grapelike or maplelike leaves with incut lobes. Frequently, the leaves have toothed edges, but they are never sharp to the touch. In addition, the leaves of many deciduous viburnums develop russet fall hues, and a few turn brilliant orange or red. And *V. opulus* 'Aureum' is noted for its yellow foliage in spring and summer.

The colorful fruits that appear on many viburnums are a bonus. Red, black, blue-black, or golden berries begin to ripen in late summer and often persist into winter. Those of *V. trilobum,* commonly (though erroneously) called the American cranberry bush, can be made into a wonderful jelly, but most others are unpalatable and some, such as *V. tinus,* are poisonous.

Site and soil
Both the winter-flowering and spring-flowering types should be set in a spot protected from cold north winds, early morning sun, and frost. However, most viburnums appreciate sun all day long; only *V. acerifolium* (the mapleleaf viburnum) and *V. lantanoides* (the hobblebush) require a shaded position.

As a rule, viburnums prefer moist soil *(V. acerifoliam* is an exception), but it may not be available in a permanently sunny site. As a compromise, set them in partial shade in ordinary, fairly deep soil.

Planting viburnums
The best time for planting evergreen viburnums is during early spring to midspring or early fall to midfall. In regions with mild

Viburnum farreri
(syn. *V. fragrans*)
(early-spring flowers)

Viburnum betulifolium
(early-fall berries)

Viburnum opulus 'Aureum'
(summer foliage)

Viburnum opulus
'Roseum'
(syn. *V.o.* 'Sterile')
snowball bush
(early-summer
flowers)

Viburnum opulus
'Xanthocarpum'
(early-fall berries)

Viburnum sargentii
'Onandaga'
(early-summer
flowers)

climates, the deciduous types can also be set out through the winter, depending on the weather.

To improve the moisture retention of free-draining soils, dig in a generous amount of organic material, such as composted manure. Then, make a planting hole large enough to accept the whole root ball and ensure that the viburnum stands at the same height in the soil as it did in the nursery. Press the soil down firmly and water the plant well.

Fruiting viburnums produce the best show when they are cross-pollinated by neighboring plants of the same species. If you have room in the garden, place two or three viburnums together. Space them at distances equal to half the ultimate spread of each.

The bushy and free-fruiting variety of the guelder rose, *Viburnum opulus* 'Compactum,' together with *V. tinus* and its cultivars, can be grown as informal hedges, which can reach up to 4

▼ **Evergreen laurustinus** One of the most popular winter-/early-spring-flowering shrubs, *Viburnum tinus* offers pink buds and white flowers followed by long-lasting blue-black berries.

ft (1.2 m) high. Space hedging plants so that they are at least 2 ft (60 cm) apart.

Aftercare

Once established, viburnums require little attention and need no regular pruning.

If plants become straggly or outgrow their allotted space, or if branches become diseased or damaged, they can be pruned back to healthy wood as necessary. For evergreen types, do this trimming in late spring. Cut out all deadwood from winter-flowering viburnums in midspring and prune summer-flowering deciduous types as soon as they have finished flowering. Don't deadhead viburnums — if you remove the faded flowers, you won't get any berries.

Most viburnums, especially *V. opulus* and *V. carlesii*, are susceptible to attack by aphids. These pests multiply rapidly, stunting the young leaves and causing them to curl. At the first sign of aphid attack, spray with a recommended insecticide or insecticidal soap. Repeat the treatment at 2-week intervals (or as recommended on the product label) until the plants are free of all signs of aphids.

Propagation

Viburnums can be grown from cuttings, 3-4 in (7.5-10 cm) long, of lateral shoots in summer or early fall. These will root better if they are taken with a heel. Insert the cuttings in a moisture-retentive but well-drained rooting medium. Summer softwood cuttings require a bottom heat of 61°F (16°C) in a propagation box. Cuttings taken in the fall from more mature wood can be rooted in a cold frame.

Once they have rooted, transplant all cuttings into 3-in (7.5-cm) pots containing well-drained potting soil and overwinter them in a cold frame or cool but frost-free spot. In midspring to late spring, place the cuttings in nursery rows outdoors and grow them on for 2 or 3 years. Transplant the young plants to their final positions from fall to spring.

Alternatively, layer long shoots in early fall and sever them a year later.

▼ **American hobblebush** On acid woodland soil, the native *Viburnum alnifolium* takes on superb fall colors that turn from yellow and orange through red to rich claret-purple. It blooms in early summer, with large white lacecap flowers.

OPULENT HYDRANGEAS

**If they are given a fairly mild, sheltered
spot and minimal attention, your hydrangeas will produce
long-lasting, showy flowers.**

Hydrangeas form a large genus of mainly deciduous shrubs — some are bushy and others are vigorous climbers. Several of the species (notably *H. paniculata)* are extremely hardy, flourishing into zone 3 or 4, although the popular hortensia cultivars do not flower well north of zone 6. As a rule, hydrangeas tolerate air pollution and coastal salt sprays. Their only demand is that their planting site should never be allowed to dry out completely; most also prefer some shade.

Flower types
One feature is common to all the hydrangeas in cultivation: their showy flowers are sterile. They consist of conspicuous white or colored sepals with no true petals or reproductive organs. Fertile flowers are present in most hydrangea heads, but they are relatively insignificant and less brightly colored.

In *Hydrangea macrophylla* cultivars, the flower heads are arranged in one of two characteristic forms. Lacecaps have broad, flat clusters consisting of an outer ring of large, sterile florets surrounding a center of small, fertile flowers. Mophead, or hortensia, types have dome-shaped heads composed almost entirely of sterile ray florets.

A third flower type is found in *H. paniculata* and its cultivars; the large pyramid-shaped cluster is made up of both sterile and fertile florets. In some types, all the florets are sterile.

Selecting colors
Hydrangea macrophylla has a unique trait among garden shrubs: With the exception of white-flowered types, the color of its blossoms can be changed from mauve/blue to pink/red just by adjusting the acidity/alkalinity of the soil surrounding the plant's roots. Clear blue flowers cannot

---

▼ **Mixed hydrangeas** The popular *Hydrangea macrophylla* group consists of two distinct types — the flat lacecaps and the huge, rounded mopheads (hortensias), both of which are excellent for drying. All thrive in light, dappled shade and moist soil.

be produced by hydrangeas planted in alkaline soils. (At best, some might turn mauve.) To get the blue forms, dress the soil liberally with an acid organic mulch and apply aluminum sulfate or a fertilizer designed for acid-loving shrubs annually.

Similarly, true pink and red blooms are unlikely to appear on hydrangeas in acid soils. To guarantee these colors, dress the soil with a handful of ground limestone per sq yd/sq m annually. But making the soil too alkaline may result in chlorosis, a condition that yellows the leaves.

Plants grown on neutral soils tend to produce rather mixed, dull flower colors.

Planting hydrangeas

Most hydrangeas will thrive in full sun or dappled shade, and they are quite tolerant of normal garden conditions. However, the *Macrophylla* cultivars require a sheltered position at the north end of their range, and young specimens of the oakleaf hydrangea (*H. quercifolia*, hardy to zone 5) will also benefit from winter protection.

In general, these shrubs appreciate loamy, moisture-retentive soils. Before planting, cultivate the soil well, digging in plenty of organic matter.

Plant hydrangeas in either early spring to midspring or midfall to late fall. Set out container-grown plants at any time. Most mature shrubs need a lot of space because they spread widely.

Dig a planting hole of sufficient size to accommodate the whole root system comfortably. When positioning the plant in the hole, check that the soil mark on the stem is level with the surrounding soil. Spread out the roots of bare-root plants in the hole. However, you must leave the root ball of container-grown plants intact (loosen any encircling roots). Refill the hole with soil, press in firmly, and water the plants.

As with bushy species, the climbing hydrangeas (*H. anomala petiolaris*) dislike dry roots, so place them at least 15-18 in (38-45 cm) away from a wall, fence, or tree trunk. Once established, they will support themselves on most rough surfaces by means of aerial roots, but for the first couple of years they will need some assistance. Insert

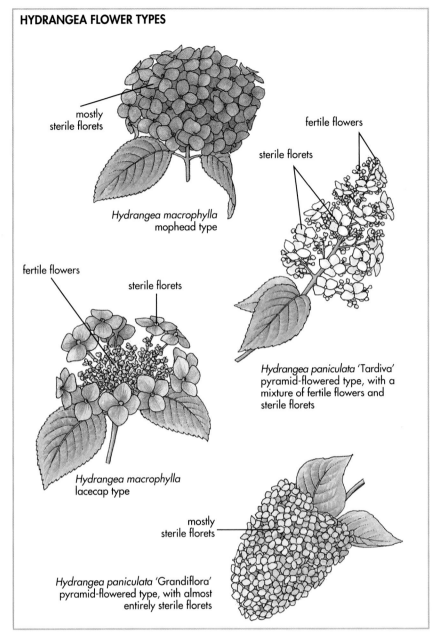

HYDRANGEA FLOWER TYPES

Hydrangea macrophylla mophead type

mostly sterile florets

fertile flowers

sterile florets

Hydrangea paniculata 'Tardiva' pyramid-flowered type, with a mixture of fertile flowers and sterile florets

fertile flowers

sterile florets

Hydrangea macrophylla lacecap type

mostly sterile florets

Hydrangea paniculata 'Grandiflora' pyramid-flowered type, with almost entirely sterile florets

stakes, slanting them toward the plant's main support, and tie in the stems loosely with garden string. Remove the stakes when the shoots are firmly established.

Routine care

Mulch hydrangeas with organic material annually in midspring and water them when dry.

For winter protection, leave faded flower heads in place. Remove them in spring, along with any dead and damaged shoots. To keep the center of the shrubs open, cut back 2- and 3-year-old stems to ground level on *H. macrophylla* varieties. In early spring, prune the previous year's shoots of *H. arborescens* and *H. paniculata* back by about half.

Propagation

Increase shrubby species by tak-

ing cuttings, 4-6 in (10-15 cm) long, of nonflowering side shoots in late summer. Root them in a moisture-retentive but well-drained rooting medium in a propagation box, with a bottom heat of 55-61°F (13-16°C), or in a cold frame.

Transplant the rooted cuttings into individual 3½-in (9-cm) pots of ordinary potting soil and overwinter them in a cold frame or other protected spot. In spring, transfer them to a nursery bed until you set them out in the garden in fall.

You can propagate climbing hydrangeas by taking cuttings, 3 in (7.5 cm) long, of vigorous side shoots in summer. Root them in a cold frame or in a cool, shaded bed and pot up singly as above. Plunge the pots into the soil outdoors and plant out in the fall.

COLORFUL BARBERRIES

**Popular for mixed borders and informal hedging,
barberries offer year-round interest, from showy spring
flowers to fall tints and massed berries.**

The genus *Berberis* consists of several hundred deciduous and evergreen shrubs. Many are native to China, Japan, and Asia, but several, including *B. darwinii* (named after Charles Darwin) come from South America. About a dozen species, together with numerous hybrids and varieties, are commonly grown in home gardens.

Berberis species are commonly called barberries. The generic name derives from the Arabic word *berberys,* meaning berries. These shrubs belong to the Berberidaceae family of flowering plants and have mahonias, epimediums, and the heavenly bamboo *(Nandina)* as relatives.

The most popular species is the well-named common barberry *(Berberis vulgaris),* an Old World native that came to North America long ago as a garden plant and now grows wild over much of the country. Because it is a host for wheat rust, this species was the target of an extensive (but

unsuccessful) program of eradication in the early part of this century. Many states still have laws that require it to be destroyed if found in the wild.

However, other barberries are harmless and offer considerable decorative value. Their leaves are arranged in rosettelike bunches on woody stems, and they have small, pendent flowers borne singly or in clusters. The berries of these plants are not poisonous, but they are not recommended for culinary use. The French, however, sometimes make a jelly from the berries of *B. vulgaris.*

Choosing barberries

Barberries are appreciated by gardeners either for their showy flowers, fall-colored foliage, bright berries, or a combination of all of these.

They range in height from just 10-18 in (25-45 cm) tall to about 7 ft (2.1 m), and so are excellent for all types of mixed or shrub borders, for specimen plantings,

and for creating informal hedging. Barberry shapes also vary, including upright or rounded types as well as spreading or prostrate ones.

Evergreen barberries provide glossy deep green foliage year round, while many deciduous types display beautiful fall colors — mainly rich red and orange. The undersides of many barberry leaves are silvery or are tinged with blue. Only 1¼ in (3 cm) long, the leaves are frequently tipped with tiny spines.

The main objection to barberries is that most species also have very sharp spines on their stems. Usually ¾-1½ in (2-4 cm) long,

▼ **Barberry variety** Stunning color contrasts in this mixed border are provided by two cultivars of the deciduous *Berberis thunbergii.* On the left is 'Aurea,' whose golden yellow foliage turns green by late summer. It is beautifully complemented by 'Rosy Glow,' which has mottled pink leaves that turn to purple as fall approaches.

Berberis darwinii
(late-spring flowers)

Berberis thunbergii
'Rosy Glow'
(early-summer color)

Berberis darwinii
(fall berries)

Berberis thunbergii
'Aurea'
(early-summer color)

they typically occur in threes.

Among the evergreen barberries, *B. darwinii* and *B.* × *stenophylla* are outstanding for their cascades of late-spring flowers; the former bears rich orange blooms, and the latter exhibits bright yellow ones. Both make wonderful, impenetrable hedges. Reaching up to 7 ft (2.1 m) tall, they need clipping only once a year, after they flower.

For fall color, few shrubs can compare with the deciduous *B. thunbergii,* a compact shrub that grows up to 4 ft (1.2 m) high. Yellow spring flowers are followed by ropes of translucent scarlet berries strung among its rich red fall foliage. Even more striking are the red-leaved cultivar 'Atropurpurea' and its dwarf form, 'Atropurpurea Nana,' only 1-1½ ft (30-45 cm) high.

Soil and site

Barberries thrive in most well-drained soils, whether acid, neutral, or alkaline. But permanently wet soils are unsuitable, and drainage of waterlogged sites is essential before planting. The shrubs usually survive short spells of drought and can be planted close to a house wall.

Deciduous types need full sun to ensure the best fall leaf colors and a profusion of colorful berries. The evergreen species do well in partial shade or full sun, although the orange-flowered and spring-blooming *B. darwinii* is most spectacular when planted in full sun.

Most barberries are very hardy, many thriving into zone 4 or even 3. Fairly tolerant of salt spray and pollution, they make good coastal- and urban-garden specimen plants and hedges.

Planting barberries

Container-grown nursery plants can be set out at any time of year. Midspring to late spring and fall are the most successful periods for planting deciduous types, while either midspring to late spring or early fall to midfall is best for evergreens.

Bare-rooted plants suitable for hedging purposes are available from some nurseries, and these should be put in their permanent sites in midspring to late spring in the case of the evergreen species, and in midfall or early spring for the deciduous ones.

The planting distance between these shrubs will depend on the ultimate spread of the chosen species or hybrids. The ideal spacing between two identical barberries is equal to the spread of each individual plant. Check with a nursery catalog when you are in doubt. If you are mixing two barberry types, add their

Berberis
× *stenophylla*
(spring flowers)

*Berberis
thunbergii*
'Dart's Red
Lady'
(fall color)

PRUNING STRAGGLY OR OVERGROWN PLANTS

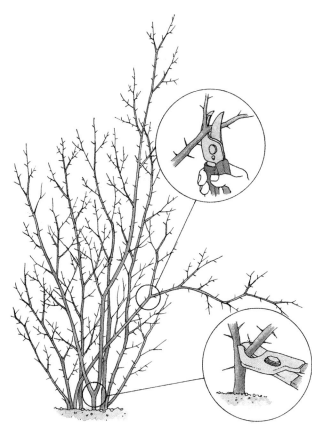

1 Barberries do not need regular pruning, but straggly or overgrown branches should be removed — trim evergreen types after flowering and deciduous ones in late winter. Use pruning shears to cut thin stems and long-handled loppers to sever thick stems or those in the center of the bush.

2 The trimmed bush should have an even outline, with a good balance of twiggy branches. A controlled shape is particularly important when growing barberries as a hedge; an annual pruning in late summer will encourage impenetrable spiny growth from the base of the plants.

ultimate spreads together and divide by 2 to calculate the planting distance. For informal hedging, space plants 12-15 in (30-38 cm) tall 1½-2 ft (45-60 cm) apart in each row.

Except on the most fertile sites, mix a spadeful of organic material into the soil at the base of each planting hole. Ensure that all barberry shrubs stand at the same height in the ground after planting as they were in the nursery.

Press shrubs in firmly and water thoroughly — never allow young plants to dry out completely. In exposed areas, provide temporary shelter in the form of a windbreak until barberries are established. If any plants become loose in the ground after severe frosts or strong winds, press them in again.

About 2 weeks after planting barberry hedges, trim off the upper quarter of each main stem. This pruning will encourage compact, bushy growth.

As soon as the soil has warmed up in spring, apply an organic mulch around the base of the young shrubs to conserve soil moisture and suppress germinating weed seedlings. Shredded leaves or shredded bark are ideal for this purpose.

Aftercare

Once established, barberries need minimal care and attention. Routine pruning is unnecessary, but overgrown or straggly plants should be trimmed to shape. Prune evergreen types immediately after flowering and cut back deciduous types in late winter or early spring. Trim deciduous barberry hedges in late summer.

Wear gloves when pruning barberries. Their spines can inflict painful wounds, and occasionally a form of dermatitis can develop around skin cut by spines or embedded thorns because of a microscopic fungus or bacteria on the plant's spines.

During prolonged periods of

drought, barberries benefit from a very thorough watering a couple of times a week.

Propagation

These shrubs can be grown from seed collected from ripe berries, but the resulting plants may not be true to type, especially if you have several different barberry species in your garden or in the neighborhood — barberries interbreed freely. Sow seeds directly in the garden soil in a nursery bed in late summer, or sow them in pots in a cold frame.

The best method of propagation is by cuttings, about 3 in (7.5 cm) long, taken from lateral shoots in late summer or early fall. You will find that cuttings with a heel root more reliably. Insert the cuttings in pots of rooting medium and place them in a cold frame.

The following midspring to late spring, transplant the rooted cuttings to an outdoor nursery bed and grow them on for another

CHOOSING BARBERRIES

For flowers

B. darwinii: golden orange flowers; evergreen; up to 7 ft (2.1 m) tall; open habit.
B. julianae: abundant yellow flowers; evergreen; up to 10 ft (3 m) tall; hardy to zone 5.
B. verruculosa: large golden yellow flowers; evergreen; up to 6 ft (1.8 m) tall; hardy in protected spots to zone 5.

For summer foliage

B. thunbergii 'Atropurpurea': purple leaves; deciduous; up to 7 ft (2.1 m) tall; upright habit.
B. thunbergii 'Aurea': golden leaves; up to 3 ft (1m) tall; bushy.
B. thunbergii 'Crimson Velvet': new foliage fuchsia-colored, darkening to smoky maroon; up to 6 ft (1.8 m) tall.
B. thunbergii 'Dart's Red Lady': purple leaves; up to 4 ft (1.2 m) tall; stiff and upright habit.
B. thunbergii 'Rosy Glow': purple-red leaves, mottled pink when young; up to 5 ft (1.5 m) tall; bushy.

For fall tints

B. koreana: reddish-purple leaves; 6 ft (1.8 m) tall; hardy, zones 3-7.
B. x mentorensis: yellow-orange-red tints; to 7 ft (2.1 m) tall; regular, rounded habit.
B. thunbergii and cultivars: mostly vivid red tints; 1-7 ft (30 cm-2.1 m) tall; variable habits. Cultivar 'Sparkle' offers compact size (to 4 ft/1.2 m tall) and brightest orange-red fall color.

For showy berries

B. darwinii: blue-purple berries; up to 7 ft (2.1 m) tall; open habit.
B. koreana: bright red berries.
B. sargentiana: red berries maturing to black; up to 9 ft (2.7 m) tall; evergreen.
B. thunbergii and cultivars: bright red berries that remain into winter; hardy from zones 4-8.

For rock gardens/edging

B. thunbergii 'Crimson Pygmy' (syn. 'Atropurpurea Nana'): red-purple leaves; fall tints; up to 1½ ft (45 cm) tall; rounded habit.

For hedging

B. darwinii, B. x gladwynensis 'William Penn,' *B. koreana, B. x stenophylla* hybrids, and *B. thunbergii* 'Redbird.'

▶ **Fall colors** The deciduous barberries display vivid fall foliage in crimsons, purples, oranges, and yellows, as well as flowers, berries, and often-colorful new growth. These features make barberry one of the hardest-working shrubs.

1 or 2 years. Transplant them to their permanent positions in fall or spring.

Evergreen types tend to dislike being moved often. After the cold-frame cuttings have rooted, they may do better if put into 4-in (10-cm) pots containing ordinary potting soil. Bury these pots in the soil outdoors for a couple of years, then plant out like container-grown nursery specimens, without disturbing the roots.

A simple way to propagate is to dig up any suckers, detach them, and replant them from midfall to early spring.

Lax-stemmed barberries may be propagated by layering in early fall to late fall. Select a non-flowering, low-growing shoot that is flexible enough to be bent to the ground without snapping. Slice off a small section of the stem's underside, about 1 ft (30 cm) from the tip. Bury the wounded area of the stem under several inches (centimeters) of soil, then anchor it with a wire peg, or else weigh it down with a large stone. Support and tie the tip of the stem upright to a stake.

Within a year, roots should develop from the buried wound. Check for rooting by removing the peg or anchor stone and gently pulling the stem — if it has rooted, you will be able to feel resistance. Sever the rooted layers and replant them immediately.

Pests and diseases

Most barberries are free of pests and diseases; unfortunately, the exception is the popular Japanese barberry *(Berberis thunbergii)*

▲ **Flowering hedges** The evergreen *Berberis* × *stenophylla* forms an impenetrable hedge with its arching, thorny branches that are covered in late spring with golden yellow flowers. You can ensure a similar display for the following year by lightly trimming it to shape immediately after blooming.

and its cultivars. It is prone to a variety of diseases, including leaf spot, anthracnose, wilt, and root rots, as well as aphids, webworms, scales, and root-knot nematodes. While spraying for insect infestations is advised, this species has the vigorous growth typical of barberries in general, and it usually copes well with afflictions unassisted. Japanese barberry is so tough, in fact, that it is widely believed to be the perfect shrub for a location where no others have succeeded.

RHODODENDRONS

**Producing stunning flower displays
in spring and summer, rhododendrons and azaleas
come in sizes to suit any garden.**

The genus *Rhododendron* encompasses hundreds of species of evergreen and deciduous shrubs, some of which grow as tall as trees, while others remain dwarf. All belong to the Ericaceae family, which includes heaths and heathers, gaultherias, pieris, pernettyas, and vacciniums.

The word rhododendron derives from the Greek *rhodon,* meaning rose, and *dendron,* a tree. In the seventeenth century, the first rhododendrons to be cultivated were the alpen roses *Rhododendron ferrugineum* and *R. hirsutum.*

The Swedish botanist Linnaeus created the genus *Rhododendron,* as well as a separate genus that he called *Azalea.* Much later, another botanist, George Don, noticed that there was no botanical difference between rhododendrons and azaleas, so the genus *Azalea* was eliminated. Nevertheless, azalea is still used as the common name for some *Rhododendron* species and hybrids.

The majority of rhododendrons are evergreen shrubs, but azaleas (in the wild at least) are mostly deciduous. This distinction is somewhat blurred by the fact that there is a large group of so-called evergreen Japanese azaleas that are popularly grown in home gardens. However, these are not true evergreens, as leaves that are formed on the lower parts of the shoots in the spring begin to fall in autumn.

Cultivated rhododendrons come mainly from the Himalayas, China, Tibet, India, Myanmar, and New Guinea, as well as the eastern United States. In addition, several types of azaleas and some rhododendrons are native to Europe.

General features

Rhododendrons and azaleas are prized for their flower clusters, which come in every color except blue. Contrasting spots or marbling may appear in the mouth of the flowers or on the petals.

Flowers are either tubular-, funnel-, bell-, or broadly bowl-shaped, and they may be borne in clusters or singly. The size of the blooms varies from ¾ in (2 cm) to 6 in (15 cm) wide, and from ¾ in (2 cm) to 4 in (10 cm) long. Most rhododendrons and azaleas blossom in spring and early summer, but *R. mucronulatum* blossoms

▼ **Spring show** Few sights are as impressive as a massed display of evergreen rhododendrons and azaleas. If they are given acid soil, shelter from winds, and dappled shade, they will bring forth brilliantly colored blooms amid handsome foliage year after year.

Rhododendron impeditum
species rhododendron

Rhododendron orbiculare species rhododendron

Rhododendron yakushimanum species rhododendron

Rhododendron 'Bow Bells'
medium-sized rhododendron hybrid

Rhododendron 'Crest' ('Hawk Crest') medium-sized rhododendron hybrid

Rhododendron 'Mrs. G.W. Leak' tall rhododendron hybrid

Rhododendron 'Sappho' very tall rhododendron hybrid

in midwinter (in mild climates), and *R. auriculatum* flowers in midsummer or late summer.

Fragrance is not common to all rhododendrons, but some have a powerful, sweet scent — for instance, *R. luteum,* a yellow azalea of eastern Europe, exudes a heavenly perfume in late spring and early summer.

Rhododendron leaves are never divided into separate leaflets. Generally oval- to lance-shaped, they are frequently crowded toward the end of each season's growth, so the lower stems tend to be rather bare. Size varies enormously, from the small leaves, 1 in (2.5 cm) long, of *R. scintillans* to the huge, leathery ones of *R. sinogrande,* which can reach 2½ ft (75 cm) long.

The undersides of rhododendron leaves are commonly covered with soft felt or fine scales. These coatings may be silvery or a rich shade of rust brown, and serve as a useful characteristic to distinguish between similar species. The surface of the leaves is usually midgreen to dark green and is often glossy. Azaleas, on the other hand, primarily have matt, rough-textured foliage.

Modern hybrid rhododendrons and azaleas are likely to have more profuse flowers or larger trusses than the true species, and these may be produced over a longer period.

Choosing rhododendrons

The Pacific Northwest, with its mild and moist climate, is the ideal region for these shrubs, and virtually every species can flourish there, if given an acid soil and proper care. The more temperate parts of the Southeast are also hospitable, especially the upland and coastal areas where summer temperatures do not rise too high. In places where the winters are cold and the summers hot, such as the Midwest, gardeners will succeed only by carefully selecting plants.

Fortunately, there has been a concerted effort to produce rhododendrons that are adapted to specific regions. Northerners have benefited from the introduction of rhododendron 'P.J.M.' and the hybrids derived from it. These compact shrubs (to 6 ft/ 1.8 m high), which bear flowers in pleasant shades of pink, lavender, and white, are reliably hardy to zone 4, and bloom well even as far north as Minnesota.

Recently, a new group of very hardy (to zone 5) hybrids has been introduced. They include 'Lodestar' (white), 'Bali' (soft pink, with cream centers), and 'Canary Islands' (deep yellow).

Residents of the Gulf and lowland South should consider deciduous azaleas, especially the Carla hybrids, the Hines hybrids, and the southern Indica types. Of the broad-leaved rhododendrons, the Shammarello hybrids, such as 'Belle Heller,' are best suited for Southerners. They thrive to zone 8.

PLANTING RHODODENDRONS

When planting rhododendrons or azaleas on level ground where annual rainfall is moderate and where soil drainage is normal, set the top of the root ball flush with the soil surface (**1**).
On sloping sites (**2**), create a level plateau of soil and build up the perimeter slightly before planting, to capture the flow of downhill runoff. Where heavy rainfall or low-lying sites create waterlogging problems, plant on a mound about 4 in (10 cm) above the surrounding soil (**3**). Stake tall, unstable plants until their roots have spread sufficiently to balance them. If rabbits and other rodents are prevalent, guard young plants from bark damage with wire netting.

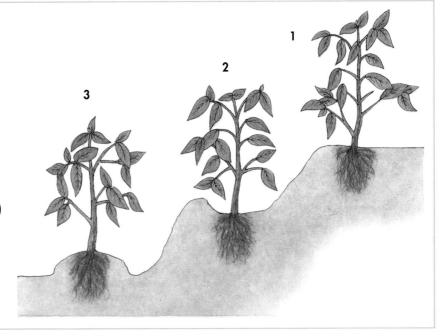

Botanists divide rhododendrons into several subgenera, but for gardeners the important categories are those that refer to the ultimate size of the plants.

Dwarf rhododendrons stand less than 3 ft (1 m) tall at maturity. They have leaves ¾-1¼ in (2-3 cm) long, and their flowers are borne in small clusters or singly at the tips of the branches. Most tolerate open sites, so they are fine for growing in a rock garden. One good choice is the species *R. campylogynum,* which has clusters of nodding, bell-like flowers, usually purple or pink. Also of interest is *R. scintillans,* a twiggy shrub with small leaves and funnel-shaped violet-blue flowers.

Dwarf hybrids are largely derived from *R. yakushimanum.* They include 'Dopey,' with red flowers; 'Hydon Ball,' with cream blossoms; and 'Pink Cherub,' with soft pink blooms.

Small rhododendrons reach 3-5 ft (1-5 m) high and are good for low mixed-bed plantings. Their flowers, which are about 1½-2½ in (4-6 cm) wide, are borne in small trusses.

Small species are available in many colors and include *R. ciliatum,* a bristly leaved, spreading shrub with profuse clusters of pale pink bell flowers; *R. haematodes,* a distinctive plant with funnel-shaped blood-red flowers and leathery leaves that have orange-brown felty undersides; and *R. racemosum,* which produces a mass of pale pink to almost white flowers against grayish leaves.

Small rhododendron hybrids are also popular, particularly 'Blue Tit,' which has pale lavender-blue flowers, and 'Chink,' which has pale yellow blossoms. If you prefer brighter colors, try the large scarlet flowers of 'Elizabeth,' the orange-red blooms of 'Fabia Tangerine,' or the violet ones of 'Blue Bird.'

Medium rhododendrons grow up to 10 ft (3 m) in height and spread to about 8 ft (2.5 m) wide. Their flowers are 1½-3 in (4-7.5 cm) wide, and their leaves are 4-6 in (10-15 cm) long. These plants add mass to mixed beds or a small wooded area.

Attractive species include the whitish-pink *R. aberconwayi* and the early-flowering primrose-yellow *R. lutescens.* Valued for its almost circular leaves, *R. orbiculare* has broad pink flowers.

Medium-sized hybrids are varied in both flower color and flower shape. For example, 'Blue Peter' bears broad cobalt-violet flowers, 'Bow Bells' carries bell-like pink flowers, and 'Crest' has wide primrose-yellow flowers.

Tall rhododendrons generally grow 10-15 ft (3-4.5 m) high and up to 12 ft (3.5 m) wide. They exhibit large flower clusters, 3-4 in (8-10 cm) wide, and have leaves that are 5-7 in (13-18 cm) long. If you have the space, these shrubs offer an eye-catching display of blossoms and provide a lush backdrop of year-round foliage.

If you need plants for informal hedges, look at *R. rubiginosum.* It is an upright shrub with lilac-pink flowers and leaves that have rust-brown scales on their undersides. Or, consider *R. thomsonii,* which has blood-red bell flowers, and *R. wardii,* with its loose clusters of yellow flowers.

There are dozens of tall hybrid rhododendrons from which to choose. The native North American species *R. catawbiense,* the Catawba rhododendron, may attain a height of 18 ft (5.4 m) over time. Though its flowers are an uninspiring lilac-purple, this species has given rise to a large number of hardy hybrids and cultivars, including 'Album' (white, hardy to zone 4), 'Boursalt' (lavender, to zone 4), 'Nova Zembla' (red, to zone 4), and 'Roseum Elegans' (lavender-pink, to zone 4). Other large rhododendrons include the blush-white 'Gomer

Rhododendron 'Blue Peter'
medium-sized rhododendron hybrid

DEADHEADING

Snap off the spent flower cluster with your hand, leaving the growth buds at the base intact. Though time-consuming, deadheading diverts energy from wasteful seed production into next year's flower and foliage buds.

Waterer,' and the peach 'Lady Clementine Mitford.'

Too expansive for the small garden, some giant rhododendrons are better set at a woodland edge or used as an evergreen backdrop to more delicate plantings. On moist but well-drained and cool soils, *R. maximum,* the rosebay, may grow into a huge 30-ft (9-m) treelike shrub. This rose-flowered evergreen is native to the central and southern Appalachian region, yet is hardy from zones 3-7. Other notable hybrids are *R. Catawbiense* 'Album,' with white flowers, and *R.c.* 'Purpureum,' which has dark pink to purple blooms.

Another possibility is *R. arboreum.* This species can also reach 30 ft (9 m) high after 20 years or more. It resembles a tree, with red, pink, or white flowers in large clusters. Likewise, many of the Exbury series hybrids can grow to substantial heights.

Deciduous azaleas are free-flowering and colorful shrubs, producing masses of clustered trumpet flowers in almost every shade of pink, red, white, or yellow and orange. Mauves and purples, however, are not common.

These plants can reach up to 12 ft (3.5 m) in height, but the majority are less than half this size. Their flowers are usually

1½-2½ in (4-6 cm) wide and may be scented. For almost any garden, *R. vaseyi* is a delightful open shrub that bears soft pink flowers on bare stems before its leaves appear; the foliage assumes fiery red tints in the fall.

There are several groups of deciduous azalea hybrids, cataloged according to parentage.

❏ Ghent hybrids were first bred in Belgium, using *R. luteum* as the main parent; many of the hybrids are scented. The tubular flowers are brilliantly colored and flare to 1½-2½ in (4-6 cm) across the mouth. Their leaves turn russet in the fall.

❏ Knap Hill and Exbury hybrid azaleas, bred in Great Britain, have been developed from many species. They are brightly colored plants with large trusses of scentless, broad-mouthed flowers, 2-3 in (5-7.5 cm) wide. Leaves often unfurl with bronze tints that turn orange-red or bronze-purple in the fall.

❏ Mollis hybrids, of Japanese parentage but first bred in Belgium and Holland, have funnel-shaped, unscented flowers in vivid colors. Their narrow, hairy leaves acquire rich fall tints.

❏ Glen Dale hybrids are a group of 400 azaleas developed at the United States Department of Agriculture (USDA) Plant Introduction Station in Maryland for use in the Middle Atlantic States. These compact plants are hardy to zone 6 and produce huge trusses of pink, purple-red, and white blossoms.

Evergreen azaleas were first bred in Japan and are sometimes called Japanese azaleas. Traditionally, their color range was more restricted than other azalea or rhododendron groups, and was limited to reds, mauves, pinks, and whites. For example, *R. kaempferi,* called the torch azalea, exhibits showy salmon to brick-red flowers. Traditional hybrid groups include:

❏ Kaempferi hybrids are showy and vigorous plants, laden with richly colored, wide-mouthed flowers that cover up the foliage.

❏ Kurume hybrids, such as the popular 'Kirin,' are smothered with pink blossoms in spring. They are mostly mound-forming shrubs with a very dense habit.

New groups of hybrids, however, are expanding into more vibrant palettes:

❏ Girard hybrids were developed in Geneva, Ohio. They offer large, colorful flowers, in whites, oranges, crimsons, and purples, and exceptional cold hardiness (to zone 5).

Suitable sites and soils

To successfully cultivate rhododendrons and azaleas, you must have acid soil, no higher than pH6, that is rich in humus. Well-drained sandy loam is the most suitable type. Do not try to grow them in alkaline soils. A thin, sandy soil will need the addition of plenty of humus-forming material, such as leaf mold, peat moss, or garden compost.

Species rhododendrons and evergreen azaleas prefer semi-shaded situations — wooded settings are ideal, but in a small garden they will thrive in dappled shade below a single tree or among other tall shrubs. However, such canopy trees or shrubs must not have shallow roots that will compete with the rhododendrons for moisture and nutrients. Although hybrid rhododendrons are more robust and tolerate open sites, they do better in semi-shade, especially in the South.

Above all, place the shrubs where they will be protected from strong, drying winds in all seasons. In coastal areas, do not expose them to sea breezes; build windbreaks to protect the plants if necessary.

Early-flowering types must not be exposed to harsh spring frosts either, so don't plant them in a frost pocket or in sites that face east. Early-morning sun after a night frost is especially dangerous to these shrubs, since sudden thawing can damage the buds.

Deciduous azaleas are somewhat less demanding shrubs and prefer an open site. Provided the soil can be kept moist (by regular

Rhododendron 'Blue Danube' evergreen azalea Vuykiana hybrid

Rhododendron 'Vuyk's Rosy Red' evergreen azalea Vuykiana hybrid

watering if necessary), scaly, small-leaved deciduous azaleas will tolerate full sun. As a rough guide, the larger and more glossy the leaves, the more shade rhododendrons and azaleas require.

Planting methods

Container-grown plants can be set out at any time of year that your climate permits. The widest selection will be available from garden centers in early spring to midspring — the most popular time for planting, though fall is also suitable. Since the roots of container-grown shrubs will not be disturbed unduly when you plant, you can wait to buy them until late spring. By then the flower buds are showing some color, ensuring that the plant matches its label and your needs.

Choose a site where soil moisture is average. Position the top of the root ball flush with the surface of the surrounding soil. Incorporate a slow-release shrub fertilizer into the soil as you fill in the space around the root ball, following the instructions on the fertilizer label.

At sites where there is a chance that the soil will become water-logged following heavy rain, plant rhododendrons with the top of their root ball about 4 in (10 cm) above the surrounding soil. Bank up the soil with a rake to form a gentle slope away from the main stem.

In dry soils, plant rhododendrons about 4 in (10 cm) deeper than the surrounding soil, leaving them in a shallow depression. Rainfall or artificial irrigation will then form a puddle in the depression, ensuring that the roots get the most water possible.

When placing rhododendrons on a sloping site, bank up the soil at the lower perimeter of the root ball to catch downhill runoff.

Spread a generous layer of

mulch of leaf mold, garden compost, or shredded bark around each shrub. Water newly planted rhododendrons frequently in spring and summer until they are well established and growing strongly.

Planting in containers If your garden has only alkaline soil, azaleas and dwarf or small rhododendrons can be planted in tubs and other large containers outdoors. Use a potting soil designed for acid-loving plants, as other blends may be too alkaline. Stand the containers in a lightly shaded spot that offers shelter from winds and morning sun.

Routine aftercare

Every year or two, mulch the plant's root-run area with leaf mold, garden compost, or shredded bark. No fertilizer is needed.

If you live in an area with hard water that contains lime, and you are growing an azalea or rhododendron in a tub, do not use it for watering. Instead, rely on rainwater, which is softer and lime-free — or even acidic, depending on the region. However, if the shrubs are set in open ground, hard tap water can occasionally be used on these shrubs.

After flowering, remove all dead flower heads. Rhododendrons and azaleas do not require regular pruning, but spindly young plants may be lightly trimmed to make them bushy. In spring, before new growth starts, prune the stems by about one-third of their length, cutting just above a bud. The buds may be very small and difficult to see.

Straggly plants, or old neglected ones that need rejuvenation, may be cut back in early spring to any point about 3 ft (1 m) above the ground. No flower buds will be visible, but shoots will grow from the stumps. After such severe pruning, it will take up to

Rhododendron vaseyi deciduous azalea species

Rhododendron kaempferi evergreen azalea species

Rhododendron luteum deciduous azalea species; flowers

Rhododendron luteum deciduous azalea species; fall foliage

Rhododendron 'Klondyke' deciduous azalea Knap Hill hybrid

Rhododendron 'Narcissiflora' deciduous azalea Ghent hybrid double-flowered

Rhododendron 'Hotspur' deciduous azalea Knap Hill hybrid

Rhododendron 'Palestrina' evergreen azalea Kaempferi hybrid

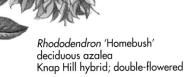

Rhododendron 'Homebush' deciduous azalea Knap Hill hybrid; double-flowered

PROPAGATING RHODODENDRONS

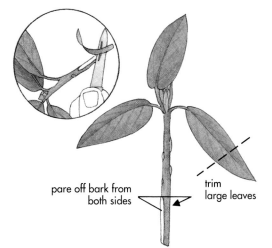

pare off bark from both sides

trim large leaves

1 Prepare semihardwood cuttings by removing shoots, 6 in (15 cm) long, from the current year's wood. If the leaves are longer than 3 in (7.5 cm), cut them in half. Pare off slivers of bark.

wounded stem

2 For layering, strip off leaves 9 in (23 cm) from a branch tip. Cut a slice out of the underside of the branch, then anchor the wounded area in a shallow peat-and-sand-filled hole and stake the tip upright.

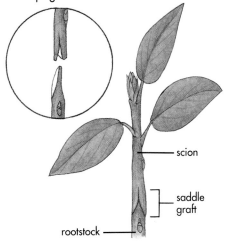

scion

saddle graft

rootstock

3 Hybrid rhododendrons that are difficult to root can be propagated by saddle grafting onto *R. ponticum* rootstocks. Bind the graft union with plastic tape.

3 years or more before flowers reappear.

Propagation

There are two main ways of propagating rhododendrons.

Layering is the simplest method and is also the fastest way to produce a new flowering plant. It is more easily done with old plants, on which the branches have become flexible, than on the new growth of young plants.

In midfall, bend a branch until it reaches the ground 9-12 in (23-30 cm) from the tip. Strip off the leaves at this point. Cut a sliver off the branch on the underside, or twist the branch to injure the surface tissue.

Dig a hole, 3-4 in (7.5-10 cm) deep, and fill it halfway with moist seed-starting mix, or equal parts by volume of peat and sharp sand. Bend the branch to the ground and set the wounded area in the hole.

Secure the branch with a bent piece of galvanized wire, 8-10 in (20-25 cm) long, and fill the hole with a potting soil used for acid-loving plants. Stake the tip of the branch upright. Cover the area around it with a 1-in (2.5-cm) mulch of garden compost.

Water the area thoroughly. After 2 years, the stem will have rooted and you will be able to sever the young plant and transplant it to a permanent position.

Semihardwood cuttings, taken in midsummer to early fall, are used to produce the greatest number of new plants.

With pruning shears, cut off shoots, 6 in (15 cm) long, that have formed in the current year, close to the parent stem. Remove all the leaves from the lower part of the shoots and cut each one straight across, just below a leaf node, so that the resulting cutting is about 2-4 in (5-10 cm) long.

Wound the lower tip of the cuttings by paring off two narrow slivers of bark, 1 in (2.5 cm) long, from each side. Dust each cutting's base with hormone rooting powder. Then, root the cuttings in pots filled with a mixture of 2 parts fine sand and 1 part peat and place them in a cold frame. When the cuttings have rooted, pot them up singly in well-drained, peat-enriched soil. Grow on for about 2 years in a nursery before planting outdoors.

Some hybrid rhododendrons are difficult to propagate by layering or cuttings. They are best reproduced in midspring by grafting a scion of the hybrid onto some vigorous rootstock such as *R. ponticum.*

▼ **Deciduous azaleas** Fully hardy and valued for their soft shades of salmon-pink, apricot, orange, and yellow, deciduous azaleas will tolerate full sun if the soil is kept moist.

DWARF CONIFERS

With evergreen foliage in many colors and textures, low-maintenance dwarf conifers make elegant focal points, graceful backdrops, and excellent ground cover.

Dwarf conifers were once grown mainly by specialists. Modern breeding techniques, however, have resulted in new types that are useful to the home gardener. They are now being seen increasingly in foundation plantings, rock gardens, and mixed beds. In addition, they make attractive specimen trees as well as focal points for window boxes and patio or rooftop planters.

Forest conifers produce tiny flowers in scalelike structures known as *strobili,* which, on female trees, mature to the well-known cones. Dwarf conifers rarely flower and fruit.

There is no clear-cut division between dwarf conifers and their tree relatives. The term dwarf refers both to truly dwarf varieties, those that are 3 ft (1 m) in height and under, and the very slow-growing types that remain of low stature for many years before reaching treelike proportions at maturity, some 20 years later.

When buying conifers, you can judge the vigor of an unfamiliar variety by the size of the plant for sale. Garden centers rarely keep plants around for too many years before selling them, so their sales stock is generally no more than 5 years old. Therefore, a nursery conifer 3 ft (1 m) tall is probably fast-growing, whereas a specimen 6 in (15 cm) tall is likely to remain dwarf.

Conifer leaves

Typically, conifer leaves are long and stiff, sometimes with a sharp tip (the reason they are called needles), but some have a much softer texture. Several genera of conifers develop two different types of foliage — juvenile and adult, although some varieties never produce the adult type. The juvenile leaves are usually long and slender, and the adult ones, tiny and scalelike.

Most conifers are evergreen, but there are several deciduous species, such as the larches *(Larix)* and the swamp cypresses *(Taxodium distichum).* These have no true dwarf forms.

Leaf color may vary, with the brightest hues appearing on young growth in spring and early summer. A few dwarf conifers acquire bronze or purplish tints on their old winter foliage.

Choosing dwarf conifers

There are dwarf types of almost every major genus of conifer: *Abies* (firs), *Cedrus* (cedars), *Chamaecyparis* (false cypresses), *Cryptomeria* (Japanese cedars), *Cupressus* (cypresses), *Juniperus* (junipers), *Picea* (spruces), *Taxus* (yews), *Thuja* (arborvitaes), and *Tsuga* (hemlocks). They can be found in a range of colors, including greens, yellows, blues, and grays. They also vary in growth habits: upright, bushy, weeping, spreading, or prostrate.

Even some huge forest conifers, such as redwood *(Sequoia),* have dwarf varieties suitable for small gardens. *Sequoia sempervirens* 'Adpressa,' for example, makes a low pyramid of gray-green foliage that takes 10 years to grow 4 ft (1.2 m) high.

If you are interested in dwarf conifers, look through plant catalogs or visit a garden center; you will find many dozens of choices. Some of these plants are valued for their wonderful foliage color; others are noted for their individual shapes and sizes.

Truly dwarf conifers are suitable for planting in rock gardens, in isolated groups in a lawn, or in any open space. You can choose the rounded *Cryptomeria japonica* 'Vilmoriniana,' whose green

◀ **Mixed conifers** Dwarf conifers look best when several are planted together to present contrasts of shapes, sizes, textures, and colors. Here, upright Lawson cypresses provide lush golden and rich greens, while a slender juniper column at the back offers a touch of gray-blue. In the foreground, a prostrate juniper spreads its apple-green branches.

Abies procera
'Glauca Prostrata'
dwarf noble fir

Chamaecyparis lawsoniana
'Minima Aurea'
dwarf Lawson cypress

Chamaecyparis obtusa
'Nana Gracilis'
dwarf Hinoki cypress

Chamaecyparis thyoides
'Ericoides'
dwarf white cypress

foliage turns red-purple in winter; the cone-shaped and golden *Chamaecyparis lawsoniana* 'Minima Aurea'; the blue-green 'Minima Glauca'; and the dense golden *Thuja occidentalis* 'Rheingold.' All of these are a good match for heathers, as are the gnarled blue-gray *Pinus pumila,* the blue-gray spruce *Picea mariana* 'Nana,' and the dark green, yellow-tipped, rounded shrub *Thuja plicata* 'Rogersii.'

Because they grow slowly, some dwarf conifers do well in window boxes and tubs. These are the dense blue-gray *Cedrus deodara* 'Pygmaea,' the narrow blue-gray *Juniperus communis* 'Compressa,' and the cone-shaped bright green *Picea glauca* 'Conica' (the dwarf Alberta spruce).

The more vigorous dwarf conifers, including *Picea abies* 'Nidiformis,' with tiered dark green branches, and the pendulous blue-green *Cedrus libani* 'Sar-

gentii,' are fine for mixed beds, as well as shrub or specimen planting. Many junipers have a creeping habit; these are often used for specimen planting and for carpeting sunny banks. Among this group are *Juniperus procumbens* 'Variegata,' with its bluish-green leaves streaked with cream; *J. horizontalis* 'Wiltoni,' which has silver-blue leaves and tolerates heat and poor soils; and *J. virginiana* 'Gray Owl,' with its silvery gray foliage.

Site and soil

Dwarf conifers grow well in sunny positions or partial shade, but the golden- and silver-leaved types do best in full sun. The dark green varieties tolerate full shade, although their foliage may become rather dull.

Most conifers favor an exposed site, but a few, such as *Chamaecyparis pisifera* 'Plumosa Rogersii,' must be positioned where

there are no cold, drying winds to burn their leaves and turn them brown. Pale, creamy yellow varieties are apt to scorch in open, sunny positions because of the strong winds that usually prevail in this type of setting. They will flourish, however, in the protection of dappled shade.

Some dwarf conifers, for instance the *Thujas,* require a moist soil, but others, especially the junipers, prefer dry conditions, and thus are invaluable to gardeners in the arid West.

Conifers generally thrive in poorer soils than many other trees. Whenever possible, though, provide them with good garden soil. Most appreciate slightly acid conditions. However, some species, such as junipers and yews, grow well on alkaline soils.

Planting

Usually, dwarf conifers are sold in plastic containers. As a result,

Juniperus squamata
'Blue Star'
dwarf juniper

Picea abies
'Nidiformis'
dwarf Norway spruce

Pinus mugo 'Mops'
dwarf mountain pine

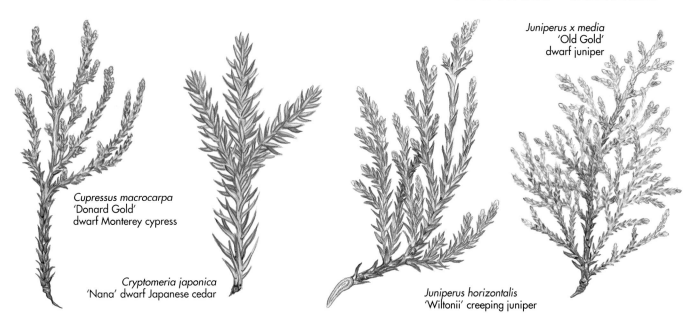

Cupressus macrocarpa
'Donard Gold'
dwarf Monterey cypress

Cryptomeria japonica
'Nana' dwarf Japanese cedar

Juniperus x media
'Old Gold'
dwarf juniper

Juniperus horizontalis
'Wiltonii' creeping juniper

they can be successfully planted at any time of year when the ground is not frozen, since the roots won't be disturbed unduly. However, avoid setting them out from late spring to early fall, as the high temperatures are liable to dry out the root ball.

Dig the planting site and remove all weeds. If you are planting in a lawn, cut out and discard a circle of turf 2 ft (60 cm) in diameter. If grass is left around the base of a conifer, it may starve the roots of moisture and nutrients, causing dieback. Poor soils benefit from the addition of organic material and a dressing of a general fertilizer.

Make the planting hole a little larger than the conifer's root ball and fork over the soil in the bottom of the hole. Knock the conifer out of its container and stand it in the hole so that the top of the root ball is level with the soil surface.

Don't disturb the main cluster of fibrous roots, but gently ease away any strong roots that are spiraling around the outside of the root ball. Face them outward so that they will anchor themselves well in the soil. If these girdling roots are left wrapped around the root ball, the plant may never securely establish itself and therefore may shift with every strong wind.

When the conifer is positioned, press fresh soil around the root ball and then water the plant well. With upright varieties that need support, insert a strong wooden stake against the side of the root ball before filling in the hole with soil. (Never push a stake through the root ball itself.) Tie the stake to the plant's stem. In exposed sites, protect newly planted conifers from winds by constructing a windbreak. In winter, bind conifers to protect them from snow.

Aftercare
In general, dwarf conifers need no routine aftercare. However, occasionally dwarf conifers must be trimmed lightly to improve their shape. Low-growing prostrate cultivars, for example, may send out overly vigorous, upward-growing shoots that ruin a uniform effect. These can be removed without harming the plant. Junipers in general become untidy with age and need trimming.

Any pruning should be done when the plant is dormant. Use pruning shears to make unobtrusive, clean cuts near the base of side branches — new shoots may not develop from the cut stems.

An upright conifer can produce two or more leading shoots; these can spoil the plant's shape. Remove any weak or poorly shaped leaders, leaving just one.

If you want to restrict upward growth, you can also cut out the

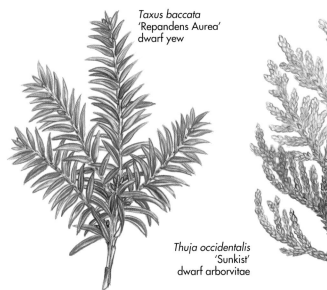

Taxus baccata
'Repandens Aurea'
dwarf yew

Thuja occidentalis
'Sunkist'
dwarf arborvitae

Tsuga canadensis
'Jeddeloh'
dwarf Eastern hemlock

PROTECTING DWARF CONIFERS

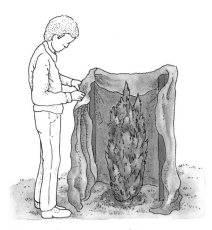

1 In windy areas, stake newly planted, upright conifers and tie them in with plastic strap-and-buckle ties. Those sold for use on roses are a better size for dwarf conifers than the larger tree ties. Or, tie the conifers loosely to stakes with soft garden twine.

2 As an alternative to staking, put up a temporary windbreak to prevent wind buffeting, which would prevent the roots from establishing themselves. Burlap stapled to wooden stakes is best. Some gentle wind movement, however, can be beneficial.

3 Protect upright conifers from snow-load damage by tying up branches with nylon or rot-resistant twine in late fall. Ensure that all the main branches are supported so that any snow that does settle cannot weigh them down and ruin the shape.

tip of the leader at any desired height. However, this type of pruning encourages side branching and changes a tapering crown into a rounded one — an undesirable feature in many firs and spruces, which have a natural cone-shaped growth habit.

Wear gloves when trimming conifers, as some types have spiny scales on their stems and the leaves may be sharp-tipped.

Also, wear old clothing when handling clippings, as the cut wood exudes sticky resin.

If a conifer has been staked at planting time, remove the support as soon as the root ball feels firm in the ground. Once the tree is securely anchored, the wind's motion actually encourages stronger rooting. In areas where heavy snowfalls are commonplace in winter, wrap upright conifers with twine in late fall. This precaution will help support the branches against snow load. Once bent, conifer branches are not likely to recover their shape.

Propagation

As a result of a genetic defect, most dwarf conifers can never attain their parents' stature. In addition, they cannot be reproduced successfully by seed; they must be cloned — a piece of the parent is removed and grafted onto a compatible rootstock in order to develop into a new (but genetically identical) specimen. This time-consuming, painstaking technique is beyond the skills of most home gardeners.

In many cases, though, dwarf conifers can be propagated successfully by rooting hardwood cuttings taken with a heel.

In late summer or early fall, insert cuttings in a moisture-retentive but well-drained rooting medium. Place them in a cold frame or bottom-heated propagation box. Hormone rooting powder may hasten rooting, but is not essential. The time it takes for roots to develop varies among the species. Some will root within weeks, others may not do so until the following spring.

◀ **Carpeting junipers** Ideal for sunny banks, the prostrate junipers thrive on alkaline and dry soils, spreading their branches wide and demanding little attention. Numerous varieties are available, with aromatic foliage in shades of green and golden yellow.

OLD AND MODERN ROSES

Roses have been long admired for their form, color, and fragrance. Today, breeding has introduced greater disease-resistance, hardiness, and a host of new selections.

The classification of roses is quite complicated and subject to change, but it is useful to know the distinguishing characteristics of the major different types.

True roses belong to the genus *Rosa* and in turn are members of the enormous Rosaceae family. Their relatives include plants as diverse as apple, cherry, cotoneaster, kerria, and raspberry.

More than one hundred rose species have been identified, but it is their innumerable varieties and hybrids that dominate our gardens today. While the modern hybrid tea rose has the best-known flower shape and growth habit, there are a remarkable number of variations within the genus *Rosa,* especially among the old garden roses that are now gaining renewed popularity.

Old garden roses

This important category encompasses a number of different types that are of extremely diverse parentage; the only requirement for membership is that the cultivar must belong to a group that originated before 1867, the year in which the first hybrid tea rose (the forerunner of our modern everblooming roses) was introduced. Once available only from a few specialist growers, old garden roses are now offered for sale in nursery catalogs.

As a result of their varied parentage, old garden roses differ greatly in flower shape and in growth habit, from tiny dwarfs to sprawling giants. Typically, however, old garden roses bloom in subtler, softer shades than modern roses, and are almost always strongly perfumed. There are only a few yellow roses among the cultivars that are hardy north of zone 8. That color was not introduced into the hardy roses until the advent of the hybrid tea. In addition, some old roses have *quartered* flowers, which means that their flattened center is composed of densely crowded petals arranged in a cross pattern.

Sadly, most cold-hardy old garden roses flower mainly in early summer, though some types, notably the hybrid perpetuals, bloom again sporadically until frost. Many of those that do not bloom again, nevertheless, are attractive in foliage, and thus are valuable in mixed flower or shrub beds or as specimen shrubs.

Alba roses have sweetly scented white or pink summer flowers; these are carried on relatively thornless stems among grayish leaves. The shrubs grow up to 6 ft (1.8 m) in height, and are suitable for training up trellises or on espaliers against walls. 'Celeste' has semidouble soft pink blooms; 'Königin von Dänemark' has quartered pink blooms.

Bourbon roses have large globe-shaped blooms packed with petals, generally in rich shades of pink; these are strongly scented and repeat-flowering. The open or floppy bushes reach 4-6 ft (1.2-1.8 m) high. 'Boule de Neige' opens from crimson buds to double white flowers; 'Mme Isaac Pereire,' one of the most fragrant of all roses, bears large, quartered deep pink blooms.

Centifolia roses, also known as cabbage or Provence roses, are tall bushes, 4-6 ft (1.2-1.8 m) in height, with floppy branches that need staking. 'Fantin Latour' has double blush-pink flowers that become deeper toward the center; 'Centifolia Variegata' has pink-and-white-striped petals.

China roses are smaller plants, usually no more than 3-4 ft (1-1.2 m) tall, with an airy growth habit. Their flowers appear among dainty leaves in succession throughout summer and fall. The clusters of semidouble pink

◄ **Colorful covering** Prostrate roses are ideal for carpeting banks and for creating weed-smothering cover. The best of these (often listed in nursery catalogs as "ground cover roses") produce a mat of foliage much denser than would be desirable on an ordinary climbing rose.

Rosa 'Silver Jubilee'
Hybrid tea rose

Rosa 'Constance Spry'
Modern shrub rose

Rosa 'Nevada'
Modern shrub rose

Rosa
'Glenfiddich'
Floribunda rose

Rosa
'Fairy Changeling'
Polyantha rose

flowers on 'Old Blush' may continue to bloom until Christmas in mild climates.

Damask roses are open and floppy in habit, with thorny stems that reach a height of 5-6 ft (1.5-1.8 m). Their strongly scented flowers are short-lived and are usually followed by long, slender, hairy hips in late summer. The popular 'Mme Hardy' bears clusters of quartered white blooms with a small green center.

Portland roses (or perpetual damasks) are similar to damasks, but they have a compact habit.

Gallica roses are fairly upright, suckering shrubs with rough textured leaves and strongly scented pink, crimson, or red-purple flowers that appear in a single flush. Varieties include the old 'Rosa Mundi,' with showy crimson flowers striped with white, and 'Tuscany Superb,' with semidouble crimson-purple flowers and golden stamens.

Hybrid perpetual roses are derived by crossing bourbons, portlands, and Chinas. They are predecessors of the modern hybrid tea roses. Although these are quite hardy, they need protection from cold winds. The upright, vigorous shrubs, 4-6 ft (1.2-1.8 m) tall, bear large double flowers, singly or in clusters, from early summer until fall. 'Reine des Violettes' is a fine choice, with mauve-purple flowers set against gray-tinged foliage; it needs hard pruning.

Moss roses can be identified easily by their mossy outgrowths on the stems and flower buds. Richly fragrant flowers, double or semidouble, are borne singly or in small clusters on shrubs that vary from compact types ('General Kleber,' fully double, soft mauve-pink) to vigorous pillar roses ('William Lobb,' double, crimson, fading to lavender).

Species roses are the wild roses from which all others have been bred. They are generally resistant to pests and diseases. These roses are deciduous, often with elegant foliage, and produce usually single blooms in one flush of flowers in summer. Many have outstanding fall hips (*R. × alba,*

Rosa rugosa 'Alba'
Rugosa rose

Rosa 'Charles de Mills'
Gallica rose

Rosa
'Baby Sunrise'
Miniature rose

Rosa xanthina 'Canary Bird'
Species rose

Rosa 'Ferdinand Pichard'
Bourbon rose

Rosa 'Eyepaint'
Floribunda

ROSE GROWTH TYPES

The classification of roses that defines features such as flower shape and parentage is of little value when choosing a rose to fill a certain space in the garden or to complement an existing grouping of plants or another garden feature.

The types of growth habit and form (the shape and the branching patterns) shown here are more important to the gardener. There are miniature roses for containers or patio plantings, medium-sized shrubs for mixed beds or focal displays, and climbers or ramblers for walls, trellises, and pillars.

Bush rose/hybrid tea
Rosa 'Wendy Cussons'

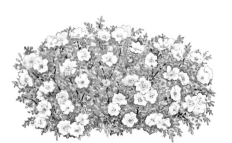

Shrub rose (modern)
Rosa 'Frühlingsgold'

Ground cover rose
Rosa 'Nozomi'

Miniature rose
Rosa 'Starina'

Pillar rose
(compact rambler)
Rosa
'American Pillar'

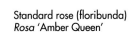

Standard rose (floribunda)
Rosa 'Amber Queen'

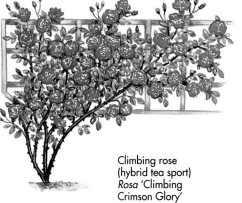

Weeping standard rose (rambler)
Rosa 'Excelsa'

Climbing rose
(hybrid tea sport)
Rosa 'Climbing
Crimson Glory'

R. × *highodensis, R. moyesii,* and *R. rugosa).*

Tea roses are not cold hardy, but are superb plants in zones 8 and 9 — areas where summers are hot and humid. They have elegant, high-centered flowers with a scent similar to that of freshly picked tea leaves. These roses are also everbloomers, producing flowers from spring through late fall if the weather is fine. This group offers many lovely yellow-flowered cultivars, such as the golden 'Lady Hillingdon.'

Modern shrub roses

Breeding work carried out during this century has increased the variety of roses enormously. In the best new roses, all the good characteristics of the old types have been selected and improved, while poor qualities, such as straggly growth, susceptibility to disease, and nonrepeat flowering, have been reduced.

Hybrid musk roses are only distantly related to the old musk rose *Rosa moschata.* They are tall, free-flowering shrubs that display large clusters of small, fragrant, single, semidouble, or double blooms from summer until fall frosts.

Rugosa roses are derived mainly from *Rosa rugosa;* they form dense, thorny bushes, 5-8 ft (1.5-2.4 m) in height, with wrinkled (rugose) leaves. Their delicately shaped single, semidouble, or double blooms appear in succession all summer and fall. Rugosas have large, rounded, and very showy hips. The shrubs are ultra-hardy (to zone 2 in some instances) and suitable for hedging.

Other shrub roses, with dozens of named varieties, grow into medium to large bushes, more than 4 ft (1.2 m) tall, and are of wide-spreading habit. They are too large for formal rose beds, but are excellent for shrubberies and mixed beds and for use as specimen shrubs. Nearly all are repeat-flowering, from early summer until fall, usually with clusters of blooms.

Modern bush roses

Recent reclassification of roses has introduced this new group. The bush roses incorporate the hundreds of roses previously listed (and still commonly referred to) as hybrid teas, floribundas, grandifloras, and polyanthas.

NEW ENGLISH ROSES

The British rose breeder and nurseryman David Austin has introduced a range of superb new roses that combine the beautiful shapes and floral forms, scents and subtle shades of old-fashioned gallica, damask, and centifolia roses with the wider color range, disease resistance, and rainproof blossoms of modern hybrid teas and floribundas.

Above all, new English roses have eliminated the most frequent criticism of old-fashioned roses, which is that they bloom only once a year — new English roses flower in succession all summer.

In this informal planting, the sweet-scented new English rose 'Graham Thomas' blends softly with aromatic sages and lavenders.

Bush roses are compact shrubs that bear flowers in succession through summer and early fall.

Floribunda roses, now called cluster-flowered bush roses, are bushy and branching plants that carry large clusters of semidouble or double flowers throughout the summer. When fully open, floribunda blooms reveal the boss of golden stamens at their center.

Floribundas usually grow to about 3 ft (90 cm) tall, but some varieties, often known as grandifloras, reach up to 7 ft (2.1 m) high and have characteristics of both floribundas and hybrid teas. Certain floribundas and grandifloras are grown as standards grafted onto a tall, unbranched main stem that carries a rounded head of branches.

The best-known grandiflora is 'Queen Elizabeth.' Its profuse pink flowers are displayed on robust stems. This rose may also be listed as a modern shrub rose.

Hybrid tea roses, now called large-flowered bush roses, are renowned for their large, elegant, high-centered, double blooms, which are generally borne one to a stem in succession. These are the best roses for cut flowers; they are especially robust, often with a powerful sweet scent.

Hybrid teas reach 2½-5 ft (75 cm-1.5 m) in height and have

upright stems. They can be grown as bushes or standards.

Polyantha roses are smaller plants, growing only to 1-3 ft (30-90 cm) in height. Large clusters of profuse small flowers bloom in two main flushes, from early summer to midsummer, and again in early fall.

Miniature roses are dwarf forms, reaching just 6-15 in (15-38 cm) tall. In early summer to midsummer, and again in early fall, they produce tiny semidouble or double flowers in clusters similar to floribundas. Miniature standards are also grown.

Climbers and ramblers

There are two groups of climbing roses: recurrent (or repeat-flowering) and nonrecurrent types (ramblers).

Climbing roses are scrambling shrubs that cling by means of hooked thorns. They have a permanent aboveground framework of stiff stems that develop lateral flowering shoots. Once mature, they exhibit little or no growth from ground level.

These roses have large double, semidouble, or single flowers that are borne singly or in clusters from early summer to fall. The plants grow to 6-30 ft (1.8-9 m) in height and spread, and are best supported on wires or a wooden trellis set against a wall or fence. In addition, they can be grown up through a tree.

Pillar roses are less vigorous varieties of climbers that are trained on free-standing pillars, posts, or other vertical structures to form an upright mass of flowering stems.

Rambling roses are similar to climbers, but they lack the permanent framework of stems. They send up fresh shoots from ground level each year to replace those that have just finished flowering, as well as to support the following year's flowers. Ramblers, therefore, need careful yearly replacement pruning. They generally produce just one large flush of single, semidouble, or double flowers in clusters or trusses in midsummer. Plants reach 9-25 ft (2.7-7.5 m) in height and spread. Some varieties are grafted onto a single upright stem to form a weeping standard.

Ground cover roses

There is no official classification for ground cover roses, but nurseries often supply plants under this group. They may also call them landscape roses.

Ground cover roses are lax-stemmed ramblers, climbers, or climbing miniatures that are allowed to sprawl across the ground instead of being trained upward. Many hybrids, as well as a couple of disease-resistant, vigorous species roses, are especially well adapted to this use. In zone 8 and southward, the evergreen, white-or yellow-flowered *Rosa banksia* makes an excellent ground cover; farther north, *Rosa wichuraiana,* the memorial rose, serves the same purpose.

Soil and site

Roses are adaptable to most soil types except waterlogged clay. For best results, grow them in a medium-rich, well-drained but moisture-retentive, and slightly acid soil (pH of 6.5). They prefer an open, sunny site, but some climbers, such as the orange-pink 'Aloha' and the sulfur-yellow 'Mermaid,' will grow happily against a north-facing wall.

Although roses need air circulation, avoid planting them in very exposed sites where winds can loosen their roots and snap their stems.

Planting roses

Container-grown plants can be set out at any time of year, climate permitting, but bare-rooted roses should be planted during their dormant season. Most mail-order and garden-center sales take place in early spring, but late-fall planting is a possibility in areas where winters are mild.

Whether container-grown or bare-rooted, roses will normally occupy their site for many years, so it is worthwhile preparing the soil thoroughly beforehand. Dig the ground to at least a spade's depth, preferably double-digging if drainage is poor. Then, fork in a layer, 3-4 in (7.5-10 cm) deep, of organic material, garden compost, or leaf mold (use much

◀ **English rose** 'Charles Austin' is a new "old" rose, bred to resemble an old-fashioned shrub rose, except that it blooms throughout the summer. The fragrant apricot-yellow flowers, crammed with petals, are 4 in (10 cm) wide. They are borne on upright bushes about 4 ft (1.2 m) tall.

PLANTING ROSES

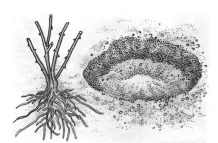

For bare-rooted roses whose roots grow in all directions, dig out circular holes, 2 ft (60 cm) in diameter and 10 in (25 cm) deep. Set the shrub in the center.

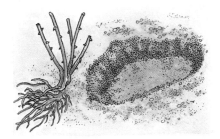

If the roots run in one direction, dig a fan-shaped hole, 1 ft (30 cm) wide, 5 in (12.5 cm) deep at the narrow stem end, and 10 in (25 cm) deep at the root end.

Stake newly planted standards by sinking a stake 2 ft (60 cm) deep; it should rise 6 in (15 cm) above the bud union.

Plant climbing roses 1 ft (30 cm) away from the base of a wall, with their roots pointing away from it, stems spread out.

▶ **Bud grafting, or budding.** Weeping standards are created by grafting scion buds of a rambler, such as 'Excelsa,' onto the rootstock and tall stem of a rugosa or briar rose. Standards are budded with bush rose varieties.

more on shallow sandy soils), with a handful of a general-purpose fertilizer, such as 5–10–5, for each sq yd/sq m. Rake the bed level and let it settle.

Try not to use a site where roses have been planted previously. Soil in which roses have been growing for more than 5 years can become "rose sick," and new roses often fail to thrive there. When no other space is available, change the soil in that area.

If bare-root roses can't be planted as soon as they arrive, unwrap and heel them into a shallow trench in the ground or keep them in a shed with a little moist soil over the roots. At planting time, make sure the roots are not dried out; if in doubt, dunk them in a mixture of mud and water or in a bucket of water for a couple of hours.

Examine the plants carefully. Using sharp pruning shears, remove any roots that are more than 10 in (25 cm) long, as well as any thick, coarse, or damaged roots. Do not trim the thin, fibrous feeding roots. In addition, cut back any dead, damaged, or weak stems to healthy wood just above outward-facing buds.

Dig out planting holes to accommodate the shape of the roots and spread a 2-in (5-cm) layer of planting mix over the base. Lay a stake across the hole to check the correct planting depth — the union of rootstock and stems on all modern shrub, bush, and climbing roses should be just below soil level (on light soil, the junction can be set as much as 2 in (5 cm) below soil level); old and species roses should be planted so that the old soil mark is level with the surrounding soil. Spread out the roots across the soil and begin to refill the hole, mixing the excavated soil with liberal amounts of some organic material, such as compost. Shake the rose gently up and down to make sure the planting mix fills all the root space, then press down the soil around the roots before filling up the hole with more planting mix.

Planting distances vary according to the type of rose. In general, bush roses should be spaced 2 ft (60 cm) apart, standards 3 ft (90 cm) apart, and shrub roses 4-5 ft (1.2-1.5 m) apart. Allow about

BUDDING: JOINING SCION AND ROOTSTOCK

1 Select as budwood a strong nonflowering shoot of the rose that you wish to propagate. (Do it in summer when the rootstock is ready.) Remove thorns and leaves, keeping ½ in (12 mm) of stalk.

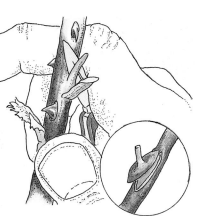

2 Make a T-shape cut, 1 in (2.5 cm) long and ½ in (12 mm) wide, in the rootstock bark just above the soil line (see step 3). Pry back the flaps. Slice an eye (inset) from the budwood of the selected stem.

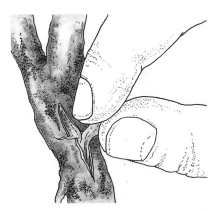

3 Holding the eye by the leaf stalk, gently remove any wood beneath its bark. Slide the eye, pointing upward, into the opened T-cut. Trim the upper edge of the eye even with the top of the T-cut.

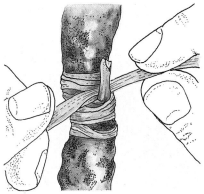

4 Close cut and wrap with raffia, knotting it on the opposite side. Successful budding shows as fresh green growth on the stem of the rootstock. In late winter, sever the new stock just above the bud.

teas and floribundas ('Etoile de Holland' and 'Iceberg'), bloom on lateral shoots of the previous year. After flowering, trim these back to strong new buds. During winter, remove any dead or weak shoots and cut leaders back to strong new extension shoots. At the same time, tie in these shoots to horizontal positions to encourage flower-bearing side shoots.

Prune ramblers in late summer or early fall; cut out their flowered shoots from the base and tie in replacement shoots, which will flower the following summer.

Old garden roses and species roses usually require only light pruning; trim them right after they finish blooming. Remove old and twiggy stems, tip the remaining shoots lightly to promote lateral growth, and shorten side shoots to about 3 in (7.5 cm).

Propagating roses
There are three ways of increasing roses — by seeds, by cuttings, and by a special grafting technique known as budding.

Only species roses breed true from seed, but they must be hand-pollinated. In the fall, extract the seeds from ripe hips, sow them in pots of seed-starting mix, and place the pots in a cold frame or other protected bed. Grow the seedlings on for a couple of years before planting them out.

Species roses and their hybrids, many old garden roses, ramblers,

7 ft (2.1 m) between vigorous climbers and 6-9 in (15-23 cm) between miniatures.

Routine maintenance
In the second year after planting, apply a commercial rose fertilizer after spring pruning and in early summer, following the manufacturer's directions. If needed, use quick-acting foliar feeds in early summer and midsummer.

Spread a 2-in (5-cm) layer of organic mulch over the root area in midspring, making sure the soil is moist. During dry spells, water the roots thoroughly, but avoid wetting open blooms.

Deadhead all roses as soon as their flowers fade, cutting the trusses back to the nearest leaf axil. Exceptions to this regime are the old roses, such as *R. rugosa,* that produce fall hips. Remove all suckers from grafted roses once they are large enough.

Pruning
Bush roses — hybrid teas, floribundas, polyanthas, standards, miniatures, and container-grown roses — should be pruned annually, in late winter or early spring. Aim to build up open-centered, well-balanced plants so that air and light can circulate. Cut back all dead, diseased, damaged, and weak stems to healthy wood, slanting all pruning cuts to outward-facing buds. Remove the weaker of two stems that cross or rub against each other.

Thereafter, reduce the stems of hybrid teas by about one-third, floribundas and polyanthas by a quarter — vigorous types need harder pruning. Standard and miniature roses are either hybrid tea or floribunda types; they should be pruned in the same way as bush types.

Climbers and pillar roses, except for climbing sports of hybrid

---

REMOVING SUCKERS

Suckers appear from the rootstock below the point of a graft union and must be removed. Scrape away the soil until the junction is unearthed, then wrench off the sucker with your gloved hand.

TAKING ROSE CUTTINGS

1 In early fall, choose nonflowering ripe side shoots — the thorns should break away easily — and cut cleanly just below a bud, with or without a heel or sliver of bark. Use a pair of pruning shears or a sharp knife.

2 Trim each cutting until it measures 9-12 in (23-30 cm) long and remove all but the upper two compound leaves. With your thumb, rub out all buds on the cutting except those in the upper leaf axils. Thorns should also be removed.

3 Dip the cuttings into hormone rooting powder and place them 9 in (23 cm) deep and 6 in (15 cm) apart in a V-shaped trench lined with sand. Fill in the trench, gently press in the soil, and leave the cuttings to root.

and miniature roses can be propagated from cuttings of lateral shoots. Rooted cuttings should be ready by the following fall.

As for budding, a growth bud of a chosen bush rose variety is joined to the rootstock of some vigorous type, such as *R. multiflora*. You can buy rootstocks compatible with your soil from rose nurseries. Plant out the rootstocks in spring or late fall. They are usually ready to receive the bud grafts the next summer.

Pests and diseases

Healthy, vigorous roses are best able to cope with the problems faced by all rose gardeners: black spot, mildew, rust, and aphids. Watch out for early signs of attack and take steps to eliminate pests and diseases before they take hold. Fungicide, for instance, is more effective when used as a preventive measure than as a cure. Begin spraying in late spring and repeat as recommended by the manufacturer. Insecticides need to be applied less frequently. One spraying in late spring, one a month later, and another in early fall should be sufficient. Some sprays give combined protection against diseases such as mildew and black spot, and pests such as aphids.

▶ **'Matangi' rose** Cluster-flowered, or floribunda, roses bloom in the middle of summer. The 'Matangi' variety, with its scented orange-vermilion flowers flecked with silver at the base and on the reverse of the petals, is particularly handsome.

HEATHS AND HEATHERS

**Heathers are among the most rewarding and versatile
plants to grow — though most demand acid soil. Their foliage is
often colorful and their flowers are long lasting.**

If you are interested in an almost trouble-free garden with color throughout the year, consider filling it with heaths and heathers. When massed together, the foliage of these shrubs makes a brilliant carpet that is practically weedproof, and when skillfully combined, the various types produce flowers almost year-round. In addition, these plants are easily propagated.

Heaths and heathers are so closely related that it is often difficult to distinguish between them. And the common names of some of these plants do not always correspond to their genus. Those plants that belong to the genus *Calluna* are correctly called heathers — or sometimes ling — but never heaths. Members of the large *Erica* genus and smaller *Daboecia* group are all known as heaths, though *Erica cinerea* is usually referred to as bell heather.

The choice of plants

Heathers *(Calluna)* are broadly grouped according to when they flower, either in summer or fall.

Heaths *(Erica),* on the other hand, bloom in winter and spring, or summer. Summer- and fall-flowering heathers need an acid soil, but the winter- and spring-flowering heaths will generally tolerate some alkalinity.

Furthermore, heathers can be divided into two groups according to size — tree heathers, which

▼ **Winter heaths** The dense flower spikes of *Erica carnea* varieties come in pure white and shades of pink and rose-purple. They form spreading carpets in marvelous bold hues.

grow up to 8 ft (2.4 m) tall, and the rest, which vary from the size of a pincushion to 4 ft (1.2 m) high. Tree heathers are valuable for adding height to an area that might otherwise be a comparatively featureless expanse. Pure heather gardens can be made more exciting by incorporating slopes, gulleys, banks, and rocks in the layout, but the addition of a few other shrubby plants gives the best visual relief.

Dwarf conifers are the traditional partners for heaths and heathers, but shrubs such as rhododendrons and azaleas, which thrive in similar soil conditions, combine well, too. Annuals can also be used to fill temporary gaps between young heathers. In large gardens, silver birch *(Betula pendula)* complements winter-flowering ericas.

In large gardens several different cultivars are often grown together. But even in a small space, single shrubs can look straggly, so try planting drifts of at least five different types. Heathers can also enhance shrub beds, mixed beds, or rock gardens, whether used as edging or intermingled with other plants. And, they can be relied on to provide a good ground cover or perhaps to make a dwarf hedge.

The dead flower heads of summer- and fall-flowering species often glow in the winter sun as richly as the blooms once did. This is also true of certain varieties of *Erica vagans,* as well as some hybrids of *E. cinerea* and *E. terminalis.*

Many of the summer-flowering heathers bring forth a second display in winter. As the frosts intensify, their foliage turns to

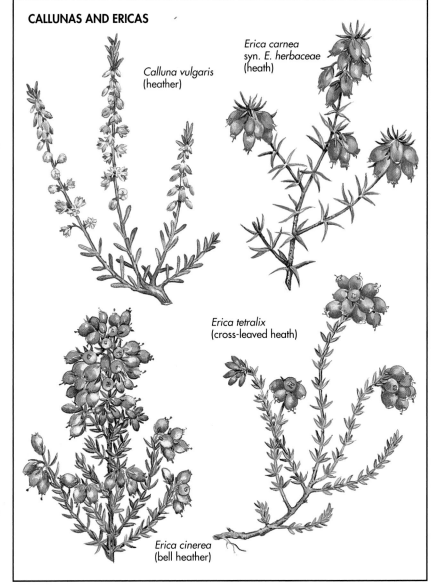

CALLUNAS AND ERICAS

Calluna vulgaris (heather)

Erica carnea syn. *E. herbaceae* (heath)

Erica tetralix (cross-leaved heath)

Erica cinerea (bell heather)

crimson, scarlet, bronze, gold, orange, yellow, silver, gray, or green.

Planting and general care
Heathers need an open position in full sun to flourish. All species do well in peaty, acid soils. Most summer- and fall-flowering types die in alkaline soil, but the winter- and spring-flowering heaths will tolerate some alkalinity in the soil.

Container plants can be set out at any time of the year, although fall and spring are best. Prepare

PLANTING HEATHERS

1 Dig the planting area thoroughly, removing all perennial weeds. Spread a layer of peat moss, about 1 in (2.5 cm) deep, and fork it in.

2 Remove plants carefully from their containers without severing the roots. Ease apart coiled roots and position plants so that their foliage rests on the soil.

3 Press in the plants and water thoroughly. To conserve water and suppress weeds, topdress the area with a layer of shredded bark or bark chips.

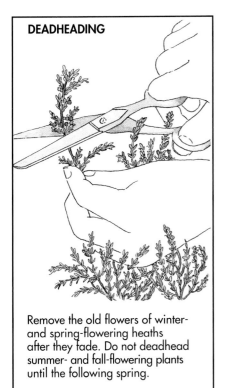

DEADHEADING

Remove the old flowers of winter- and spring-flowering heaths after they fade. Do not deadhead summer- and fall-flowering plants until the following spring.

for planting by digging the ground to one spade's depth and removing all traces of perennial weeds. On acid soils, spread a layer of peat moss, about 1 in (2.5 cm) thick, on the ground and lightly fork it in. Alkaline and heavy soils need additions of acid organic matter. On poor soils, sprinkle a small handful of bone meal over every sq yd/sq m.

Next, decide on the spacing between each shrub. To obtain quick ground cover, the small varieties should be planted 9 in (23 cm) apart, and the taller, spreading ones 1½ ft (45 cm) apart. If you are producing individual plants, double these spacings. For tree heathers, allow a distance of about 3-4 ft (90-120 cm) between plants. Mark out the planting distance using wooden stakes.

With a trowel, dig a hole slightly deeper than the container holding the heather. Remove the plant from the container and ease the roots apart. If tough roots are growing through the drainage holes in the bottom of the container, you may have to break or cut the container. Be careful not to sever the roots because you will upset the balance between root growth and top growth, and the plant may die back as a result. Lower the heather into the hole and refill with the peat-enriched soil. Except for tree heathers, ensure that the entire stem is buried so

that the foliage rests on the soil.

Press in the plant with your fingers, then water it thoroughly. Cover the entire surface of the soil with a mulch of bark chips. This layer conserves moisture and controls weeds.

In general, no staking is necessary; however, some mature tree heathers may need staking if planted in exposed sites.

For the first few months after planting, see that the soil is never allowed to dry out, especially during early spring, when winds can dry the surface rapidly. Apply water in the evening so that the plants can absorb it during the lower nighttime temperatures.

After fall or winter planting, press in all plants after a period of heavy frosts. Shake off any snow that accumulates in the branches of tall species, because the load can permanently distort the shape or break the branches.

Young shrubs that do not grow well and develop brown leaves a month or so after planting have usually been set in badly — the roots are probably in a tight ball. Lift the shrubs, ease the roots apart, then replant and saturate them with water.

A mulch of garden compost or fine bark chips may be applied each spring, but no annual fertilizer is required. Heaths and heathers are natives of areas with poor soil, and so are not used to a rich supply of nutrients. In fact, overfeeding with nitrogen will inspire a burst of weak, straggly, and disease-prone growth, which may kill the plant. Established heathers need only be watered during dry spells.

Remove weeds regularly between heathers for the first few years, using a hoe or hand fork. Take care not to damage the heather's shallow surface roots. Once a ground cover has been established, it will suppress most weeds.

Deadheading and pruning
Winter- and spring-flowering heaths, and dwarf forms of others, rarely need pruning. With pruning shears, remove dead flower heads immediately after they fade, cutting the growth just below the spent flower spikes.

The dead flower heads of summer- and fall-flowering heathers can often provide attractive color in winter, so postpone any dead-

heading until the next spring.

Summer- and fall-flowering heathers may become straggly with age and their flower spikes may lose vigor. In spring, cut back the old woody stems with pruning shears. They can be cut back as far as you like, and no damage will be done to the plant, though generally only light pruning is necessary. Make the cuts diagonally across the stems.

To prevent legginess, trim tall-growing species lightly with pruning shears either in late fall or before new growth starts.

Propagation
Nearly all of the heaths and heathers grown in gardens are cultivated varieties and will not breed true from seed. Vegetative propagation — by layering or cuttings — is the only reliable method of getting plants that resemble their parent.

Layering A well-established plant can be layered at any time of the year, but the quickest results are obtained in spring. First, separate a low-lying branch from the rest of the plant. Place several handfuls of a mixture of

LAYERING

1 In spring, separate a low-lying branch from the rest of the plant, then cover the main stem of the branch with a mixture of peat and sharp sand.

2 Anchor the layered branch with a heavy stone, and repeat with other branches. Once rooted, sever from the old stem and lift the new plant.

equal parts of peat and sharp sand over the main stem of the plant. Alternatively, cover with a potting soil for acid-loving plants.

Press the layered branch down with a heavy stone and leave it in place. Repeat this operation with as many branches as required.

Spring layers should have rooted by fall, and fall layers in about a year's time. Sever the old stems with pruning shears and lift the new plants with a trowel. Set them out in the normal way.

Cuttings In late summer or early fall, snip off branches that include side shoots of the current year's growth. They are softer, thinner, and paler green than the old growth. In the case of summer-flowering heathers, take cuttings from nonflowering shoots.

Cover the base of a 5-in (12-cm) pot with a layer of gravel and almost fill the pot with a mixture of equal parts screened peat moss and sharp builder's sand. Moisten well and press down with the base of another pot. Spread a thin layer of dry sand over the surface of this rooting medium.

Pull a side shoot of the current year's growth from the branch. Trim the tip of the shoot so that the cutting is 1 in (2.5 cm) long, remove the lower leaves, and dust the base with hormone rooting powder. A 5-in (12-cm) pot will hold about 20 cuttings spaced ¾ in (2 cm) apart. With a pencil or other sharp stick, make planting holes that are half the depth of the cuttings. Then, insert the cuttings and press them in with your fingers.

Cuttings root better if they are covered with clear plastic. Make a cover by inserting two wire hoops into the pot. Place a plastic bag over the hoops and fasten it with an elastic band. Stand the pot in a shady part of a cold frame or another cool but frost-free location. When new growth appears, the cuttings have rooted. Raise the plastic bag to let in some air. A week later, completely remove the plastic bag. Keep the cuttings in the same protected spot through the winter.

By midspring, the cuttings should be ready for potting into their own 3-in (7.5-cm) pots filled with a moist, acid potting soil. Ensure that the growth is clear of the surface of the soil, then stand the pot outside in a partly shaded place. Do not let the soil dry out. The heathers should be ready for planting out in their flowering positions in the fall.

Pests and diseases

Heaths and heathers are generally resistant to pests and diseases. However, Japanese beetles, two-spotted mites, and oyster-shell scale may attack the shrubs and must be treated with an appropriate pesticide.

If there is too much lime in the garden soil, the plants may suffer from chlorosis, a condition in which the foliage — particularly the young tips — becomes suffused or mottled with yellow, and may turn brown and die. Water the plants during the growing season with chelated iron (often sold as "plant tonic") and mulch well with bark chips.

Wilt, or dieback, produces graying foliage that begins to droop and eventually turns brown and dies. Dispose of infected plants, but keep the remaining ones vigorous by applying a general fertilizer and a deep acid mulch.

TAKING CUTTINGS

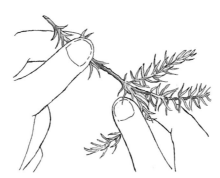

1 In late summer or early fall, snip off a branch that includes side shoots of the current year's growth — usually softer, thinner, and paler green than the growth of previous years.

2 Pull off the side shoots and trim the tips to make cuttings about 1 in (2.5 cm) long. Cuttings from summer-flowering heathers should be taken from nonflowering side shoots.

3 In a pot containing a moistened rooting medium of peat and sharp builder's sand, topped with a layer of sand, set the cuttings in holes ½ in (1.2 cm) deep and ¾ in (2 cm) apart.

4 Cover the cuttings with a plastic bag supported on wire hoops and secure it with an elastic band. Stand the pot in a cool, shady cold frame. New growth indicates successful rooting.

5 By spring, the cuttings should have rooted and should be ready for potting into their own individual pots. Ease out the tiny plants with your fingers or with a plastic plant label.

6 Put each plant in a 3-in (7.5-cm) pot, making sure that the foliage is clear of the soil. Press in the plant, water it thoroughly, and stand in a lightly shaded spot outdoors. Plant out in the fall.

GLOSSARY

Amendment: Materials that improve a soil's *tilth* or nutrient value.

Bare-root: A plant sold without soil around its roots.

Basal growth: Arising from the base or lower part of a plant.

Bract: A modified leaf that helps a tiny flower attract pollinators.

Bud, axillary: An embryonic shoot, leaf, or immature flower that develops in an angle between a leaf and a stem.

Bud, terminal: An embryonic shoot, leaf, or immature flower at the tip of a stem or side shoot.

Bulb: A swollen underground organ that stores food during the plant's rest period, or dormancy.

Bulbils: Bulblike growths, usually originating from a leaf axil or a flower head.

Bulblets: Small, immature *bulbs* produced at the base of a parent bulb.

Cloche: A cover of glass, plastic, or landscape fabric used to protect young plants from cold weather.

Cold frame: An unheated plastic- or glass-covered frame used to protect plants from cold weather and wind.

Compost, garden: Decayed vegetable matter used as an *amendment.*

Cooperative Extension Service: A free information service.

Corm: A swollen, solid stem base, without scales, found underground.

Crown: The growing point of an herbaceous plant where the roots and shoots are joined.

Culm: The stem of a plant, particularly the hollow jointed stems of grasses and bamboos.

Cultivar: A plant, often named, that originated under cultivation.

Deadhead: To remove dead flower heads to prevent seed formation and encourage continued blooming.

Epigeal: Producing seed leaves above the ground in germination.

Family: A group of related plants that may contain one *genus,* or many.

Flowers, semidouble: Flowers with more than one layer of petals, one of which is incomplete.

Forcing: Bringing a flower into bloom ahead of its natural season by artificially controlling heat and light.

Genus: Plants with the same characteristics within a *family* of plants.

Grafting: Propagation by joining different parts of two separate plants to make a single plant.

Habit: The general appearance of a plant; the way it grows. Examples are spreading, upright, and trailing.

Harden off: Gradually acclimate young plants to the outdoors.

Hardiness: The degree to which a plant can endure cold weather.

Heel: The small piece of old wood and bark that is retained when a shoot is pulled from the parent plant instead of cut.

Heel in: To plant temporarily to keep the roots from drying out while the final site is chosen and prepared.

Humus: Decayed *organic material* that improves the soil by increasing its ability to retain water, and helps a plant absorb nutrients.

Hybrid: A plant derived by cross-fertilizing two or more genetically different parents. An F1 hybrid is a first-generation cross of two pure-bred plants. An F2 hybrid is a second generation cross of two F1 hybrids.

Inflorescence: The arrangement of an individual flower or group of flowers on a plant stem or branch.

Lateral: A side shoot or bud arising in the leaf axil of a larger stem.

Layering: Propagation by covering a lower section of a stem with soil.

Loam: Rich, fertile soil containing neither an excess of sand nor of clay.

Microclimate: The temperature, humidity, and airflow around a single plant or small group of plants.

Mulch: A protective inorganic or *organic material* applied to the top of the soil to protect a plant and suppress weeds.

Naturalize: Encourage a garden plant to establish itself in a wild or nongarden setting.

Node: A stem joint where buds and side shoots emerge.

Offset: A small plant produced at the base of the parent or on short stolons. It can be planted on its own.

Organic material: Decayed plant or animal matter.

Ovary: The female flower part that holds the seeds after fertilization.

Panicle: A flower head with several opposite or alternate branches.

Petiole: The stalk of a leaf.

pH factor: The degree of acidity or alkalinity in the soil: Seven is neutral; 8-14 is increasingly more alkaline; 6-1 is increasingly more acid .

Phosphorus: Available as potash, a nutrient for good root development.

Pinching: Gently pulling off the soft growing tips of shoots to induce side shoots.

Potassium: Available as phosphate, an element responsible for flower and fruit development.

Prick out: Transplant seedlings to allow them more room to grow.

Propagation box: Shallow pot or flat for starting plants from seed.

Rhizome: An underground stem that has reserve food material and produces shoots and grows roots.

Root-run: An area of soil occupied by a plant's roots.

Rootstock: The part of a plant onto which a shoot of another plant is grafted.

Runner: A trailing stem that forms roots wherever a node touches the soil; it then produces a small plant.

Scion: A bud or shoot taken from one plant that is, or has been, *grafted* onto another plant.

Seed-starting mixture: A sterile blend, such as equal parts of vermiculite, milled sphagnum moss, and perlite, which promotes good root development.

Sepal: The outer part of a flower that protects the petals.

Sharp builder's sand: A coarse-grade sand that is used for aerating potting mixtures.

Side-dressing: Additional fertilizer applied beside, not on top of, the roots to boost growth.

Soilless mixture: A growing or starting material that contains the proper nutrients and physical conditions, but does not include soil.

Spathe: A prominent modified leaf or *bract,* usually surrounding a small spike of tiny flowers.

Species: A group of plants with common characteristics, but distinct from others of the same *genus.* Abbreviation: sp., plural, spp.

Spike, flower: An *inflorescence* of a long, unbranched flower head.

Spur: A tubular or saclike projection of a petal or *sepal.* A short lateral twig of a fruit tree that bears flowers and fruits.

Stamen: The male part of a flower. Pollen is carried on two anther lobes attached to a filament.

Stigma: Part of the female reproductive organ that receives pollen.

Stipule: A small leaflike structure that is usually found in pairs at the base of a leaf *petiole.*

Stolon: A horizontal stem, at or below ground level, that roots at its tip to produce a new plant.

Sucker: A shoot arising from below the soil surface, usually from the plant's roots.

Thatch: A mass of dead grass roots and stems that may build up between living grass and soil.

Tilth: The physical suitability of land for sowing seeds or planting. Soil in good tilth is friable, well-drained, and porous.

Topdressing: Replacing the top two inches of soil with either fresh soil or a nutrient, without digging it in.

Umbel: A flower head in which the individual flower stalks arise from a common point.

Variety: The variations in a plant arising through accidental cross-breeding or mutation in the wild.

INDEX

ACKNOWLEDGMENTS
Photo credits
Heather Angel/Biofotos 57(b), 105; Patricia J. Bruno/Positive Images 31(b); Karen Bussolini/Positive Images 49; Brian Carter 43, 111, 113(b); Eric Crichton 28(b), 32(t), 57(t), 63, 91, 95, 100, 104, 119, 122, 137, 140, 145, 150(t), 151, 157; EWA 21, (Jerry Harpur) 34, 70; Garden Picture Library (Brian Carter) front cover, 32(b), 147, (John Glover) 6-7, (Marijke Heuff) 98; John Glover 118(t), 132, 134; Neil Holmes 94, 112(b), 116(t); Derek Fell 4-5, 31(t), 50(b); Margaret Hensel/Positive Images 12; Jerry Howard/Positive Images 8, 9, 11, 50(t);

Lamontagne 13, 28(t), 35, 110(b), 161; Andrew Lawson 109; John A. Lynch/Photo/Nats 61; Robert E. Lyons/Photo/Nats 51; Tania Migdley 17, 39, 71, 141, 150(b),156; Natural Image/Bob Gibbons 164; Philippe Perdereau 127; Photos Horticultural back cover, 16, 42, 77, 83, 87, 108, 112(t), 115, 116(b), 117(t), 118(b), 121, 123, 127, 136, 144, 160, 165, 166, 168; Harry Smith Collection 2-3, 25, 53, 101, 110(t), 113(t), 117(b), 126, 143; David M. Stone/Photo /Nats 29; Margaret Turner 45.

Illustrators
Sarah DeAth 111; Elisabeth Dowle 22-23, 26-27(t), 39, 46-48, 54-56, 66-68, 72-73, 78-82, 84-85, 78-82, 84-85, 92-93(b), 96-97, 102-103, 104-105, 120, 124-125, 128-130, 138, 142-143, 152-153, 154-155, 158-160, 162-163, 166-167, 170-172; Christina Hart-Davies 14-15, 18-20, 24, 26-27(b), 37-38, 43-44, 60, 62-64, 74-76, 93(t), 99, 122, 132-133, 139, 146, 148-149; Nigel Hawtin 153(t), 154, 156; Marilyn Leader 36; Marianne Markey 52, 60(c), 90(br); Reader's Digest/Sally Smith 109, 114; Ray Skibinski 10, 30, 32; Ann Winterbotham 88-90.